69

D1086295

BUDDHISM

BUDDHISM

Its Essence and Development

by

EDWARD CONZE

WITH A PREFACE BY ARTHUR WALEY

HARPER TORCHBOOKS ▾ The Cloister Library

HARPER & ROW, PUBLISHERS

NEW YORK

BUDDHISM: ITS ESSENCE AND DEVELOPMENT
Printed in the United States of America

Reprinted by arrangement with Bruno Cassirer Limited,
Oxford, which published the original edition in 1951.

First HARPER TORCHBOOK edition published 1959

Library of Congress catalog card number: 59–10345

CONTENTS

PREFACE

by Arthur Waley

INTRODUCTION

I
COMMON GROUND

II
MONASTIC BUDDHISM

III
POPULAR BUDDHISM

IV
THE OLD WISDOM SCHOOL

V
THE MAHAYANA, AND THE NEW WISDOM SCHOOL

VI
BUDDHISM OF FAITH AND DEVOTION

VII
THE YOGACARINS

APPENDICES

TABLE OF DATES

DIAGRAM

New Wisdom School, Yogacarins, Tantra

PREFACE

by

ARTHUR WALEY

THERE is not at present in English or any other language so comprehensive and at the same time so easy and readable an account of Buddhism as is to be found in Dr. Conze's book.

You probably know the story of the king who asked the blind men what an elephant was like. One, feeling its trunk, said 'Like a chariot-shaft'; another, feeling its ear, said 'Like a winnowing-fan', and so on. The parable might well be applied to European attempts to write the history of Buddhism. Not that the historians were to blame. Early in the 19th century the only accessible documents were those representing medieval Buddhism in Nepal. So great was the sensation created by the subsequent recovery of a much earlier Canon in Ceylon that the Pali scriptures (those found in Ceylon) were taken as embodying the whole of early Buddhism. Even as recently as 1932 Mrs. Rhys Davids, in her *Manual of Buddhism for Advanced Students* (a rather ambitious title) makes little use of anything but the Pali scriptures. A year later a more comprehensive account was given by E. J. Thomas in his *History of Buddhist Thought*; but his work is addressed to specialists rather than to the general public. Other books, such as Keith's *Buddhist Philosophy*, are simply lists of views held by people felt to be wholly remote and "lacking in both system and maturity." To Dr. Conze the questions that Buddhism asks and answers are actual, living, questions, and he constantly brings them into relation both with history and with current actuality.

Books are, to my mind, valueless unless they express a point of view, and they must do this not by distorting the facts, but by making apparent to the reader the Author's emotional and intellectual reaction to these facts. Dr. Conze's book, more than any of its kind that I have read for a long time, succeeds in doing this.

AUTHOR'S NOTE

THE idea of this book originated with friends of mine in 1941, when I lived in Godshill in Hampshire, and attempted to find out how much of Buddhist meditation could actually be practised in this present age. The first chapters represent lectures which I gave some years ago in Oxford at St. Peter's Hall, and some traces of the spoken word still cling to them. In 1948, Dr. William Cohn, of Oxford, suggested to me that a work covering the whole range of Buddhist thought would be much appreciated, and encouraged me to complete the book. Dr. Cohn, and, at a later stage, Mr. Arthur Waley and Mr. Christmas Humpheys, have eliminated many errors. Mr. Claud Sutton and Mr. Arthur Southgate have watched over the English style. Discussions with various scholars have, I hope, put me right on a number of difficult and controversial points. In this connection, I must mention, with gratitude, Prof. F. W. Thomas, Dr. E. J. Thomas, Prof. Murti of Colombo, Prof. Lamotte of Louvain, Prof. Demieville of Paris, Prof. Tucci of Rome, and Dr. Pott of Leyden. Many of the texts on which my account is based have never been translated into English. It may one day be possible to offer the reader a Selection from the main Documents of Buddhist thinking, which would substantiate much that is merely stated here.

SAFFRON CLOSE,   EDWARD CONZE
EWELME.
January, 1951.

INTRODUCTION

Buddhism as a Religion

BUDDHISM is an Eastern form of spirituality. Its doctrine, in its basic assumptions, is identical with many other teachings all over the world, teachings which may be called 'mystical.' The essence of this philosophy of life has been explained with great force and clarity by Thomas a Kempis, in his *Imitation of Christ*. What is known as 'Buddhism' is a part of the common human heritage of wisdom, by which men have succeeded in overcoming this world, and in gaining immortality, or a deathless life.

During the last two centuries, spiritual interests have in Europe been relegated into the background by preoccupations with economic and social problems. The word 'spiritual' seems vague nowadays. It is, indeed, not easy to define. It is easier to state by what means one gets to the spiritual realm than to say what it is in itself. Three avenues of approach to the spiritual are, I think, handed down by the almost universal tradition of the sages :

to regard sensory experience as relatively unimportant ;

to try to renounce what one is attached to ;

to try to treat all people alike—whatever their looks, intelligence, colour, smell, education, etc.

The collective effort of the European races during the last centuries has gone into channels which by this definition are not 'spiritual.'

It is often assumed that there is some fundamental and essential difference between East and West, between Europe and Asia, in their attitude to life, in their sense of values, and in the functioning of their souls. Christians who regard Buddhism as unsuitable for European conditions forget the Asiatic origin of their own religion, and of all religions for that matter. A religion is an organisation of spiritual aspirations, which reject the sensory world and negate the impulses which bind us to it. For 3,000 years Asia alone has been creative of spiritual ideas and methods. The Europeans have in these matters borrowed from Asia, have adapted Asiatic ideas, and, often, coarsened them. One could not, I think, point to any *spiritual* creation in Europe which is not secondary, which does not have its ultimate impulse in the East. European thought has excelled in the elaboration of *social* law and organisation, especially in Rome and England, and in the *scientific* understanding and control of sensory phenomena. The indigenous tradition of Europe is inclined to affirm the will to live, and to turn actively towards the world of the senses. The spiritual tradition of mankind is based on the negation of the will to live, and is turned away from the world of the senses. All European spirituality has had to be periodically renewed by an influx from the East, from the time of Pythagoras and Parmenides onwards. Take away the Oriental elements in Greek philosophy, take away Jesus Christ, Saint Paul, Dionysius Areopagita, and Arabic thought—and European spiritual thinking during the last 2,000 years becomes unthinkable. About a century ago the thought of India has begun to exert its influence on Europe, and it will help to revivify the languishing remnants of European spirituality.

Some features distinguish Buddhism from other forms of wisdom. They are of two kinds :

Much of what has been handed down as ' Buddhism ' is due not to the exercise of wisdom, but to the social conditions in which the Buddhist community existed, to the language employed, and to the science and mythology in vogue among the people who adopted it. One must throughout distinguish the exotic curiosities from the essentials of a holy life.

There are a number of methods for winning salvation by meditation, of which Buddhist tradition gives a clearer and fuller account than I have found elsewhere. This is, however, largely a matter of temperament.

Properly studied, the literature of the Jains, of the Sufis, of the Christian monks of the Egyptian desert, and of what the Catholic Church calls 'ascetical' or 'mystical' theology, yields much of the same kind.

To a person who is thoroughly disillusioned with the contemporary world, and with himself, Buddhism may offer many points of attraction—in the transcending sublimity of the fairy land of its subtle thoughts, in the splendour of its works of art, in the magnificence of its hold over vast populations, and in the determined heroism and quiet refinement of those who are steeped into it. Although one may originally be attracted by its remoteness, one can appreciate the real value of Buddhism only when one judges it by the results it produces in one's own life from day to day.

The rules of wholesome conduct which are recommended in the Buddhist Scriptures are grouped under three headings : *Morality*, *Contemplation* and *Wisdom*. Much of what is included under *Morality* and *Contemplation* is the common property of all those Indian religious movements which sought salvation in a life apart from ordinary everyday society. There we have, in addition to rules of conduct for the laity, regulations for the life of the homeless brotherhood of monks ; many Yoga practices—rhythmical and mindful breathing, the restraint of the senses, methods for inducing trance by staring at coloured circles, stages of ecstasis, the cultivation of un-limited friendliness, compassion, sympathetic joy and even-mindedness. Further, meditations of a generally edifying character, which could be found in any mystical religion, such as meditation on death, on the repulsiveness of the functions of this material body, on the Trinity of the Buddha, the Dharma (Truth), and the Samgha (Brotherhood). Few could be expected to practise all those methods in one life-time. There are many roads to emancipation. What is common to all of them is that they aim at the extinction of the belief in individuality.

When taken in its present-day vagueness, the word 'individuality' does, however, fail to convey the Buddha's

meaning. According to Buddhist teaching, as we shall
see in more detail later on, man, with all his possible
belongings, consists of five ' heaps,' technically known
as *Skandhas*. They are :

The Body

Feelings

Perceptions

Impulses and Emotions

Acts of Consciousness.

Anything a person may grasp at, or lean on, or appropriate,
must fall within one of those five groups, which make up
the *stuff* of ' individuality.' The *belief* in individuality
is said to arise from the invention of a ' self ' over and
above those five heaps. The belief expresses itself in the
assumption that any of this is ' mine,' or that ' I am '
any of this, or that any of this ' is myself.' Or, in other
words, in the belief that ' I am this,' or that ' I have
this," or that " this is in me,' or that ' I am in this.'
The fact of individuality disappears with the belief in
it, since it is no more than a gratuitous imagination. When
the individual, as constituted by an arbitrary lump taken
from those five heaps, ceases to exist, the result is Nirvana—
the goal of Buddhism. If one wishes to express this by
saying that one has found one's " true individuality," the
word ' individuality ', as understood at present, is elastic
and vague enough to permit this. The Buddhist Scriptures
do, however, distinctly avoid this, or any equivalent,
expression.
The various schools of Buddhism spring, as I will try to
show, from differences in the approach to the Buddhist
goal. Already in the early Order, men of different temperament and endowment are reported to have reached
the goal by different roads. Sariputra was renowned for
his wisdom, Ananda for his faith and devotion, Maudgalyayana for his magical potency. In later times, different-
minded people formed different schools, and, in addition,
the spread of the doctrine led to geographical separation
and to separate organisations. Some of the methods for
achieving de-individualisation, which we shall discuss in

the later chapters of this book, are not mentioned at all in the oldest strata of the tradition as it has come down to us, or are no more than dimly foreshadowed. But, as many of the later Buddhists would have argued, in his love for beings the Buddha would have excluded nothing that could help anyone who wanted the right thing. A great deal of this book will be devoted to explaining what each of the chief schools stood for, what method it chose as its own particular way, how it can be thought to lead to the same goal as the others, and how it fared in the world of history.

Buddhism as a Philosophy

Philosophy, as we understand it in Europe, is a creation of the Greeks. It is unknown to Buddhist tradition, which would regard the enquiry into reality, for the mere purpose of knowing more about it, as a waste of valuable time. The Buddha's teaching is exclusively concerned with showing the way to salvation. Any ' philosophy ' there may be in the works of Buddhist authors is quite incidental. In the ample vocabulary of Buddhism we find no word to correspond to our term ' philosophy.' An analogy may clarify the position. The Chinese language, as the Chinese understood it, did not contain any grammar, and it was taught in China without any grammatical instructions. Some European philologists, on the model of our Latin grammatical categories, have constructed a ' grammar ' for the Chinese language. It does not fit particularly well, and the Chinese continue to dispense with it. The Latin-style grammar, with its familiar categories, may, however, help some Europeans to learn the Chinese language more easily. In a similar way, an attempt to define Buddhist thought in the philosophical terminology current in Europe may facilitate the approach to it. Buddhism, as a ' philosophy ' could then be described as a " dialectical pragmatism " with a " psychological " turn. Let us consider these three items one by one.

In its origin and intention a doctrine of salvation, Buddhism has always been marked by its intensely practical attitude. Speculation on matters irrelevant to salvation is discouraged. Suffering is the basic fact of life. If a man were struck by an arrow, he would not refuse to have it extricated before he knew who shot the arrow, whether that man was married or not, tall or small, fair or dark. All he would want, would be to be rid of the arrow. The Buddha's last injunction to his disciples ran : *All conditioned things are impermanent. Work out your salvation with diligence.* In their long history, the Buddhists have never lost this practical **bent.** Innumerable misunderstandings would have been avoided if one had seen that the statements of Buddhist writers are not meant to be propositions about the nature of reality, but advice on how to act, statements about modes of behaviour, and the experiences connected with them. 'If you want to get there, then you must do this.' 'If you do this, you will experience this.'

We can, therefore, say with some truth that Buddhist thinking tends in the direction of what we call *Pragmatism.* The value of a thought is to be judged by what you can do with it, by the quality of the life which results from it. Wherever one finds evidence of such qualities as detachment, kindness, serene self-confidence, etc., one would be inclined to believe that the ' philosophy' behind such an attitude had much to say in its favour. *Of whatever teachings you can assure yourself that they conduce to dispassion, and not to passions ; to detachment and not to bondage ; to decrease of worldly gains, and not to their increase ; to frugality and not to covetousness ; to content and not to discontent ; to solitude and not to company ; to energy and not to sluggishness ; to delight in good and not to delight in evil, of such teachings you may with certainty affirm : This is the Norm. This is the Discipline. This is the Master's Message.*

As Buddhism developed, its pragmatism became even more explicit. One came to see that anything one may say is ultimately false—false by the mere fact that one says it. *Those who say do not know ; those who know do not say.* The *Aryan silence* alone did not violate the Truth. If one says something—and it is astonishing to find how much the supporters of the Aryan silence had to say—it is justified only by what they called " skill in means." In other words, one says it because it may help other people at a certain stage of their spiritual progress.

The holy doctrine is primarily a medicine. The Buddha is like a physician. Just as a doctor must know the diagnosis of the different kinds of illness, must know their causes, the antidotes and remedies, and must be able to apply them, so also the Buddha has taught the *Four Holy Truths*, which indicate the range of suffering, its origin, its cessation, and the way which leads to its cessation (see pp. 43—48). If one, however, isolates the Buddha's statements from the task they intend to perform, then they become quite meaningless, and lose all their force.

Meditation is in Buddhism easily the chief means of salvation. The stress is throughout far less on " doing something " by overt action, than on contemplation and mental discipline. What one aims at is the control of mental processes by meditating on them. In consequence, Buddhist thought is impregnated with what we call *Psychology*. It mixes metaphysics and psychology in a way to which we have no parallel in the West.

In addition to pragmatism and psychological emphasis, Buddhist thought is inclined to what we may call *Dialectics*. Dialectics is a form of logic, associated in Europe with such names as Zenon of Elea and Hegel. It stands for the belief that, if you think properly and deeply on anything, you arrive at contradictions, i.e. at statements which to some extent cancel each other out. Buddhist thinkers loved paradox and contradiction. I may illustrate this by two quotations from the *Diamond Sutra*, a treatise written probably about 350 A.D., which has had more readers than any other metaphysical work. There the Buddha says : " ' *Beings,' ' beings,' O Subhuti, as ' no-beings ' have they been taught by the Tathagata. Therefore are they called ' beings.' *" Or again : " *As many beings as there are in these world systems, of them I know, in my wisdom, the manifold trends of thought. And why ? ' Trends of thought,' ' trends of thought,' O Subhuti, as ' no-trends ' have they been taught by the Tathagata. Therefore are they called ' trends of thought.' And why ? Past thought is not got at ; future thought is not got at ; present* *thought is not got at.*"

By defeating thought, contradictions are set free. Another fetter of existence has been cast off, and the vastness of the unlimited space of truth opens itself up. In a more secular way, some people get a similar feeling from reading nonsense literature. In Buddhism, the ordinary rules of logic are defied in the name of the freedom of the Spirit which transcends them. In addition, it is the introduction of the notion of the Absolute which here, as also with Zenon, Nicholas of Cues and Hegel, makes self-contradictory statements appear permissible.

Self-extinction, and the Doctrine of Not Self

The specific contribution of Buddhism to religious thought lies in its insistence on the doctrine of '*not-self*' (*an-attā in Pali, an-ātman in Sanskrit*). The belief in a 'self' is considered by all Buddhists as an indispensable condition to the emergence of suffering. We conjure up such ideas as 'I' and 'mine,' and many most undesirable states result. We would be perfectly happy, quite blissfully happy, as happy as, according to some psychologists, the child is in the womb, if we first could get rid of our selves. The assertion that one can be really happy only after one is no longer there, is one of the dialectical paradoxes which to the man in the street must appear just as plain nonsense. In any case, it is fairly obvious that unhappiness requires that I should identify myself with other things, in the sense that I think that what happens to them happens to me. If there is a tooth, and there is decay in that tooth, this is a process in the tooth, and in the nerve attached to it. If now my 'I' reaches out to the tooth, convinces itself that this is 'my' tooth—and it sometimes does not seem to need very much convincing—and believes that what happens to the tooth is bound to affect *me*, a certain disturbance of thought is likely to result. The Buddhist sees it like this : Here is the idea of 'I,' a mere figment of the imagination, with nothing real to correspond to it. There are all sorts of processes going on in the world. Now I conjure up another figment of the imagination, the idea of ' belonging,' and come to the conclusion that some, not particularly well defined, portion of this world ' belongs ' to that ' I,' or to ' me.' In this approach Buddhism greatly differs from some of our traditions in the West. In the philosophy of Aristotle, for instance, this idea of ' belonging ' (hyparkhein) is quite uncritically treated as an ultimate datum of experience, and the entire logic and ontology of Aristotle is built upon it.

This doctrine of Anatta is very deep. One assumes that it will need more than one life-time to get to the bottom of it. As it is handed down by Buddhist tradition, it really comprises two statements. The two propositions which we must distinguish are :

It is claimed that nothing in reality corresponds to such words or ideas as ' I,' ' mine,' ' belonging,' etc. In other words, the self is not a fact.

We are urged to consider that nothing in our empirical self is worthy of being regarded as the real self (see pp. 110sq.)

The second of these propositions will become clearer in the course of this book. We must now have a look at the first one.

We are urged to struggle against the intellectual conviction that there is such a thing as a ' self,' or a ' soul,' or a ' substance,' or such relations as ' belonging ' or ' owning.' It is not denied that the self, etc., are data of the world as it appears to commonsense. But as facts of ultimate reality, we must reject the ' self,' and all kindred ideas. This step has an important corollary. If there is no such thing as a 'self,' there is also no such thing as a ' person.' For a ' person ' is something which is organised round a supposed inner core, a central growing point, a ' self.'

In my book, *Contradiction and Reality*, I have attempted to re-state in modern terms the Buddhist arguments against the objective validity of the notion of ' self.' Their repetition would lead us too far here. Whatever arguments there may be against the idea of ' self,' it is obvious that we habitually speak of it, and find it difficult to dispense with the word. In England, Hume's denial of the existence of the ego, as an entity distinct from mental processes, comes very near the Anatta-doctrine. From the purely theoretical point of view Buddhism has in this respect little to teach that one cannot find as well, and probably in a more congenial form, in Hume and kindred thinkers, like William James. The difference between the Buddhist and the European and American philosophers lies in what they do with a philosophical proposition once they have arrived at it. In Europe, we have become accustomed to an almost complete gap between the theory of philosophers and their practice, between their views on the nature of the universe and their mode of life. Schopenhauer and Herbert Spencer, for instance, at once come to mind as particularly striking examples. If a philosopher here has proved that there is no ego, he is apt to leave it at that, and to behave very much as if there were one. His greed, hate and attachment remain practically untouched by his philosophical arguments. He is judged by the consistency of his views, not with his life, but with themselves, by his style, his erudition—in short, by purely intellectual standards. It just would not do to 'refute' a philosopher by pointing out that he is insufferably rude to his wife, envies his more fortunate colleagues, and gets flustered when contradicted. In Buddhism, on the contrary, the entire stress lies on the mode of living, on the saintliness of life, on the removal of attachment to this world. A merely theoretical proposition, such as 'there is no ego' would be regarded as utterly sterile, and useless. Thought is no more than a tool and its justification lies in its products.

Not content with the intellectual conviction that there is no ego, a Buddhist aims at an entirely new attitude to life. Day in, day out, in all the many functions and bothers of daily life, he must learn to behave as if there were no ego. Those who look to Buddhism for startlingly new and unheard-of ideas on the problem of self, will find little. Those who look to it for advice on how to lead a self-less life, may learn a great deal. The great contribution of Buddhist 'philosophy' lies in the methods it worked out to impress the truth of not-self on our reluctant minds, it lies in the discipline which the Buddhists imposed upon themselves in order to make this truth into a part of their own being.

'Radical Pessimism'

The other side of the Anatta-doctrine, which consists in the repudiation of everything which constitutes or attracts the empirical self, has earned for Buddhism the reputation of being a ' pessimistic ' faith. It is true that this world, i.e. everything conditioned and impermanent, is emphatically regarded as wholly ill, as wholly pervaded with suffering, as something to be rejected totally, abandoned totally, for the one goal of Nirvana. I am not quite sure, however, that ' radical pessimism ' is really a good word for this attitude to the world. Observers of such Buddhist countries as Burma and Tibet record that their inhabitants are spontaneously cheerful, and even gay—laymen and monks alike. It is rather puzzling that the pessimistic gloom which one reads into the Buddhist doctrine of universal suffering should reflect itself in a cheerful countenance. This world may be a vale of tears, but there is joy in shedding its burden. It must be renounced. But if there is a kingdom of God to win by renouncing it, the gain infinitely outweighs the loss. In any case, the best thing we can do with such a word as ' pessimism ' is to discard it and look the problem straight in the face.

The negative attitude of Buddhist thinkers to this world is obviously bound up with the question of the meaning of life, and the problem of the destiny of man. However difficult this problem may be, however unscientific it may be to concern ourselves with it, we must come to a decision on it, because the entire happiness and fruitfulness of our lives depends on the answer. The views on the nature and destiny of man, or the meaning of human existence, fall roughly into two classes. According to some, man is a product of the earth. The earth is his home. His task is to make himself at home on the earth. Self-preservation is the highest law, and even duty, of man. Others, however, believe that man is a spirit ill at ease, a soul fallen from heaven, a stranger on this earth. His task is to regain the state of perfection which was his before he fell into this world. Self-denial is the highest law and duty of man.

Our modern civilisation favours the first view-point, Buddhism the second. It would, of course, be futile to contend that such issues can be decided by argument alone. In all decisions on values one must be careful not to exalt one's own personal tastes, temperament, and preferences to the dignity of an objective and natural law. One should only define one's position, and not coerce others into it. The Buddhist point of view will appeal only to those people who are completely disillusioned with the world as it is, and with themselves, who are extremely sensitive to pain, suffering, and any kind of turmoil, who have an extreme desire for happiness, and a considerable capacity for renunciation. No Buddhist would assume that all men are either able or willing to understand his doctrine.

The Buddhist seeks for a total happiness beyond this world. Why should he be so ambitious ? Why not be content with getting as much happiness out of this world as we can, however little it may be ? The answer is that in actual practice we are seen not to be content. If increase in physical comfort and earthly satisfactions would make us content, then the inhabitants of the suburbs of London should be immeasurably more radiant and contented than Chinese koolis or Spanish peasants. The exact opposite is the case. Our human nature, according to the Buddhist contention, is so constituted that we are content with nothing but complete permanence, complete ease, complete security. And none of that can we ever find in this shifting world.

The discoveries which philosophers and psychologists have made in recent years about the central importance of anxiety at the very core of our being, have quite a Buddhist ring about them. According to the views elaborated by Scheler, Freud, Heidegger and Jaspers, there is in the core of our being a basic anxiety, a little empty hole from which all other forms of anxiety and unease draw their strength. In its pure form, this anxiety is experienced only by people with an introspective and philosophical turn of mind, and even then only rarely. If one has never felt it oneself, no amount of explanation will convince. If one has felt it, one will never forget, however much one may try. It may come upon you when you have been asleep, withdrawn from the world ; you wake up in the middle of the night and feel a kind of astonishment at being there, which then gives way to a fear and horror at the mere fact of being there. It is then that you catch yourself by yourself, just for a moment, against the background of a kind of nothingness all around you, and with a gnawing sense of your powerlessness, your utter helplessness in the face of this astonishing fact that you are there at all. Usually, we avoid this experience as much as we possibly can, because it is so shattering and painful. Usually, I am very careful not to have myself by myself, but the I plus all sorts of other experiences. People who are busy all the time, who must always think of something, who must always be doing something, are incessantly running away from this experience of the *basic* or *original* anxiety. What we usually do is to lean and to rely on something else than this empty centre of ourselves. The Buddhist contention is that we will never be at ease before we have overcome this basic anxiety, and that we can do that only by relying on nothing at all.

Immortality

With their exalted view of the nature of man, Buddhists regard it as a reasonable and sensible thing for us to strive for immortality. The aim of Buddhism, like that of many other religions, is to gain immortality, a deathless life. The Buddha, after he had become enlightened, claimed to have opened up the *doors to the Undying*. It is obvious that there is a great difference between the perpetuation of this individuality on the one side and immortality on the other. Immortality is just the opposite of this life, which is bound up with death, and inseparable from it. We start dying the moment we are born. The rate of metabolism in our bodies begins to slow down immediately after conception. Birth is the cause of death. All the circumstances which may bring about actual death are but its occasions. The act of birth, or conception, to be more accurate, is the decisive cause which makes death inevitable. I sometimes believe that the English persist in the gentle habit of executing criminals by hanging, because this form of execution affords such a close parallel to the course of human life. At the moment of conception we jump, as it were, off a board, with a noose round our necks. In due course, we will be strangled—it is only a matter of sooner or later. We are all the time aware of our perilous condition, whether we dare face it or not. How *can* one be at one's ease in the interval ? Immortality is therefore not a desire to perpetuate an individuality which is bought at the price of inevitable decay, but a transcending of this individuality.

Now suppose that Mr. John Smith is fed up with this state of affairs in which everything is just produced for a short time in order to be destroyed again. Suppose he wishes to become immortal. Then he has no choice but to deny himself throughout the whole length and breadth of his being. Anything impermanent in himself he has to get rid of. Just try to think of what is left of Mr. Smith after he has become immortal. His body would obviously be gone. With the body his instincts would have disappeared—since they are bound up with his glands, with the needs of his tissues, in short with the body. His mind also, as he knows it, would have to be sacrificed. Because this mind of ours is bound up with bodily processes, its operations are based on the data provided by the bodily organs of sense, and it reveals its impermanence by incessantly and restlessly jumping from one thing to another. With the mind would go his sense of logical consistency. As a matter of fact, Mr. John Smith, turned immortal, would not recognise himself at all. He would have lost everything that made him recognisable to himself and to others. And he could be born anew only if he had learned to deny all that clutters up the immortal side of his being—which lies, as the Buddhists would put it, outside his five skandhas—if he would deny all that constitutes his dear little self. Buddhist training consists, indeed, in systematically weakening our hold on those things in us which keep us from regaining the immortality which we lost when we were born. The body is subdued, the instincts are weakened, the mind is calmed, logical thinking is baffled and exhausted by absurdities, and sensory facts are thought little of, the eye of faith and the eye of wisdom replacing the eyes of the body. It comes really to the same as the precept of John Wesley, when he urged a disciple of his *to kill himself by inches.*

But, as I have said, it all depends on one's view on the nature of man. Those who regard man as a creature of the earth only, will be inclined to compare this Buddhist yearning for immortality with the snail which leaves its house in order to go on a flying expedition. Those who regard man as an essentially spiritual being will prefer the Buddhist simile of the mountain swans who, when they have left their mountain lake, go from puddle to puddle, without making their home anywhere, until they are back to their true home in the clear waters of the mountain lake.

Survival Values

How ever eloquent the sages may be on this issue, common-sense cannot help feeling that this kind of unworldliness is all very well and noble, but certainly quite unsuitable for anyone who has to live in this world, and on this earth. We are all of us nowadays unconscious Darwinians, and the survival value of an unworldly doctrine seems to be fearfully small. How could it ever keep its footing on the earth ? Historical facts, however, are rather disconcerting to common sense. The Buddhist community is the oldest institution of mankind. It has survived longer than any other institution, except the kindred sect of the Jains. Here you have the big bullying empires of history, guarded by hosts of soldiers, ships and magistrates. Scarcely one of them lasted longer than perhaps three centuries. There you have a movement of deliberate beggars, who always

prized poverty more than wealth ; who were sworn not
to harm or kill other beings ; who spent their time in
dreaming superb dreams, and inventing beautiful never-
never-lands ; who despised whatever the world valued ;
who valued whatever the world despises—meekness,
generosity, idle contemplation.　And yet, where these
mighty empires, built on greed, hatred and delusion,
lasted just a few centuries, the impulse of self-denial
carried the Buddhist community through 2,500 years.
I suppose that quite a number of conclusions could be
drawn from this fact.　The one which I would like to
point out is that Darwinism, and the other philosophies
behind the big empires are very shallow ; they have their
day—it is really a very short day, and not a very restful
one while it lasts.　Whereas the great and universal wisdom
tradition of mankind goes deep down to the very roots,
the very breath and rhythm of life.　It is the meek that
will inherit the earth, it is the meek that *have* inherited
the earth—because they alone are willing to live in contact
with it.　The Chinese philosopher Laotse expressed this
very beautifully in the *Tao te king* (chapter 7) :

" Heaven is lasting and earth enduring.
The reason why they are lasting and enduring is that they
　　do not live for themselves ;
Therefore they live long.
In the same way the Sage keeps himself behind and he is in
　　the front ;
He forgets himself and he is preserved.
Is it not because he is not self-interested
That his self-interest is established ? "

I

COMMON GROUND

The Flavour of Dharma

THE historian who wants to determine what the
Buddha's doctrine actually was, finds himself confronted with literally thousands of works, which all
claim the authority of the Buddha, and yet contain
the most diverse and conflicting teachings. Some influential writers, bred in a Nonconformist tradition, have
recently contended that one must seek for the true Buddhist
doctrine only in what Gautama Buddha actually said
about 500 B.C. This thesis has led to some acrimoniousness.
The truth is that the oldest stratum of the existing
scriptures can only be reached by uncertain inference and
conjecture. One thing alone do all these attempts to
reconstruct an 'original' Buddhism have in common.
They all agree that the Buddha's doctrine was certainly
not what the Buddhists understood it to be. Mrs. Rhys
Davids, for instance, purges Buddhism of the doctrine of
'not-self,' and of monasticism. To her, some worship
of "The Man" is the original gospel of Buddhism. H. J.
Jennings, in cold blood, removes all references to re-
incarnation from the Scriptures, and claims thereby to
have restored their original meaning. Dr. P. Dahlke,
again, ignores all the magic and mythology with which
traditional Buddhism is replete, and reduces the doctrine
of the Buddha to a quite reasonable, agnostic theory.
In this book I set out to describe the living tradition of
Buddhism throughout the centuries, and I confess that
I do not know what the 'original gospel' of Buddhism
was. To regard all later Buddhist history as a record of
the 'degeneration' of an 'original' gospel is like regarding
an oak tree as a degeneration of an acorn. In this book I

assume that the doctrine of the Buddha, conceived in its full breadth, width, majesty and grandeur, comprises all those teachings which are linked to the original teaching by historical continuity, and which work out methods leading to the extinction of individuality by eliminating the belief in it.

The Documents

Throughout the book we will have to refer to the Scriptures as the essential documents of Buddhist history. A general survey of Buddhist literature must be inserted at this point, and we must briefly consider the various divisions of the scriptures, their age, and the collections in which they are preserved.

From early times onwards, the scriptures were divided into *Dharma* and *Vinaya*. *Vinaya* deals with monastic discipline, *Dharma* with doctrine. At a later time, we find a threefold division, into *Vinaya*, *Dharma* or *Sutra*, and *Abhidharma*. The *Abhidharma* deals with more advanced doctrines (see pp. 105 sq.).

Another important division is that between *Sutra* and *Shastra*. A sutra is a text which claims to have been spoken by the Buddha himself. It always begins with the words, *Thus have I heard at one time. The Lord dwelt at . . .* The ' I ' here means the disciple Ananda, who recited the entire Buddha-word immediately after the Buddha's death. Many sutras were composed centuries after the death of the Buddha. The actual authors of the sutras which were not spoken by the historical Buddha himself, are, of course, unknown. The Buddhists themselves were sharply divided as to the value of these later sutras. One fraction, known as the *Hinayana*, or *Lesser Vehicle*, held that works composed a substantial time after 480 B.C. and not recited at the first Council immediately after the Buddha's death, could not be authentic, could not be the Buddha's own words, could be no more than mere poetry and fairy tale. The other section, however, known as the *Mahayana*, the *Great Vehicle*, asserted, in the face of all chronological difficulties, that even these later sutras

come from the Buddha's own mouth. The time lag in
publication was accounted for in various ways. One
well-known story, for instance, runs that the *Prajñaparamita
Sutras*, the texts dealing with perfect wisdom, were revealed
by the Buddha himself, but that they were too difficult
to be understood by his contemporaries. In consequence,
they were stored in the palace of the Serpents, or Dragons,
called Nagas, in the Nether world. When the time was
ripe, the great doctor Nagarjuna went down into the
Nether world, and brought them up into the world of
men. This tale is not meant to be believed by everyone.
In their desire to adapt themselves to the various dis-
positions of different people, the Buddhists were ever
ready to give a mythological explanation to people who
thought in mythological terms, and at the same time a
philosophical explanation for those used to philosophical
ways of thinking. The philosophical justification of the
later Sutras makes use of the doctrine of the ' three bodies '
of the Buddha, which we shall explain soon. It maintains
that the old Sutras were taught by the Buddha's ' form-
body,' and the later ones by his ' enjoyment-body ' (see
p. 171).

A *Shastra* is a treatise written by an author who is generally
known by name, who endeavours to be more systematic
than the Sutras usually are, and who quotes the Sutras as
authorities. Many Shastras by the doctors of the Church,
such as Nagarjuna, Vasubandhu, and others, are preserved
for us.

The total literary output of the Buddhists was enormous.
Only fragments have reached us. Our history of Buddhism
must therefore always remain fragmentary and tentative.
For about 400 years the tradition was transmitted only
orally, by schools of Reciters. Some features of the older
scriptures are clearly those of an oral tradition, such as the
many repetitions, and a fondness for verse and for numerical
lists. Owing to this preference for oral transmission, many
just of the oldest documents are now lost.

About the *age* of the Scriptures we are somewhat in the
dark. Buddhism is a body of traditions in which few names
stand out, and in which fewer dates are precisely known.

It is indeed most exasperating when we try to apply our
current ideas of historical criticism. Langlois and Seignobos,
in their text book of historical method, state that " *a
document whose author, date and provenance cannot be determined, is just good for nothing.*" Alas, that is the case
with most of the documents on which we build a ' history '
of Buddhism. Hindus have always shown an almost
complete indifference to historical dates. Historical change
is considered as quite unimportant compared with the
unchanging Truth. The Indian Buddhists shared this
attitude. Even with regard to a date as fundamental as
that of the life-time of the Buddha, their estimates varied
substantially. Modern scholars generally place the death
of the Buddha at 483 B.C. In India, Buddhist tradition
put forward many other dates, for instance 852 B.C.,
or 652, or 552, or 353, or even 252. Without a firm framework of dates, a great deal of what we say about the temporal
sequence of events in Buddhist history can be no more
than plausible guess work. We should, however, admit
that the Buddhist attitude to dates, exasperating though
it is to the historian, is not quite as wrong-headed as it
seems. The Dharma itself has no history. What changes
are only the external circumstances in which it operates.
And much of what is really important from a spiritual
and religious point of view has no place in an historical
book at all. Most of the experiences of the sages and saints
of old in their solitude elude the historian.

The Buddhists also preserved few names, because it was,
in the best periods, bad form for a monk to make a name
for himself by literary work. It did not matter to them
who said something, but whether it was true, helpful and
in keeping with tradition. Originality and innovation
were not encouraged, and anonymity was a concomitant
of sanctity. This attitude has its compensations. If a
persistent collective effort is made, over a long time, by
a great number of people devoted singly to their emancipation, to work out a system of spiritual healing, the result
after, say, ten centuries, is likely to be fairly imposing.

In addition, even where names are mentioned, they cannot
be always taken at their face value. The great names of

men like *Ashvaghosha*, *Nagarjuna* and *Vasubandhu*, often attracted to themselves so many works, that later pious tradition sometimes extended the life-time of their holders over many centuries, while modern historical criticism has had the greatest difficulties in distinguishing the different persons behind the one name.

Nevertheless, some rough dating of literary works is possible. The *Sutta Nipata*, for instance, seems to contain some of the oldest texts we possess, partly because of its archaic language, and partly because a commentary of a part of it is included in the Canon of the Theravadins. Our conjectures as to the relative dates of Buddhist writings may be based on linguistic, or doctrinal grounds. With regard to the latter, one is faced with the danger—not often avoided in the past—that one forms some arbitrary conception of ' primitive ' Buddhism, and then dates everything in reference to that. The Chinese translations are a great help to us, because they always meticulously record the date, and allow us to infer that the book in question must have been composed in India some time before that date. But even then, we find that the composition of just the most important works seems to have extended over a long period. Works like the *Mahavastu* and the *Lalitavistara* contain materials which may range from 200 B.C. to 600 A.D. In a book like the *Lotus of the Good Law*, or the *Perfection of Wisdom in* 8,000 *Lines*, the last chapters are centuries later than the first.

What has survived of the scriptures exists now in 3 great collections :

I. *The Pali Tripitaka*

This contains the scriptures of one of the Hinayana schools, the Theravadins. The scriptures of other Hinayana schools are partly preserved in Sanskrit and Chinese, but the greater number of them is lost. For future reference I give a short survey of the chief divisions of the Hinayana Canon.

II. *The Chinese Tripitaka*

Its composition is less rigidly fixed, and it has varied in

the course of time. The oldest Catalogue, of 518 A.D., mentions 2,113 works, of which 276 are still in existence. In 972 the Canon was printed for the first time. The latest Japanese edition, the *Taisho Issaikyo*, 1924-1929, gives 2,184 works in 55 volumes of ca 1,000 pages each.[1]

III. *The Tibetan Kanjur and Tanjur*

The Kanjur is a collection of the Sutras, and it comprises either 108, or 100 volumes. Of these, 13 deal with Vinaya or monastic discipline ; 21 with Prajñāpāramitā, or " Perfect Wisdom " ; 45 with various Sutras, and 21 with Tantric texts. The Tanjur, in 225 volumes, gives the commentaries and the Shastras. The Tanjur falls into three parts : The first, of one volume only, gives 64 hymns ; the second, 2,664 commentaries on Tantric texts, in 86 volumes. The third part is less homogeneous. It gives, first of all, 38 commentaries to the Prajñāpāramitā in 15 volumes ; then the Shastras of the Madhyamika School (vol. 16–33) ; then commentaries to a variety of sutras (vol. 34–43) and the Shastras of the Yogacarins (vol. 44–61). This concludes the Mahayana texts. Then follow ca 30 volumes of scientific works belonging to the Hinayana. With volume 94 of part 3, the distinctly Buddhist Shastras come to an end. They are followed by 30 volumes devoted to the translations of sanskrit works dealing with accessory subjects, such as Logic, Grammar, Medicine, various arts and crafts and social economics, and, finally, by 13 volumes of Tibetan works on technical subjects.

IV. A number of *Sanskrit* works are preserved, but there exists no collection or Canon of them.

In this book all the treatises enumerated under these four headings are regarded as authentic sources of Buddhist thought. The choice has been made in the past by men wiser than myself, and I have no reason to dispute it. The greater part of this book will be devoted to the

---

[1] The *Taisho Issaikyo* is composed as follows :
    21 vols. Sutras ; 3 Vinaya ; 8 Abhidharma ; 12 Chinese commentaries ; 4 Chinese and Japanese schools ; 7 histories, catalogues, dictionaries, biographies.

THERAVADINS (Pali)	SARVASTIVADINS (Chinese)	MAHASANGHIKAS
I. Vinaya Pitaka, 1564 pp.	I. Vinaya, ca 3000 pp.	I. Vinaya (Chinese) Mahavastu, from Vinaya (Sanskr.)
II. Sutta-Pitaka :	II. Sutra :	II.
1. Digha-nikaya, 904 pp.	1. Dirghagama	1. —
2. Majjhima-nikaya, 1092 pp.	2. Madhyamagama	2. —
3. Samyutta-nikaya, 1686 pp.	3. Samyuktagama	3. —
4. Anguttara-nikaya, 1840 pp.	4. Ekottaragama (only partly preserved)	4. Ekottaragama (Chinese)
5. Khuddaka nikaya : 15 works, e.g.	5. Kshudraka, e.g.	5. —
Dhammapada, 95 pp.	Dharmapada (Sanskr.)	—
Sutta Nipata, 226 pp.	Jatakas	—
Jataka	Many Avadanas (Sanskr.)	—
Apadana, 613 pp.		Lalitavistara (Sanskr.)
III. Abhidhamma Pitaka : 7 works, e.g.	III. Abhidharma : 7 works, e.g.	III.
Dhammasangani, 264 pp.	Dharma-Skandha-Pada 232 pp.	—
Vibhanga, 436 pp.	Jñana-Prasthana, 554 pp.	—
Patthana, 3120 pp.		—

discussion of beliefs and practices shared only by a section of the Buddhist community, which is divided into monks and laymen, Hinayana and Mahayana, and various schools of thought. A few beliefs have, however, been common ground for the whole Buddhist movement in all its forms and it is with them that we must now begin. We must, first of all, say a few words about the beliefs held concerning the Buddha, and in connection with that, discuss the supposed ' atheism ' of the Buddhist faith. Secondly, a few points of doctrine are common to all Buddhists. They concern either the essence of the spiritual life, and are laid down in the " four holy truths." Or they concern the structure and evolution of the world, and are derived from Hinduism.

The Buddha

As the beliefs concerning the Buddha do not form part of our cultural heritage, they are anything but obvious to most people, and require careful explanation. The Buddha can be considered from three points of view :

> *As a human being*
> *As a spiritual principle*
> *As something in between the two.*

1. *As a human being*, the Buddha Gautama lived probably between 560 and 480 B.C., in the north-east of India. The historical facts of his life cannot be isolated from the legend which all Buddhists accept. The existence of Gautama, or Shakyamuni (*The sage from the tribe of the Shakyas*), as an individual is, in any case, a matter of little importance to Buddhist faith. The Buddha is a type that has been embodied in this individual—and it is the type which interests the religious life. While it is possible, though by no means certain, that ordinary believers may have thought sometimes of the Buddha as a personal being, the official Buddhist theology does nothing to encourage such a belief. In the official theory, the Buddha, " the Enlightened," is a kind of archetype which manifests itself

in the world at different periods in different personalities, whose individual particularities are of no account whatsoever.

It is obvious to Buddhists, who believe in re-incarnation, that Gautama did not come into the world for the first time at 560 B.C. He had, like everyone else, undergone many births, had experienced the world as an animal, as a man, as a god. During his many rebirths, he would have shared the common fate of all that lives. A spiritual perfection like that of a Buddha cannot be the result of just one life. It must mature slowly throughout the ages. His had been a long journey, of a length which staggers the imagination. It took slightly more than three immense aeons (kalpas, see p. 49) according to the usual reckoning. In terms of years that would be about 3×10^{51} years, or at least some number of that order of magnitude. During all that time, the future Buddha practised all virtues in all possible ways. The *earth-witnessing posture* of so many Buddha statues symbolises the Buddha's long preparation for Buddhahood. The legend tells us of Shakyamuni's struggle with Mara, the Evil One, the Lord of this world, just before his enlightenment. Shakyamuni tells Mara that he has proved his contempt for worldly power and grandeur when he sacrificed wealth, limbs and life so many times in so many lives. He points to the earth as his witness, and the deity of the earth rises out of the ground, to confirm his statement. She also bore witness to the fact that Shakyamuni had fulfilled the complete discipline and duty of a Bodhisattva. This parable hides a deep spiritual truth. Mara, who corresponds to Satan, is the Lord of this world and of this earth. He claims therefore that the Bodhisattva, representing that which is beyond this world and irredeemably hostile to it, has no right even to the piece of ground on which he is seated in meditation. The Bodhisattva, on the other hand, claims that through his innumerable deeds of self-sacrifice in his former lives, he has won a right to this little bit of earth.

2. If the doctrine of the Buddha had been just the saying of some person or individual, it would lack in compelling

authority. As a matter of fact, it emanated from the *spiritual principle*, from the Buddha-nature, which lay hidden in that individual Shakyamuni, and which as we might say 'inspired' him to understand and to teach the truth. When the Buddhists consider the Buddha as a spiritual principle, they call him the *Tathāgata*, or speak of his *Dharma-body*. The original meaning of the word 'Tathāgata' is no longer known. Later commentaries explain the term as composed of the two words 'Tathā,' 'Thus,' and the past participle 'āgata,' 'come,' or 'gata,' 'gone.' In other words, the Tathagata is one who has come or gone 'thus' i.e. as the other Tathagatas have come or gone. This explanation stresses the fact that the 'historical Buddha' is not an isolated phenomenon, but that he is just one in an endless series of innumerable Tathagatas, who appear throughout the ages in the world and always proclaim the same doctrine. The Tathagata is, therefore, essentially one of a group. Sets of seven, or twenty-four, or a thousand, Tathagatas were particularly popular. In Sanchi and Bharhut, for instance, the seven Tathagatas, i.e. Shakyamuni and his six predecessors, are represented in art by the seven stupas which contained their relics, or by the seven trees under which they won enlightenment. In Gandhara, Mathura, and Ajanta, the seven Buddhas are shown in human form, one practically undistinguishable from the other.

3. We must now consider the Buddha in his *glorified body*. When he walked about as a human being, Shakyamuni naturally looked like any other human being. But this ordinary human body of the Buddha was nothing but a kind of outer layer which both enveloped and hid his true personality, and which was quite accidental and almost negligible. It was not at all an adequate expression of the Buddha's own being. Hidden behind this outer shell was another kind of body, different in many ways from that of ordinary mortals, which could be seen only with the eye of faith. The Buddhists variously called it, 'the enjoyment body,' 'the unadulterated body,' 'the body which expresses the Buddha's own true nature.' A list of 32 'marks of a superman,' often supplemented

by a list of 80 'subsidiary marks,' described the most
salient features of the Buddha's 'glorious body.' The
list of the 32 marks is common to all schools, and it must
be fairly old. The paintings and statues of the Buddha
which we find in Buddhist art, never depicted the human
body visible to all, but they always try to represent the
'glorious body' of the Buddha.

Far from being invented only in the later stages of
Buddhist history, the idea that various signs on the body,
known only to the wise, indicate a person's destiny, stature,
and future, is very much older than Buddhism itself.
The 32 signs of the superman are derived from a pre-
Buddhistic manual of astrology. The Buddha's 'glorious
body' did not suffer from the physical limitations of an
ordinary body. It can move about in a space which is
not bigger than a mustard grain, and, on one occasion, the
Buddha rose in three steps to the heaven of Indra, which
is very distant indeed.

It would lead us too far to discuss all the traditional
signs of a superman in detail, although an understanding
of Buddhist art is quite impossible without a thorough
acquaintance with them. The Buddha's 'glorious body'
was 18 feet high, and many of the statues of the Buddha
have attained that height. The body was golden in colour.
"Between the Lord's eyebrows there was a woolly curl
(Urna), soft like cotton, and similar to a jasmine flower,
to the moon, to a conch-shell, to the filament of a lotus,
to cow's milk, to a hoar-frost blossom." Many-coloured
light radiates from this hair-tuft, which is as white as
snow or silver. Sculptures usually represent the Urna
by a simple dot or by a jewel. In the later stages of
Buddhism the Tantra, under the influence of Shivaism,
interpreted the Urna as a third eye, the 'eye of wisdom.'
We have here to deal with a tradition which owes much
to Yoga practices. It is usual for Yogis to concentrate
on an invisible centre above and between the eyebrows,
and the Yoga doctrine has always assumed that some
centre of psychic or spiritual force is located in that part
of the forehead.

Two other features of the Buddha's 'glorious body' are

particularly conspicuous and important. There is the
Ushnisha, literally ' turban,' a kind of ' cowl on the head,'
which is shown on statues as a growth or protuberance
on the top of the head. It is round in Gandhara, conic
in Cambodia, pointed in Siam and on Bengal miniatures
of the 11th century, and of the shape of a flame in Laos.
In addition, light emanates incessantly from the Buddha's
body. Rays of light issue from him and illuminate a vast
space. "*Around the body of the Buddha there is always a
light, a fathom wide, on all sides, which shines constantly
day and night, as brilliantly as a thousand suns, and resembling
a mountain of jewels in movement.*" According to common
Indian tradition, a kind of fiery energy radiates from the
bodies of great men, and the habit of meditation increases
it. Very often this magical power is represented by flames
which emanate from a halo round the figure of the Buddha,
and sometimes from his shoulders. In Java, the small
flames which issue from the halo behind Buddha statues
are in the shape of the sacred syllable OM, i.e. in the
shape of an inverted question mark with a spiral tail.
Round the head of the Buddha there is a nimbus which
signifies divinity and sanctity. In the art of Gandhara
the nimbus is also given to Gods and Kings, and Christian
art adopted this symbol in the 4th century.

Whenever the word Buddha is used in the Buddhist
tradition, one has this three-fold aspect of the Buddha
in view. To the Christian and agnostic historian, only
the human Buddha is real, and the spiritual and the magical
Buddha are to him nothing but fictions. The perspective
of the believer is quite different. The Buddha-nature
and the Buddha's ' glorious body ' stand out most clearly,
and the Buddha's human body and historical existence
appear like a few rags thrown over this spiritual glory.

Is Buddhism atheistic?

It has often been suggested that Buddhism is an atheistic
system of thought, and this assumption has given rise to
quite a number of discussions. Some have claimed that
since Buddhism knew no God, it could not be a religion;

others that since Buddhism obviously was a religion which knew no God, the belief in God was not essential to religion. These discussions assume that *God* is an unambiguous term, which is by no means the case. We can distinguish in this context at least three meanings of the term. There is firstly a personal *God* who created the Universe ; there is secondly the *Godhead*, either conceived as impersonal or as supra-personal ; there are thirdly a number of *Gods*, or of *angels* not clearly distinguished from Gods.

I. As for the first, Buddhist tradition does not exactly deny the existence of a creator, but it is not really interested to know who created the Universe. The purpose of Buddhist doctrine is to release beings from suffering, and speculations concerning the origin of the Universe are held to be immaterial to that task. They are not merely a waste of time but they may also postpone deliverance from suffering by engendering ill-will in oneself and in others. While thus the Buddhists adopt an attitude of agnosticism to the question of a personal creator, they have not hesitated to stress the superiority of the Buddha over Brahma, the God who, according to Brahminic theology, created the Universe. They represent the God Brahma as seized by pride when he thought to himself : " *I am Brahma, I am the great Brahma, the King of the Gods ; I am uncreated, I have created the world, I am the sovereign of the world, I can create, alter, and give birth ; I am the Father of all things.*" The Scriptures are not slow in pointing out that the Tathagata is free from such childish conceit. If indifference to a personal creator of the Universe is Atheism, then Buddhism is indeed atheistic.

II. We are, however, nowadays, if only through the writings of Aldous Huxley, familiar with the difference between God and Godhead as an essential feature of the *Perennial Philosophy.* When we compare the attributes of the Godhead as they are understood by the more mystical tradition of Christian thought, with those of Nirvana, we find almost no difference at all. It is indeed true that Nirvana has no cosmological functions, that this is not God's world, but a world made by our own greed and stupidity. It is indeed true that through their attitude the Buddhists express a more radical rejection of the world in all its aspects than we find among many Christians. At the same time, they are spared a number of awkward theological riddles and have not been under the necessity to combine, for instance, the assumption of an omnipotent and all-loving God with the existence of a great deal of suffering and muddle in this world. Buddhists also have never stated that God is *Love*, but that may be due to their preoccupation with intellectual precision, which must have perceived that the word " Love " is one of the most unsatisfactory and ambiguous terms one could possibly use.

But, on the other hand, we are told that Nirvana is permanent, stable, imperishable, immovable, ageless, deathless, unborn, and unbecome, that it is power, bliss and happiness, the secure refuge, the shelter, and the place of unassailable safety ; that it is the real Truth and the supreme Reality ; that it is the *Good*, the supreme goal and the one and only consummation of our life, the eternal, hidden and incomprehensible Peace.

Similarly, the Buddha who is, as it were, the personal embodiment of Nirvana, becomes the object of all those emotions which we are wont to call religious.

There has existed throughout Buddhist history a tension between the Bhaktic and the Gnostic approach to religion, such as we find also in Christianity. There is, however, the difference that in Buddhism the Gnostic vision has always been regarded as the more true one, while the Bhaktic, devotional, type was regarded more or less as a concession to the common people (see pp. 144 sq.). It is generally found in philosophical thought that even philosophical abstractions are clothed with some kind of emotional warmth when they concern the Absolute. We have only to think of Aristotle's description of the Prime Mover. In Buddhism, however, in addition, a whole system of ritual, and of religious elevation is associated with an intellectually conceived Absolute in a manner which is not logically very plausible, but which stood the test of life for a long time.

III. We now come to the thorny subject of Polytheism. The Christian teaching which has to some extent pervaded our education, has made us believe that Polytheism belongs to a past period of the human race, that it has been superseded by monotheism, and that it finds no response in the contemporary mind. In order to appreciate the Buddhists' toleration of Polytheism, we must first of all understand that polytheism is very much alive even among us. But where formerly Athene, Baal, Astarte, Isis, Sarasvati, Kwan Yin, etc., excited the popular imagination, it is nowadays inflamed by such words as *Democracy*, *Progress*, *Civilisation*, *Equality*, *Liberty*, *Reason*, *Science*, etc. A multitude of personal beings has given way to a multitude of abstract nouns. In Europe the turning point came when the French deposed the Virgin Mary and transferred their affections to the Goddess of Reason. The reason for this change is not far to seek. Personal deities grow on the soil of a rural culture in which the majority of the population are illiterate, while abstract nouns find favour with the literate populations of modern towns. Mediaeval men went to war for Jesus Christ, Saint George and San José. Modern crusades are in aid of such abstractions as Christianity, The Christian Way of Life, Democracy and The Rights of Man.

Literacy, however, is not the only factor which differentiates our modern Polytheism from that of ancient times. Another factor is our separation from the forces of Nature. Every tree, every well, lake or river, almost every type of animal, could once bring forth a deity. We are now too remote from Nature to think that. In addition, our democratic predilections make us less inclined to deify great men. In India, kings were held to be Gods and, ever since the days of Egypt, the despotism of a divine ruler has been a most efficient way of keeping vast empires together—in Rome, in China, in Iran and in Japan. However much people may think of Hitler, Stalin and Churchill, they are disinclined to grant them *full* divinity. The deification of great men is not confined to political figures. The inveterate Polytheism of the human mind broke out in Islam and Christianity, through the crust of an official Monotheism in the form of the worship of saints. In Islam again the saints fused with the spirits which since ancient times had inhabited different localities. Finally, we must realise that religious people everywhere expect also immediate advantages from their religion. I saw, recently, in an Anglican shop window in Oxford, that at present Saint Christopher seems to be the only saint who appeals to those circles. His medals protect from car accidents. Similarly, the Buddhist expected from his religion that it would protect him from illnesses and fire, that it would give him children and other benefits. It is quite obvious that the one God, who soars above the stars and has the entire Universe to look after cannot really be bothered with such trifles. Special needs, therefore, engender special deities to provide for them. At present, we have developed a kind of confidence that Science and Industry will provide those needs, and our more ' superstitious ' inclinations are reserved for those activities which contain a large element of chance.

Among the populations which adopted Buddhism almost all activities contained a large element of chance, and a great number of deities were invoked for protection and help. The Buddhists would find no objection whatsoever in the cult of many Gods because the idea of a jealous God is quite alien to them ; and also because they are imbued with the conviction that everyone's intellectual insight is very limited, so that it is very difficult for us to know when we are right, but practically impossible to be sure that someone else is wrong. Like the Catholics, the Buddhists believe that a Faith can be kept alive only if it can be adapted to the mental habits of the average person. In consequence, we find that, in the earlier Scriptures, the deities of Brahmanism are taken for granted and that, later on, the Buddhists adopted the local Gods of any district to which they came.

If Atheism is the denial of the existence of a God, it would be quite misleading to describe Buddhism as atheistic. On the other hand, Monotheism has never appealed to the Buddhist mind. There has never been any interest in the origin of the Universe—with only one exception.

About 1000 A.D. Buddhists in the North-West of India came into contact with the victorious forces of Islam. In their desire to be all things to all men, some Buddhists in that district rounded off their theology with the notion of an *Adibuddha*, a kind of omnipotent and omniscient primeval Buddha, who through his meditation originated the Universe. This notion was adopted by a few sects in Nepal and Tibet (see pp. 190 sq.).

The Four Holy Truths

Next to the Buddha, the Dharma. The essence of the doctrine, accepted by all schools, has been laid down in the four Holy Truths, which the Buddha first preached at Benares immediately after his enlightenment. I will first give the formula of this basic teaching, and then comment on it.

1. *What then is the Holy Truth of Ill? Birth is ill, decay is ill, sickness is ill, death is ill. To be conjoined with what one dislikes means suffering. To be disjoined from what one likes means suffering. Not to get what one wants, also that means suffering. In short, all grasping at (any of) the five skandhas (involves) suffering.*

2. *What then is the Holy Truth of the Origination of Ill? It is that craving which leads to rebirth, accompanied by delight and greed, seeking its delight now here, now there, i.e. craving for sensuous experience, craving to perpetuate oneself, craving for extinction.*

3. *What then is the Holy Truth of the Stopping of Ill? It is the complete stopping of that craving, the withdrawal from it, the renouncing of it, throwing it back, liberation from it, non-attachment to it.*

4. *What then is the Holy Truth of the steps which lead to the stopping of Ill? It is this holy eight-fold Path, which consists of: Right views, right intentions, right speech, right conduct, right livelihood, right effort, right mindfulness, right concentration.*

Systematic meditation on the four Holy Truths, as on the basic facts of life, is a central task of the Buddhist life. I must confine myself here to the first Truth. A survey of some of its implications will greatly help us to see the Buddhist doctrine in its proper perspective.

The first part presents little intellectual difficulty, and anybody can assent to it. It merely enumerates seven well-known aspects of life which are fraught with suffering. Our intellectual resistance will begin only with the second part, which infers the universality of suffering. We must, however, reckon with an emotional resistance which acts as a powerful obstacle to the full appreciation even of the first part. Most of us are inclined by nature to live in a fool's paradise, to look on the brighter side of life, and to minimise its unpleasant sides. To dwell on suffering runs normally counter to our inclinations. Usually, we cover up suffering with all kinds of ' emotional curtains.' For most of us life would be intolerable if we could see it as it is, and if our mental perspective would emphasise its distasteful features as much as its gratifying ones. We like to keep distressing facts out of sight. This is illustrated by the widespread use of ' euphemisms,' which is nothing but the avoidance of words that call up disagreeable associations. A vague or round-about expression covers up a fact which is disagreeable or taboo. There are, in all languages, hundreds of euphemisms for death, deformity, disease, sex, the processes of digestion, and domestic troubles. A man does not ' die,' but he ' passes away,' ' breathes his last,' ' goes to sleep,' ' leaves the world behind,' ' joins his Maker,' etc. A special effort of meditation is needed to face the full reality of death. It is common practice to shut one's eyes to unpalatable facts, to pass over them, to minimise their importance, or to prettify them. Middle-aged women are not gladly reminded of their age. When people see a corpse, they often shudder and look away. As subjects of conversation, the distressing and disheartening aspects of life shock the ' nice people,' and frighten the others. Again, special meditation is needed to bring to the fore that which is usually glossed over. I cannot show here in detail how this flight from displeasing reality is partly caused by concern for narcissistic self-love, and chiefly by fear, coupled with a desire to protect the personality from ideas which threaten its integrity. The overwhelming majority of people cannot live joyfully without adopting some kind of ostrich attitude to life. In this sense the first Truth is not self-evident. To understand it, we must do violence to our ingrained habits of thought. In the desire to impress the unattractive aspects of life on a reluctant mind, the Buddhist Yogin will therefore repeatedly contemplate in great detail one by one the seven items of the formula.

At the end of the formula, the Buddha has stated that everything in this world is bound up with suffering. The 'skandhas' have been mentioned before (p. 14). It is now said that it is impossible to 'grasp' at matter, or at feelings, perceptions, impulses and acts of consciousness, without getting involved in suffering. Buddhaghosa explains the Buddha's meaning by a set of well-chosen similes. " *As in the case of the fire and the fuel, of the weapons and the target, of gadflies, mosquitoes, etc., and a cow's body, of the reapers and the field, of the village robbers and a village— so here also birth, etc., trouble the five grasping skandhas, in which they are produced, just as grass and creepers grow on the earth, or as flowers and fruits sprout on trees.*"

The universality of suffering does not immediately stand out as a self-evident fact. We tenaciously cling to the belief that some happiness can be found in this world. Only the accomplished saint, only the Arhat, can fully understand the first Truth. As the Buddha put it : " *It is difficult to shoot from a distance arrow after arrow through a narrow key hole, and miss not once. It is more difficult to shoot and penetrate with the tip of a hair split a hundred times a piece of hair similarly split. It is still more difficult to penetrate to the fact that ' all this is ill.'* "

As a matter of fact, the insight into the universality of suffering gradually extends with our spiritual growth. There is much obvious suffering in the world. A great deal of it, however, is concealed, and can be perceived only by the wise. Obvious suffering is recognised by the unpleasant and painful feelings which are associated with it, and by reactions of avoidance and hate. Concealed suffering lies in what seems pleasant, but is ill underneath.

It is sufficient to mention four kinds of concealed suffering, the understanding of which depends on the maturity of our spiritual insight :

1. *Something, while pleasant, involves the suffering of others.*
One is usually rather blind to this aspect of one's enjoyments. As our capacity for compassion grows, it widens the field of the sorrow which we feel as our own. Roast duck is pleasant as long as one ignores the feelings of the duck. Our unconscious mind has a greater sense of solidarity with other people than we often realise. When we buy pleasure by depriving someone else of happiness, we are apt to feel that pleasure as a kind of privilege which is coupled with an unconscious sense of guilt. This is well illustrated by the attitude of the wealthy to their wealth. Few of the wealthy people I have met did not fear to become poor. They feel unworthy of their wealth, as is shown by the efforts they make to prove that they deserve it. Since they got their wealth at the expense of the poor, they wish to shut the poor out from their sight, or buy them off, or tread mentally upon them by contemplating their unworthiness. Repressed compassion results in an unconscious sense of guilt. One easily compares oneself with an afflicted person, poor or deformed, and often puts oneself in their place. Some of us feel that they did nothing to deserve being better off than their ill-fated fellow-men. On the contrary, we may feel we richly deserve to be punished, and that there is really nothing that can protect us from a similar fate. Acute mental distress is avoided by shutting out the unpleasant experience. We also have to bear in mind that our social conscience is never quite extinct. Those who are better off are always inclined to blame themselves for the misery of the others. They therefore invent a picture of the social world in which misery is either minimised, or justified, or prettified. " Nobody need go without food in England." " Everybody can find work if he only wants to." " Beggars are simply lazy, and often they are quite wealthy. Did you not see the case in the papers recently . . . ? " " The

poor would be better off if they did not drink so much, or smoked fewer cigarettes." All this may be quite true, but why this elaborate superstructure if there is no sense of guilt at the bottom of it?

2. *Something, while pleasant, is tied up with anxiety, since one is afraid to lose it.*
Buddhists call this 'suffering from reversal,' and most, if not all, things are liable to it. Anxiety and worry are inseparable from attachment. This becomes fully obvious only when one dares to be free from attachment, and tastes the bliss and fearlessness which result.

3. *Something, while pleasant, binds us still further to conditions which are the ground on which a great deal of suffering is inevitable.*
What terrors are we not exposed to by the mere fact of having a body! Much pleasure is followed by bad karmic consequences (punishment), and by fresh craving which ties us to this world. There is suffering inherent in the mere fact that our existence is conditioned. We are usually quite unable to see that, and our eyes are only opened to the extent that we gain, through prolonged meditation, some understanding of the Unconditioned as our original home (see p. 110 sq).

4. *The pleasures derived from anything included in the 'skandhas' are worthless to satisfy the inmost longings of our hearts.*
They are short-lived, riddled with anxiety, coarse and vulgar. It is absurd to try and build any real ease on anything as shifting, trivial and insignificant as this world has to offer. This becomes more and more obvious as one acquires an experience of spiritual bliss. Compared with that, sensory pleasures seem unsatisfying, even pernicious, because they shut out the calm which comes from the rejection and extinction of craving.

> " *The joy of pleasures in the world,*
> *And the great joy of heaven,*
> *Compared with the joy of the destruction of craving*
> *Are not worth a sixteenth part.*

> *Sorry is he whose burden is heavy,*
> *And happy is he who has cast it down ;*
> *When once he has cast off his burden,*
> *He will seek to be burdened no more."*

As for the second and third Truths, their meaning is fairly obvious. They assert that craving is the cause of suffering, and that the abolition of craving will abolish suffering. The mechanism which inevitably links suffering to craving has been stated in an important corollary to the Four Holy Truths, which is known as the formula of *Conditioned Co-production*. Beginning with Ignorance, it enumerates a set of 12 conditions, with decay-and-death as the last, which comprise everything that happens in this world. The discovery of the 12 links of Conditioned Co-production was hailed as the greatest deed of the Tathagata. One verse sums up the Credo of all Buddhist schools, and it is found everywhere on temples, stones, statues, steles, and manuscripts throughout the whole world of Buddhist influence. " *The Tathagata has expounded the cause of all those dharmas which spring from a cause, and also their cessation. That is the teaching of the Great Ascetic.*" The actual interpretation of the formula of the 12 links differs, however, greatly in the various schools. The details fall outside the scope of this book. The practices comprised in the eight-fold Path will be discussed in detail in the following chapters. Here it is sufficient to note that *Right Views* means the ' Four Holy Truths,' *Right Intentions*, a desire for self-extinction and the welfare of others, paraphrased by Buddhaghosa in the three terms " Renunciation, Absence of Ill Will and Inoffensiveness," and that *Right Effort* refers to one's endeavours to abandon all unwholesome dharmas, and to gain, increase and develop instead states which are wholesome.

Cosmology

The Four Holy Truths state the essence of the specific religious doctrine of Buddhism. In their views on the structure and evolution of the universe, the Buddhists were, however, content to borrow from the traditions of contemporary Hinduism. Hindu cosmology is largely mythological, and differs greatly from our own. One must say a few words about some of its essential features. We will confine ourselves to explaining the notion of *Aeons* and *World Systems* on the one hand, and the six *Conditions of living Existence* on the other.

Before the Copernican revolution and the invention of the telescope the European mind was confined into a universe but tiny in its dimensions. Galilei, when he became blind in 1638, wrote to his friend Diodati : " *Alas, your dear friend and servant Galileo has been for the last month hopelessly blind ; so that this heaven, this earth, this universe, which I by marvellous discoveries and clear demonstrations had enlarged a hundred thousand times beyond the belief of the wise men of bygone ages, hence-forward for me is shrunk into such small space as is filled by my own bodily sensations.*" Europeans in the 17th century were quite unaware that " *the wise men of bygone ages* " in India had for a long time already done justice to the immensity of time and space, not, however, through *marvellous discoveries and clear demonstrations*, but through the intuitions of their cosmic imagination.

First, as regards the extent of *Time*, they measured cosmic time not in years, but in *Kalpas* or *Aeons*. A kalpa is the duration of time which elapses between the origin and the destruction of a world system. The length of a kalpa is either suggested by way of simile, or reckoned by way of number. Suppose there is a mountain, of a very hard rock, much bigger than the Himalayas ; and suppose that a man, with a piece of the very finest cloth of Benares once every century should touch that mountain ever so slightly—then the time which it would take him to wear away the entire mountain would be about the time of an aeon. As for numbers, some say that a kalpa lasts only 1,344,000 years, others reckon 1,280,000,000 years, and no general agreement has been arrived at. In any case, a very large and almost incomputable stretch of time is intended.

During the course of one kalpa, a world system completes its evolution, from its initial condensation to the final conflagration. One world system follows the other, without beginning and end, quite interminably. A *World System* is a conglomeration of many suns, moons, etc. Innumerable world systems reach out into space, immeasurably far. In a way, modern astronomy has an analogous idea when it speaks of 'island universes,' billions of which are already known, many of them billions of light years away. Each such 'spiral nebula' consists of thousands of millions of stars rotating round a common centre. Their shape is often that of a mill-wheel, just as the Buddhists had asserted. The earth forms part of the 'Galactic system,' which would correspond to what the Buddhists called "*This Saha-world*."

In regard to the size of the universe, Buddhist views are borne out by recent discoveries, and their vast cosmic perspective cannot fail to be salutary to spiritual growth. It would, however, be idle to pretend that the detailed description which the Buddhist scriptures give of the constitution and composition of a world system can be harmonised with the conclusions of modern science. Almost all the traditional assertions must appear fabulous to us. We hear, in particular, a great deal about the 'heavens' and 'hells' attached to each world system, and the account of the earth's geography is quite at variance with the picture presented by a modern atlas. Buddhists assume, by the way, as a matter of course, that life is not confined to this earth, that living beings dwell in many of the stars, and the later Buddhism of the Mahayana laid great stress on the Buddhas and Bodhisattvas who worked to release suffering beings in world systems other than our own (see p. 154 sq.).

Now to the classes of living beings. At present, we distinguish three kinds of life : men, animals and plants. Buddhist tradition counts six : The six *planes of life* are the Gods, the Asuras, Men, Ghosts, Animals and Hells. Some authors count only five 'worlds,' omitting the Asuras. There was much disagreement on details, but the general scheme was accepted by all schools. All the innumerable beings in the world fall into one of those six, or five classes. The merit one has acquired in the past decides on the place where one can choose one's rebirth.

The ' Gods ' (Devas) are ' above ' us in the sense that their material constitution is more refined than ours, that their emotions are less coarse, that their life-span is much longer, and that they are less subject to suffering than we are. They resemble the Olympian Gods, but with the important difference that they are not ' immortal.' In some ways they are more ' angels ' than ' Gods.' Buddhist tradition gives an elaborate classification of the Gods which we can omit here. The *Asuras* are also celestial beings. They are furious spirits who continually fight with the Gods. Some authors count them among the Gods, and others again among the Ghosts.

The animal world, the world of ghosts, and the hells, are the three *Dismal Destinies*, or *States of Woe*. The term ' Ghosts ' (Preta) referred orginally to the ' Spirits of the Departed,' but the more developed Buddhist theory attempts to systematize under this heading a great deal of the folklore current in India. The ' hells ' are very numerous, and usually divided into hot hells and cold hells. Since life in hell comes to an end some day, they are more like the Purgatory of the Catholic Church, than like the Hell of orthodox Christianity.

Suffering is the common lot of life in all its forms. The Gods suffer because they are bound in due course to fall from their exalted condition. Men have much sorrow and little joy, and they often fall into a worse rebirth. The Pretas are incessantly tormented by hunger and thirst, and the pains of the beings in hell are almost unthinkable. Faced with this vast ocean of suffering, one trained in the doctrine will feel compassion, and he will reflect : " Even if I would give the greatest happiness in the world to these beings, that happiness must end in suffering. It is only through the eternal bliss of Nirvana that I can do good to all. I must therefore first win true wisdom, and then I can work the weal of other beings." Rebirth as a *man* is, however, essential for the appreciation of the Dharma. Gods are too happy to feel dislike for conditioned things, and they live too long to appreciate impermanence. Animals, ghosts and the damned lack in clarity of mind. Once he has gained a certain height of spirituality, a man can never again be reborn in the ' states of woe.' He may, however, in the view of all Buddhist schools, voluntarily seek rebirth in them, in order to help beings by the teaching of the dharma. Thereby he gladdens and heartens those beings, and also increases both his disgust for existence, and his patience.

MONASTIC BUDDHISM

The Samgha

THE first, and the most fundamental, division among Buddhists is that between monks and householders. In this chapter I intend to describe the essential virtues of the monastic life, proceed in the next chapter to a survey of popular Buddhism, and then devote the remainder of the book to an outline of the various schools of Buddhist thought.

The core of the Buddhist movement consisted of monks. A monastic life alone will normally provide the conditions favourable to a spiritual life bent on the highest goal. The monks either lived in communities, or, as hermits, in solitude. The entire ' brotherhood ' of monks and hermits is called the *Samgha*. The Samgha naturally always formed only a small minority of the Buddhist community. Its proportion to the householders varied greatly with social conditions at different times. China, for instance, knew 77,258 monks and nuns in 450 A.D., and 2,000,000 seventy-five years later, in 525. Ceylon, in 450 A.D. had 50,000 monks, but only 2,500 in 1850, and again 7,300 in 1901. In Japan, in 1931, there were 58,400 priests to 40,000,000 laymen. In Tibet, one third of the entire male population lived at times in the monasteries.

The monks are the Buddhist elite. They are the only Buddhists in the proper sense of the word. The life of a householder is almost incompatible with the higher levels of the spiritual life. This has been a conviction common to all Buddhists at all times. They differed only in the strictness in which they adhered to it. The Hinayana was, on the whole, disinclined to grant any exceptions. The *Questions of King Milinda*, it is true, somewhat grudgingly

admit (p. 265) that also a layman can win Nirvana, but
add at once that he must then either enter the Order, or
die. In any case, a layman could attain Nirvana in this
life only if he had pursued a monastic life in some former
existence (p. 353). The Mahayana went further, and
granted that householders could be Bodhisattvas, i.e.
first-class Buddhists. Vimalakirti is a famous example from
literature. In order that he should not be contaminated
by home and family, a Bodhisattva must preserve a correct
and watchful attitude towards sense pleasures. He must
feel disgust for them, and fear them, " *just as someone
in the middle of a wilderness infested with robbers, would
eat his food in trembling, and with the ever recurring hope
of getting away from this dreadful place.*"

The continuity of the monastic organisation has been
the only constant factor in Buddhist history. Monastic
life was regulated by the rules of the *Vinaya*. The term
is derived from ' vi-nayati,' ' to lead away,' from evil,
' to discipline.' The monks were apt to attach extraordinary
importance to the observance of the Vinaya rules. Monastic
discipline was codified in the *Pratimoksha* rules. Different
sects count between 227 and 253 of them. They are very
similar in all sources, and must therefore be very old,
older than the independent development of the schools.
The word ' prati-moksha ' either means to ' abandon sin,'
or it may mean ' equipment, armour.' The rules must
be recited twice a month in an assembly of the chapter.

Poverty

Poverty, celibacy, and inoffensiveness were the three
essentials of monastic life. A monk possessed almost no
private property at all. He was allowed to have his robes,
an alms bowl, a needle, a rosary, a razor with which to shave
the head every fortnight, and a filter which served to
remove little animals from his drinking water. Originally,
the dress consisted of rags which were taken from the
rubbish heaps in the villages, and which were stitched
together and dyed a uniform saffron colour. Later on
the cloth for the robes was usually donated by the faithful.

In theory and intention a monk should be without a home or permanent shelter. The life of the monk is described as the *homeless life*, and in order to enter upon it he had to *leave the home, filled with faith*. The original rigour of the monastic rules seems to have demanded that a monk lived in the forest, in the open, at the foot of a tree. The Vinaya speaks of the dwelling in convents, sanctuaries, temples, houses and grottos as of a luxury, permissible, but nevertheless full of dangers. Food should be obtained by begging.

As a matter of fact, a monk should really rely on begging for all his needs. A number of monks, who wanted to lead a particularly strict life, conformed to this rule. Others seem, from very early times onwards, to have accepted invitations into the houses of the faithful. The possession of money was forbidden for a very long time. About 100 years after the foundation of the order, some monks of Vaisali tried to break this rule, and their conduct led to the first real crisis in the order. The ' Second Council of Vaisali ' settled the matter in favour of the strict observance of the rules, but in later times a great deal of laxity about the possession of money, land and other property set in.

The begging-bowl was the Buddha's badge of sovereignty. Many statues show the Buddha holding his begging-bowl, indicating that he obtained it as the reward of rejecting the position of a world ruler. Teachers often gave their begging-bowl to their successor as a sign of the transmission of authority. It must, of course, be remembered that in Asiatic countries begging has always been an accepted mode of earning one's living. We are apt to forget that, during the Middle Ages, all through Europe monastic orders maintained themselves by begging, and it was really only the economic system of rising industrialism which found that begging was incompatible with its needs for industrial workers, and passed the Vagrancy Laws as one of its first measures. When we consider history, we find that all the more developed forms of society seem to have a great deal of surplus wealth to spend. The Egyptians used it for the building of pyramids. At present, only too much of it goes into wars, female vanity, and drugs, i.e. beer, tobacco, cinemas, fiction. In Buddhist countries it is spent on maintaining the Samgha, and on manufacturing innumerable objects of worship such as stupas and statues. The Buddhists considered the practice of begging as a breeding ground for many virtues. The monk had no sense of inferiority about this mode of livelihood. He felt that he was not idle by any means, but led a strenuous life, in curbing his desires and developing his meditations. Since generosity is one of the prime virtues, the monks felt that by accepting alms they gave the householder an opportunity for gaining merit. At present, society is inclined to regard contemplatives as parasites. From the Buddhist point of view, the existence of contemplatives is the only justification of human society.

On their begging rounds the monks often met with humiliating experiences. They were called ' bald-pate,' and similar names, and the curbing of pride is counted among the advantages of begging. In addition, one learns to have few desires, to be easily contented, and to restrain the sentiments of anger and disappointment. The results of begging are uncertain and one trains oneself in doing, for a time, even without the necessities of life. The indifference of the begging monks to worldly advantages, their calm and dignified behaviour, helps to convert unbelievers and to strengthen the faith of the believers.

The practice of begging gives ample opportunities to *watch well over the body, control the senses, and to repress thoughts.* The monk must go from house to house without making a distinction between those of the poor and those of the wealthy. He must pay no attention to what he gets, and must be neither pleased nor displeased. If a woman hands him his food *he must not speak to her, or look at her, or observe her beauty or ugliness.* The food which was given to the monks was not always either ample or dainty, or even wholesome. Gastric troubles were the professional disease of the monastic communities. The experiences of the Buddhist monks were to some extent paralleled by those of Saint Francis of Assisi, who had once been a prosperous man, and who had been ' dainty in his father's home.' After his great renunciation of all property, he took a bowl and begged scraps of food from door to door. As the legend says : " *when he would have eaten that medley of various meats, at first he shrank back, for that he had never been used willingly even to see, much less to eat, such scraps. At length, conquering himself, he began to eat ; and it seemed to him that in eating no rich syrup had he ever tasted aught so delightsome.*"

Finally, the absence of ties, the great independence, the ability to come and go freely was one of the greatest advantages of begging. Compared with the life of the wandering monk, the home life of the householder seemed cramped and stuffy. Even the more settled life of monastic communities contained many *afflictions and distractions*, which distract the mind and *impede the practice of the path. One must obey the rules of the monastery, interrupt one's meditations to receive guests, help to administrate the affairs of the community, accept duties and fulfil functions.*

The Hinayana treats begging chiefly as a school of self-discipline. The Mahayana, which largely abandoned the practice of begging, stressed its altruistic aspects. This instance confirms, I think, the general observation that the profession of altruistic sentiments is often a means to cover up some personal advantage. The Mahayanist in any case, should use his begging round as an opportunity to cultivate his love for his fellow beings.

In the course of time, particularly outside India, the practice of begging was discontinued. The reasons which Asanga in his *Yogashastra* gives for the abrogation of the ancient poverty, are very noble and altruistic ; they are, at present, heard frequently among well-to-do Christians. According to Asanga, monks may possess wealth and property, even gold, silver, and silken clothes, because such possessions allow them to be more useful to others and to help them. At present the habit of begging has totally disappeared from China, Korea, and Annam. In China, under the T'ang dynasty, a special sect, the Vinaya sect, was founded for the purpose of reviving the old practice of begging, and enforcing the strict rules of the Vinaya in general. Under the Sung dynasty, the Ch'an monks practised begging and this practice persists among the Zen monks in Japan. It is in Japan, however, not the chief source of livelihood but only a disciplinary exercise for novices, or a mode of collection on special occasions and for charitable purposes.

Monastic Celibacy

Celibacy was another cornerstone of the monastic life. Innumerable and meticulous rules hedged in the conduct of a monk towards the women he met on his alms rounds, or whom as nuns he had to instruct. Unchastity was an offence which automatically led to expulsion from the order. Chastity, called *Brahmacarya*, or *Conduct worthy of a Brahmin or a holy man*, was a great ideal from which the monk must not swerve even at the cost of his life. The orthodox decried sexual intercourse as the ' bovine ' or ' bestial ' habit, and they cultivated a certain contempt for women. This contempt is, of course, easily understood as a defence mechanism, since women must be a source of perpetual danger to all celibate ascetics—especially in a hot climate. The monk was warned to be perpetually on his guard, and a short dialogue admirably sums up the attitude of the early Buddhists :

Ananda : ' *How should we behave to women ?* ' Lord : ' *Not see them !* ' Ananda : ' *And if we have to see them ?* ' Lord : ' *Not speak to them !* ' Ananda : ' *And if we have to speak to them ?* ' Lord : ' *Keep your thoughts tightly controlled !* '

The reasons for this rejection of the sexual impulse are not far to seek. A philosophy which sees the source of all evil in craving for sensuous pleasure, would not wish to multiply the occasions for indulgence in sensual pleasure. " *As long as even the slightest thought of lust of a man towards women remains undestroyed, so long is his mind tied, even as the sucking calf is bound to its mother.*" It is very difficult to have sexual relations with women without becoming fond of one or the other of them. Such attachment would be fatal to a man's freedom. In its later development, in the Tantra, the initiate was bidden to expose himself to this danger, and to indulge in sex without polluting his mind thereby. For more than 1,000 years such audacity would have seemed an almost blasphemous foolhardiness to the monks. Furthermore, sexual relations may lead to children, and children would be a terrible tie to one who wished to live outside society in carefree independence. There is, however, a much deeper reason why the saints of all ages have viewed the sexual impulse with particular suspicion. Sexual intercourse is apt to produce a certain rapturous calm and relaxation. Neurotics are known to use it for the purpose of warding off their mental conflicts for the time being. In this respect, the better is the foe of the good. In his practice of Trance the monk possessed a far more efficacious method for inducing inward quietude. Meditation and sexual intercourse have in common the goal, and the force which they use. For the simple reason that one cannot use the same force twice, complete suppression of sexual behaviour is indispensable to success in meditation.

Psychologists have often observed the similarity between mystical states and the experiences of our sexual life. The sexual imagery in some mystical writers has been widely discussed. On the whole, psychologists are inclined to derive the spiritual from the sexual, and to regard meditation as a kind of sublimated or attenuated sexuality, as an aim-inhibited and object-inhibited sexuality, or in other words, as a lesser version of something else. A practising mystic, on the other hand, would be inclined to say that we are as true to ourselves in meditation as in sexual intercourse, if not much more so. He would agree to the considerable similarity between enlightenment and sexual union, but he would, with Plotinus, regard the spiritual activity as primary, and the sexual as secondary and derived. It is illuminating to quote Plotinus in this context, when he says: "*There is in ecstatic union no space between the soul and the highest. There are no longer two, but both are united in one. They cannot be separated from each other as long as one is there. This union is imitated in our world by lovers and loved when they wish to unite in one being.*" Following this line of argument, the transfer of the meditational force to sexual activity would amount to a fall, a degradation, a dulling of that energy. By indulging in sex one would make an absurd and unworthy use of it. Sex would be a 'bovine' and abortive attempt to gain the union of enlightenment and its emotional satisfaction, but in its essence it would be a miscarriage or misuse of the longing for reunion with the Absolute.

For more than 1,000 years, these views remained predominant in the order. After that a section of the Community, swayed by other considerations, came to believe that sexual life was not incompatible with monkhood. Married monks are reported for Kashmir about 500 A.D., and from about 800 A.D. onward the Tantra sanctioned the marriage of monks in the districts which came under its influence. In the left-handed Tantra, as we shall see later on (Chapter VIII), there was nothing shameful about sexual intercourse, but it was, on the contrary, one of the means of winning enlightenment. Padma Sambhava, *the Lotus-born*, who, about 770 established Buddhism in Tibet and who is considered as a second Buddha, accepted from the Tibetan king the gift of one of his five wives, and many paintings represent Padma Sambhava flanked by his two chief wives, Mandarava and Yé-ses-rgyal. Marpa, the translator (born 1011), one of the greatest teachers of Tibet, married when 42 years old, and he also had *eight other female disciples, who were his spiritual consorts*. Quite different is the motivation of the Shin School in Japan (founded about 1200). Its adherents claim that they are so 'low and inferior' that they cannot be expected to follow the Buddha's precepts. They thus habitually lead a married life and eat meat. The bonze Kenryo Kawasaki has succinctly expressed the motives of this School : " *It is not at all necessary to withdraw from the world and to practise special austerities in order to become a perfect Buddhist. Our founder, the Shonin Shinran, was married and lived as the world does. It is our duty to live according to the moral code of our environment, of our family, profession or nation, and not to distinguish ourselves from other people by external acts or manifestations.*" We will have occasion to return to this argumentation.

It is sufficient here to have explained the attitude which the majority of the monks adopted towards celibacy, and at the same time to have illustrated the fact, astonishing to the Western mind, that on some questions the Buddhist religion does not speak with one voice. When facing this, or any other vital issue, Buddhism has, like a proper Janus' head, consistently looked into the two opposite directions. It has attempted to arrive at the truth, not by excluding its opposite as falsehood, but by including it as another form of the same truth.

Inoffensiveness

About 500 B.C. two religions came to the fore in India which placed " *No Harming* " into the very centre of their doctrine—the one being Jainism and the other Buddhism. This special emphasis on the prohibition of doing harm to any living being was presumably a reaction against the increase in violence, which marked human relationships as a consequence of the invention of bronze and iron. It was directed in India not only against the massacres which marked tribal warfare, but also against the enormous slaughter of animals which accompanied the Vedic sacrifice, and to some extent against the cruelty which marks the attitude of peasants to animals. The doctrine of Jains and Buddhists is based on two principles :

1. The belief in the kinship of everything that lives, which is further strengthened by the doctrine of reincarnation, according to which the same being is to-day a man, tomorrow a rabbit, after that a moth, and then again a horse. By ill-treating an animal one might thus find oneself in the invidious position of ill-treating one's deceased mother or one's best friend.

2. The second principle is expressed in the Udana, where the Buddha says : " *My thought has wandered in all directions throughout the world. I have never yet met with anything that was dearer to anyone than his own self. Since to others, to each one for himself, the self is dear, therefore let him who desires his own advantage not harm another.*" In other words, we should cultivate our emotions so that we

feel with others as if they were ourselves. If we allow the virtue of compassion to grow in us, it will not occur to us to harm anyone else, any more than we willingly harm ourselves. It will be seen that in this way we diminish our sentiment and love of self by widening the boundaries of what we regard as ours. By inviting, as it were, everybody's self to enter our own personality, we break down the barriers which separate us from others.

Through this attitude, Buddhism can be said to have had an immense humanising effect on the entire history of Asia. It is the kindness of everyone which strikes the observers in countries saturated by Buddhism, such as Burma. King Asoka was converted to Buddhist faith repenting the slaughter which had won him his empire. It was he who made Buddhism into a world religion. Sir Charles Bell's book on *The Religion of Tibet* shows again and again how Buddhism softened the rough warrior races of Tibet and Mongolia, and nearly effaced all traces of their original brutality.

In this context, we must consider two kindred problems, the attitude of Buddhism to vegetarianism and its attitude to religious persecution. Since it is impossible to eat animals without harming them, a Buddhist should be a vegetarian. But if he is a monk, who begs his food by going round a village from house to house, and if this village is inhabited by non-vegetarians, he comes up against a serious difficulty. In order that he should have no attachment to food, he is bidden to eat everything and anything which is thrown into his bowl ; and the Venerable Pindola has been held up to the reverence of posterity for calmly eating a leper's thumb which had fallen into his bowl. Monastic discipline would be undermined if monks would start to pick and choose their food. In consequence, a compromise has been arrived at, and in actual practice Buddhists who take their religion seriously, avoid eating meat unless compelled to do so.

One often argues against Buddhist vegetarianism, that it is quite futile because, while a few hens and cows might be kept alive who otherwise would have been killed, nevertheless the normal pursuit of our ordinary life involves a considerable amount of destruction of life which cannot be avoided while we live. By merely washing our hands, we kill as many living creatures as there are human beings in the whole of Spain. So we are faced with the alternative of either killing ourselves to save others, or of killing others to save ourselves. The taking of life seems to be inseparable from life itself. The Buddhists have always been fully aware of the gravity of this objection. They advise us, at least, to diminish the involuntary slaughter, for instance, by being careful about what we tread on when walking in the woods. In addition, the Buddhists believe that it is very salutary for us to realise what a calamity there is involved in the mere fact of our being alive, and a contemplation of the extent of this calamity should induce us to be more energetic in our efforts to escape from a condition in which our own suffering can be perpetuated only by inflicting a great deal of suffering on other creatures also. When Calderon once said that the greatest sin of all is that we were born, he expressed a typically Buddhist thought. Some people only see what they call ' pessimism ' in such a thought, but it also involves a recollection of the more noble side of our nature which deplores the thoughtless way in which we crush other beings all the time in order to perpetuate our own miserable existence.

It goes without saying that there would be little room in Buddhism for religious persecution—for Crusades, or Inquisitions. If the Buddha were insulted, a Buddhist would see little reason to torture or kill the person who ' insulted ' him. "*Why become indignant when the Buddhas are insulted ? The Buddhas are not touched by blasphemies.*" It would appear incongruous to a Buddhist to convince someone of the superior quality of his great benevolence by burning him alive. It would, of course, be an exaggeration to claim that Buddhist writings are entirely free from invective and vituperation. Even in some of the most sacred writings, such as the Prajñā-pāramitā and The Lotus of the Good Law, we find a somewhat deplorable inclination on the part of the writers to consign fellow Buddhists, who think differently from them, to Hell for long periods of time. What has, however, prevented this

natural exuberance of theological spite from hardening
itself into deliberate intolerance, has been the strong sense
of individual and temperental differences with which the
Buddhists are normally strongly imbued. The Dharma
is not really a dogma, but it is essentially a path. If dogma
is placed into the centre of religion, and if one believes
that a statement is either true or false, and that a man's
salvation depends on his acceptance of a true statement
as true, then one's benevolence may easily come to destroy
the bodies of others in order to save their souls. According
to the Buddhists, however, it is very difficult, if not impossible to make any positive statement at all which is
not false and inadequate owing to the mere fact of its
being made (see p. 133). All statements made in words
are at the best half-truths, and their only value lies in
inducing one to adopt a certain path of action. Just as
we are told in the Bible that in Our Father's House there
are many mansions, so it is not unlikely that more than one
path leads to the heavenly city. According to their dis-
positions, different people have different needs—what is
food for one is poison for another ; and it would be coming
near to an almost insensate presumption if one were to
be quite certain about the needs of others. As a result
of this conviction, the history of Buddhist thought is
marked by a bold and almost boundless experimentation
with spiritual methods which were tested merely prag-
matically, merely by the results attained. In Tibet,
there is a proverb that every Lama has his own religion,
and that there are as many Buddhisms as there are Lamas.
It has been said that this boundless tolerance has been
responsible for the decline of Buddhism. As a matter of
fact, Buddhism has lasted longer than most historical institutions. In any case, little would be gained by per-
petuating the forms of its worship at the expense of its spirit.

We shall see that royal patronage has been one of the
chief causes for the spread of Buddhism. Royal power
is obviously based on brutality and violence, and equally
obviously the conversion of the rulers has sometimes been
incomplete. It would therefore be an exaggeration to
say that Buddhist rulers have never used violence for

furthering the cause of religion. As soon as the monks became, through the friendship of emperors and kings, invested with social and political power, they were also open to some contamination from power. Finally, we would expect that in a country in which Buddhism provides all the terminology of culture, popular rebellions would avail themselves of its ideas to express their social aspirations, just as the Lollards and German peasants did with Christianity.

In their desire to express disapproval of Christianity, many authors have painted the record of Buddhism too white, and it will be necessary to admit that on occasion the Buddhists were capable of behaviour which we usually regard as Christian. In Tibet, for instance, there was a bad king Lang Dar-ma, who about 900 A.D. persecuted the monks. A Buddhist monk murdered him. The official Tibetan history praised him for his *compassion for the king who was accumulating sins by persecuting Buddhism*, and later generations, far from disapproving, have canonised the monk. Nearly all European histories praise the Yellow church, which has dominated Tibet for the last 300 years. They suggest that the ascendancy of this sect over the older Red sects was due to the great learning of Tsong-kha-pa, to the purer morality of its adherents, and to their comparative freedom from magic and superstition. This may be true to some extent, but some of the success of the *Ge-lug-pa* was due to the military support of the Mongols, who, during the 17th century, frequently devastated the monasteries of the rival Red sects, and who throughout supported the Dalai Lama, the head of the Yellow Church. In Burma, King Anuruddha, in the 11th century, made war on the neighbouring kingdom of Thaton in order to seize a copy of the Holy Scriptures, which the king of Thaton refused to have copied. In a warlike country like Japan, the monasteries during the Middle Ages were a source of constant turmoil, and the monks were in the habit of invading Kyoto in vast armed hordes from their mountain retreats. The Boxers were an example of a popular movement resorting to violence and employing Buddhist terminology. This fusion of popular discontent with Buddhist beliefs is fairly old in China, and the predecessors of the Boxers, such as the White Lotus sect, have had a powerful influence on Chinese history. In Burma, the English offended the religious feelings of the Burmese, for instance by licensing and promoting the sale of liquor. They also destroyed monastic discipline by suppressing the hierarchy of the Church. In consequence, a kind of political Buddhism spread more and more, since there was nothing to check it. Saya San, a popular leader, for instance, issued in 1930 a proclamation which, according to M. Collis (*Trials in Burma*, 206), read : " In the name of Our Lord and for the Church's greater glory, I, Thupannaka Galon Raja, declare war upon the heathen English who have enslaved us."

These examples could be multiplied indefinitely. On the whole, the Buddhists would deplore such incidents as lapses from Grace and as due to the inherent corruption of human nature. In India itself the monks offered no resistance when the Hephtalitic Huns, and later on the Mohammedans sacked the monasteries, killed their inhabitants, burned the libraries and destroyed the sacred images. Organised Buddhism, as a consequence of this persecution, was extinguished first in Gandhara, and then in the whole North of India. But the essence of the doctrine, as expressed in the Prajñāpāramitā and Nagarjuna, has lived in India until to-day, and, under the name of Vedanta, it is still the official doctrine of Hinduism on its highest level.

The main currents of Monastic Thought

The development of monastic *thought*, or of the metaphysics of spirituality, will be described later on in chapter IV to IX. The main lines of division are shown on the appended *Diagram*, in explanation of which I will say a few words here.

The basic division is that between *Hinayana* and *Mahayana*. In the Hinayana there is, first of all, the *Old Wisdom School*, which, about 200 years after the Buddha's Nirvana, split into two branches : In the East of India the

Theravadins, who at present still dominate Ceylon, Burma and Siam ; and in the West the *Sarvastivadins*, who flourished for 1,500 years, with Mathura, Gandhara and Kashmir as their centres. In addition, there were a number of *other schools*, of which almost no record is preserved. The *Mahasanghikas*, in Magadha and in the South round Amaravati, organised from ca 250 B.C. onward, the dissenters from the Old Wisdom School into a separate sect, which perished only when Buddhism was destroyed in India.

The more liberal Mahasanghika version of the Buddhist tradition soon developed into a new trend, called the *Mahayana*. The Mahayana divided itself into different schools, not immediately, but after about 400 years. Each of the schools stressed one of the many means of emancipation. The *Madhyamikas*, founded about 150 A.D. by Nagarjuna, expected salvation from the exercise of wisdom understood as the contemplation of emptiness. Because they formulated their doctrines in deliberate contrast to those of the ' Old Wisdom School,' we speak of a ' New Wisdom School.' Another school of thought, closely connected with the Madhyamikas, placed its trust in *faith* in the Buddhas and Bodhisattvas, and in devotion to them. The systematisation carried out by the Madhyamikas neglected, however, some of the ideas current in the early Mahayana, which later on received greater weight from parallel developments in Hinduism. The influence of the Samkhya-Yoga philosophy shows itself in the *Yogacara* school, founded about 400 A.D. by Asanga, which relied for salvation on introspective meditation known as Yoga. Finally, after about 500 A.D., the development of the Tantra in Hinduism furthered the growth of a magical form of Buddhism, called the *Tantra*, which expected full enlightenment from magical practices. The Tantra became very influential in Nepal, Tibet, China, Japan, Java and Sumatra. Outside India, a few genuinely new Schools developed from the fusion of the Mahayana with indigenous elements. Noteworthy among them are, in China and Japan, the *Ch'an* (meditation) school, and *Amidism*, and in Tibet the *Nyin-ma-pa*, who absorbed much of the Shamanism native to Tibet.

The creative impulse of Buddhist thought came to a halt about 1,500 years after the Buddha's Nirvana. During the last 1,000 years no new school of any importance has sprung up, and the Buddhists have merely preserved, as best they could, the great heritage of the past. It is possible to believe that the lotus of the doctrine has, after 1,500 years, fully unfolded itself. Perhaps there is no more to come. The conditions of our industrial civilisation, however, offer a challenge which may lead to a new synthesis. Unless our present civilisation perishes soon from its own violence, Buddhism will have to seek some accommodation with it. The Dharma cannot be heard in a world dominated by modern science and technical progress. A great deal of adaptation is needed, and a great change is bound to take place in the exposition of the doctrine. So far the vague beginnings of such a change are discernible in various parts of the world, but they are not yet sufficiently definite to merit inclusion in this historical treatise.

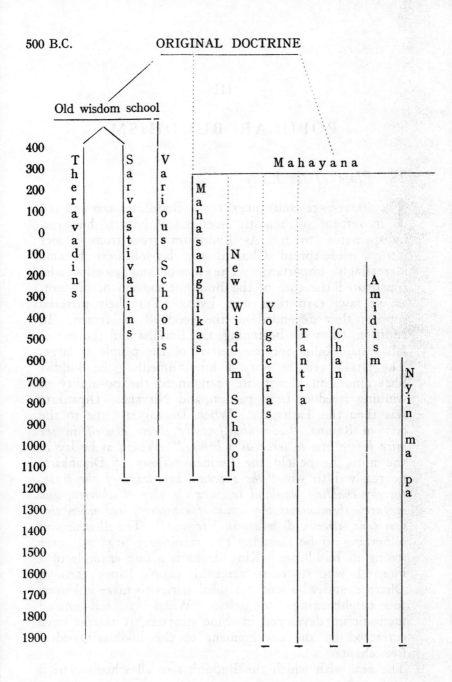

500 B.C.   ORIGINAL DOCTRINE

Old wisdom school

400									
300	T	S	V			Mahayana			
200	h	a	a						
100	e	r	r	M					
0	r	v	i	a					
100	a	a	o	h	N				
200	v	s	u	a	e			A	
300	a	t	s	s	w	Y		m	
400	d	i		a		o		i	
500	i	v	S	n	W	g	T	d	
600	n	a	c	g	i	a	a	i	
700	s	d	h	h	s	c	n	s	N
800		i	o	i	d	a	t	m	y
900		n	o	k	o	r	r		i
1000		s	l	a	m	a	a		n
1100			s			s			m
1200					S				a
1300					c				p
1400					h				a
1500					o				
1600					o				
1700					l				
1800									
1900									

III

POPULAR BUDDHISM

The Place of the Laity

IN its essence and inner core, Buddhism was and is a
movement of monastic ascetics. A laity is, however,
indispensable to it. As Buddhism grew from a sect
into a wide-spread Church, the lay-followers became
increasingly important. The monks and ascetics who
constituted the core of the Buddhist movement did not,
as we saw, earn their own living. For their material
support they depended on the goodwill of laymen. In
addition, from the beginning, the Buddha and the monks
felt responsibility for the welfare of the people at large.
The Jatakas tell the story of how Sumedha—the Buddha
Shakyamuni in a past life—renounced the possibility of
winning freedom from passion, and Nirvana. Dipankara
was then the Tathagata. When Dipankara came to the
city of Ramna, " *Sumedha joyfully threw himself in the
mire before him to serve as a bridge.*" When, as he lay in
the mire, he beheld the Buddha-majesty of Dipankara,
he resolved to win " *the supreme knowledge of the truth,
thereby enabling mankind to enter the ship of dharma, and
so carry them across the ocean of existence, and when this
was done, afterwards to attain Nirvana.*" The dharma was
something to be shared. The missionary urge was ever
strong in Buddhism. King Asoka is a fine example of a
monarch who strove to make his people happy through
Dharma, and who sent out missionaries to make it known
to neighbouring countries. When a self-centred
monasticism developed in some quarters, it was at once
corrected by the development of the Bodhisattva-ideal
(see chapter V).
The zeal with which the Buddhists of all schools carried

their gospel all over Asia, and the qualities that enabled them to do so, is well exemplified by the story of Pūrna, one of the earliest apostles of the dharma. He asked permission of the Buddha to go as a missionary to a barbarous country, called Sronāparāntā. The Buddha tried to dissuade him, and the following dialogue developed :

Buddha : *" The people of Sronaparanta are fierce, violent and cruel. They are given to abusing, reviling and annoying others. If they abuse, revile and annoy you with evil, harsh and false words, what would you think ?"*

Purna : *" In that case I would think that the people of Sronaparanta are really good and gentle folk, as they do not strike me with their hands or with stones."*

Buddha : *" But if they strike you with their hands or with stones, what would you think ? "*

Purna : *" In that case I should think that they are good and gentle folk, as they do not strike me with a cudgel or a weapon."*

Buddha : *" But if they would strike you with a cudgel or a weapon, what would you think ? "*

Purna : *" In that case, I would think that they are good and gentle folk, as they do not take my life."*

Buddha : *" But if they kill you, Purna, what would you think ? "*

Purna : *" In that case, I would still think that they are good and gentle folk, as they release me from this rotten carcass of the body without much difficulty. I know that there are monks who are ashamed of the body, and distressed and disgusted with it, and who slay themselves with weapons, take poison, hang themselves with ropes or throw themselves down from precipices."*

Buddha : *" Purna, you are endowed with the greatest gentleness and forbearance. You can live and stay in that country of the Sronaparantas. Go and teach them how to be free, as you yourself are free."*

It is often asserted that the Hinayana had less missionary zeal than the Mahayana. This is not the case. The Hinayana, like the Mahayana, was carried to Ceylon, Burma, Tibet, China, Java and Sumatra. If the Mahayana alone survived in Tibet and China, it was because it was

more adapted to non-Indian populations than the
Hinayana. The king of Tibet, for instance, invited about
750 the Hinayana sect of the Sarvastivadins—flourishing
at that time in Kashmir and Central Asia—to establish
themselves in Tibet. The masses of the people, however,
wanted a religion which was impregnated with magic,
and for that reason the Sarvastivadins soon died out in
Tibet. Thus, Buddhists of all shades of belief, were ever
ready to spread the good news about the Dharma.

At the same time, wherever the Dharma has been a living,
social reality, Buddhist theory has combined lofty metaphysics with a willing acceptance of the magical and
mythological beliefs of the peasants, warriors and merchants
among whom it took roots. If they wanted to be true to
their ideals of compassion, the monks had to win followers.
If they wanted to exist, they needed alms from their lay-
followers, or from rulers. Two questions must therefore
be considered : 1. What did the monks do for the masses
of their adherents, or for their royal patrons ? And,
2. how did the concern for the needs of the laity in its
turn influence Buddhist thought ?

Buddhism and the Temporal Power

Without the support of kings and emperors, the triumphant
spread of the Dharma throughout Asia would have been
impossible. It was one of the greatest rulers of India,
King Asoka (274–236 B.C.), who first made Buddhism
into a world-religion, spread it through the length and
breadth of India, brought it to Ceylon, Kashmir and
Gandhara, and even sent missions to the Greek princes
of his time—Antiochos II of Syria, Ptolemy Philadelphos
and Antigonos Gonatas of Macedonia. After Asoka, the
Buddhists were favoured by another great conqueror,
the Scyth Kanishka (78–103 A.D.), who ruled over the
North of India, by Harshavardhana (606–647), and by the
Pala dynasty (750–1150) which ruled over Bengal. Outside
India, Chinese emperors and empresses were often converted to Buddhism, so were Mongol Khans, so in Japan
a statesman of the calibre of Shotoku Taishi (572–621).

In Further India, we find an abundance of Buddhist dynasties at various times.

Only very few of the monarchs just mentioned were Buddhists to the exclusion of other religious leanings. The Palas and the rulers of Ceylon and Burma were the exceptions. Buddhism does not require the exclusive allegiance of its adherents. Kadphises I—a Kuchana king (25–60 A.D.)—calls himself *constant adept of the true Dharma.* The money which he issues shows, on the one side, a seated Buddha, on the other the Zeus of the city of Kāpisa. Kanishka adorned his money with Gods from Iran—Verethraghna, Ardokhcho, Pharso—with the Hindu Shiva, and with the Buddha—shown either standing or in the lotus seat, with his name in Greek characters as Boddo, or Boudo. Gupta kings favoured both Vishnuism and Buddhism, the kings of Valabhī (490 onwards), though " devotees of Shiva," protected Buddhism, Harshavardhana combined Buddhist piety with a cult of the Sun, etc., etc. Similarly, outside India. The great Khan Mongka (ca 1250) favoured Nestorians, Buddhists and Taoists, in the belief that, as he said to the Franciscan William of Rubrouck, " *all religions are like the fingers of one hand*,"—although to the Buddhists he said that Buddhism was like the palm of the hand, the other religions being the fingers. Kublai Khan combined leanings towards Buddhism with a partiality for Nestorianism.

Since it is the purpose of rulers to rule, it is unlikely that their conviction of the spiritual value of the Buddhist doctrine would be the only, or even the chief, motive for the protection which they extended to the Buddhist religion. In what manner, then, could the seemingly other worldly and anarchic doctrine of Buddhism increase the security of a ruler's power over his people ? It does not only bring peace of mind to the other-worldly, but it also hands over the world to those who wish to grab it. In addition, the belief that this world is ineradicably bad and that no true happiness can be found in it, would tend to stifle criticism of the government. Oppression by government officials would appear partly as a necessary concomitant of this world of birth-and-death, and partly as a punishment for one's own past sins. The stress which Buddhism lays on non-violence would tend to pacify a country and to make the position of its rulers more secure. In addition, if the people regard this world as none too important, their cheerfulness will not be impaired by lack of possessions, and it is preferable to rule over a cheerful rather than a sullen people. In Buddhist society, a simple life would be held most in keeping with the religious doctrine, and people would want to be ' poor ' in the sense in which Burmans were poor. M. Collis (*Trials in Burma,* p. 214) makes the following apt comment on the British contempt for the Burmans on account of their poverty :

" *A Burman who had, as many of the villagers had, his own house and his own farmland, a wife, and lots of children, a pony and a favourite actress, a bottle of wine and a book of verse, racing bullocks, and a carved teak-cart, a set of chess, and a set of dice, felt himself at the summit of felicity, and ignored the English view that he was a poor man because his cash income was about ten pounds a year.*"

Buddhism would everywhere discourage the accumulation of material wealth in the hands of individuals, and encourage people rather to give away any material wealth, and to invest it in works of piety, as has been the case in Burma and Tibet for so many centuries. If we consider that the encouragement of a desire for material possessions and for a higher ' standard of living ' among the European masses has not only destroyed all despotic forms of government, but has undermined all steady and permanent governmental authority in Europe, we can understand why Buddhism should appear as a blessing to the habitually despotic rulers of Asia.

Ever since the Neolithic Age, rulers, particularly where they had to cope with large and heterogeneous empires, were to some extent deified. This idea of the divinity of Kings is quite familiar from Egypt, China and Japan. It played its rôle in Rome and Byzantium, has been superseded by democratic ideas only quite recently, and still shows a surprising vigour in the attitude which a number of Germans adopted to Hitler, or in some of the pronouncements made about Josef Stalin in the Soviet Union. In

India the divinity of the Rajahs, however small their domain, has always been a commonplace of popular belief. The moral authority of a king would grow immensely if and when his will could appear as the will of God. It was particularly among the great conquerors that Buddhism found favour. The Buddhists actively increased the prestige of such a monarch by their theory of the *Wheel-turning King*, in Sanscrit *Cakravartin*. The Scriptures give a somewhat idealised portrait of such a ruler. Here is the description from the Divyavadana (548–9): "*He is victorious at the head of his troops, just (dhārmiko=dikaios), a king of dharma, endowed with the 7 treasures, i.e. a chariot, an elephant, a horse, a jewel, a wife, a minister and a general. He will have* 100 *sons, brave and beautiful heroes, destroyers of the enemies' armies. He shall conquer the whole wide earth to the limits of the ocean, and then he will remove from it all the causes of tyranny and misery. He will rule without punishing, without using the sword, through Dharma and peacefulness.*"

It has been a fiction among Buddhists that the rulers who favoured them lived more or less up to this ideal conception. When later on the Mahayana elaborated a new pantheon of deities, Buddhist kings received some of the reflected glory. Rulers in Java, Cambodia and also in Ceylon in the 10th century, were regarded as Bodhisattvas. In Cambodia, at the end of the 12th century, Jayavarman VII consecrated a statue of his mother as Prajñāpāramitā, *Mother of Buddha*. In the 20th century, the King of Siam is still *The Holy Master Buddha* (PHRA PHUTTICCHAO). In an Uigur inscription of 1326, Chengis Khan is called a *Bodhisattva in his last birth*. Kublai Khan became in Mongol tradition, a *Cakravartin*, a sage and a saint (*Hutuktu*). Travellers often refer to the rulers of Mongolia and Tibet as 'living Buddhas.' This is a misnomer and does not express the sense in which the Dalai Lama is regarded as an incarnation of the Bodhisattva Avalokitesvara, or the Hutuktu of Urga as a manifestation of Amitāyus. The Buddhist idea is that the Buddhas and the Bodhisattvas conjure up phantom bodies which they send to different parts of the world, and that those dignitaries are such phantom bodies. Whatever the exact connotation, the prestige value of such suggestions is obvious. It will not only increase the docility of the population, but it will also induce the monks to act as spiritual policemen for the government. It is one of the curiosities of history that, outside India, under Buddhist influence, real theocracies on the Egyptian model were built up, in Indo-China, in Java, in Tibet.

In all pre-industrial societies one believed that the prosperity and welfare of the state depended on the harmony with the invisible and celestial forces which were the true rulers of the Universe. At every step in the Odyssey the fate of Odysseus is decided by a decision made on Olympus. By being friendly with the Buddhist monks a ruler would try to keep on good terms with the invisible forces, and a monk who could claim particular familiarity with them might rise to high office as a responsible adviser. So we read in Wei Shou's (c. 550 A.D.) account of Buddhism in China of a Kashmirean monk of c. 400 A.D., who was *" clever in fortune-telling, in preventive magic, and spoke in detail of the fortunes of other states, much of which came true. Mêng-Hsün often consulted him on affairs of state."*

The motives which we have explained so far would, of course, induce rulers to support not only Buddhism, but any other religion which would support their authority. There were, however, two factors which favoured Buddhism in particular. In many cases it was not Buddhism alone which was introduced into countries like Japan or Tibet, but the new religion was coupled with many advantages of a superior civilisation. In the case of Japan, for instance, the entire apparatus of Chinese civilisation was carried across the sea at the time when Shotoku Taishi decided to adopt the Buddhist faith. The Tibetans, together with the Buddhist dharma, also took over the secular sciences of India—such as grammar, medicine, astronomy and astrology. Secondly, there is something cosmopolitan and international about Buddhism, which would recommend it to monarchs who wished to unify large areas. There is nothing, or almost nothing, in the Buddhist interpretation of spiritual truth which ties it to any soil or any climate, to any race or tribe. Hinduism as compared with it is full of tribal taboos. In Buddhism there is nothing which cannot easily be transported from one part of the world to another. It can adapt itself as easily to the snowy heights of the Himalayas as to the parched plains of India, to the tropical climate of Java, the moderate warmth of Japan and the bleak cold of outer Mongolia. Indians, Mongols, and the blue-eyed Nordics of Central Asia could all adjust it to their own needs. Although it is essentially hostile to industrialism, in Japan it managed during the last 40 years, to adjust itself even to the highly uncongenial industrial conditions. A creed as flexible and adaptable as that would be valuable to men who have to rule vast empires, because it would help to unify heterogeneous populations through giving them common beliefs and practices, and through the mutual contact which monks of different regions would cultivate. As far as the spread of Buddhism from Indian to non-Indian countries was concerned, merchants and traders played a prominent part. The strict caste rules of Hinduism made it difficult for orthodox Hindus to leave the country ; special sea-voyages were frowned upon and held to pollute so that travellers on their return had to be purified. In consequence, a great deal of the external trade of India during the Middle Ages was in the hands of Buddhists who carried their religion wherever they went.

Having considered the problem of the services Buddhism rendered to the temporal power, we can now ask what it did for the masses and its lay followers.

The Samgha's Services

The accounts which we have of the early years of the order indicate that the Buddha showed great sagacity in his dealings with the laity, and was ever ready to meet their needs and their legitimate grievances. In order to keep the religion alive for more than 2,500 years, the small élite of the monks must have done something for the lay followers which they could appreciate. The needs of the laity which Buddhism catered for were, I think threefold : *Spiritual, Mythological, and Magical.*

1.　Even those who in general pay no attention to spiritual values, are intermittently afflicted by a sense of the futility of the life they lead.　They feel that their present condition does not allow them an adequate expression of their true self, and that escape from the world might bring them into their own.　To the world-weary, the monks could offer a coherent account of the origin and destiny of man, of his place in the world, of the meaning of his life, and of the means by which a better life could be obtained. In this way, the doctrine as preached was a window out of the world.　And in their lives, many of the monks gave examples of that kindliness, self-possession and detachment from circumstance which people feel they need to pull themselves out of the world.　They were happy, although they treated as nothing the things other people worry about all the time.

2.　In chapter I (p. 41 sq.) we showed why mythology seems to satisfy some deep-rooted need of the human soul.　The world, as we see it, is too small to hold all the love and faith that are in the heart of man.　According to Buddhist theory, faith is the step in the direction of Buddhism, and for the laymen faith is bound to cover more or less the sum total of their religious aspirations. *Faith* would in this context not be an acceptance of definite dogmas, but its essence would consist in some measure of detachment from this world, and a partial turning-away from the visible to the invisible, without, however, quite reaching it.　What then would the *Faith* of a Buddhist layman consist in ?

He would have respect for the Buddha, for his doctrine (the Dharma), and for the community of monks.　He would be convinced that these *Three Treasures* were helpful to him, that a person's good or bad fortune depends on his deeds, and that to acquire merit matters more than anything else.　It appears, indeed, that the acquisitive instincts of men were deliberately canalised into the acquiring of *Merit*.　Merit is gained, for instance, by giving gifts, particularly to priests and holy men, by leading a pure life, by remaining patient when insulted, by being friendly to others.

Westerners seem often to have difficulties in understanding what the Buddhists mean by 'Merit.' The advantage of 'Merit' is supposed to lie in that it either gives you a more happy or comfortable life in the future, or, what is more important, a life which is more abundant in spiritual opportunities and in spiritual achievements. To be reborn in a better world could be regarded as either a good thing in itself, or as a means of obtaining more favourable conditions for attaining enlightenment in a future life. For instance, a very wicked person would be reborn as a fish, and among the fish the religion of the Buddha would be completely unknown. In the perspective of a householder, Nirvana was too remote to aim at in this life. The burden of his past deeds was too heavy for him to climb so high. No one who believes in a separate individuality— and who would be a householder if he did not ?—could win Nirvana ; but the belief in individuality does not, it is taught expressly, hinder rebirth in heaven. Our records show that a hope to be reborn in the heavens as a reward for a life of purity and devotion animated large numbers of Buddhist laymen during many centuries.

Faith is a longing for things not of this world, and it expresses itself in worship. Buddhists are in the habit of worshipping the Relics and footprints which were the visible traces of the Buddha's presence on earth. They also worship what is technically known as *Caityas*. A Caitya is a general name for any sanctuary or shrine. It is always connected with the person of the Buddha himself, although the connection may be a very indirect one. The Caitya may contain a relic of the Buddha's physical body, a tooth, or other bone ; it may contain something which the Buddha had worn on himself or used, like his robe, which was preserved at Hadda, or his alms-bowl, which was shown at Peshawar; or it may contain portions of the Dharma-body of the Buddha, in other words, of the Scriptures. Some years ago some very ancient Buddhist manuscripts were found in Gilgit in Kashmir, where they had lain in a stone mound or *Stupa* for 1,500 years. In some cases, however, the Caitya just commemorates an incident in the life of the Buddha. Bodh-gaya, the most sacred place of world Buddhism, for instance, centres round the tree under which the Buddha obtained en-lightenment.

By what actions, and in what spirit, then, were sacred objects *worshipped* by the Buddhists ? *Worship* (Pūjā) requires that one should make offerings of food, garlands of flowers, umbrellas (which are the symbols of royalty) and sometimes of money. At the same time a reverential attitude is indicated by *Circumambulation*—one goes round the image or temple, always keeping it to one's right.

Images were important objects of contemplation and fruitful sources of merit. To produce and to multiply sacred images was held to be highly meritorious, and in periods of exalted faith, the manufacture of images almost assumed the profusion of a natural force. At the same time it is believed that the prosperity of a nation depends on honouring those images. It would, of course, never have occurred to a Buddhist that an image was the deity himself. Protestant missionaries often believe that the heathen mistake their idols for Gods, but among the heathen no support has been found for this assumption. The image is :

a. A very imperfect symbol of a divine force, and an inadequate support to one's contemplation of it.

b. An object charged with magical power. The image is meant to call to mind the spiritual force represented by a Buddha or Bodhisattva, but it does not claim to possess a material or sensory similarity to them. For 500 years, the Buddhists refrained from representing the Buddha after his enlightenment in human form, because he had, strictly speaking, outgrown all humanity. They were content, in the scenes from his life which were carved in stone, to remind the onlooker of his presence by means of a tree, of a wheel (a symbol of the dharma), a throne, a stupa containing his relics. We do not yet know the motives which induced them to change this convention, and to carve and paint the Buddha in a human form.

While on the one hand images symbolised spiritual forces, they were also regarded as a kind of magical power station. The magical force inherent in them became manifest to the faithful by the miracles which habitually occurred in connection with Caityas, Stupas or Images. The theory was, according to the Hinayana, that these miracles were not produced by the Buddha or by the relics, but that they were the result either of the grace of Arhats and deities, or of the resolute faith of the devotee. So *The Questions of King Milinda* (p. 309). The Mahayana, on the other hand, assumes that the supernatural power of the Buddha's grace continues to work in his relics and in the places where they are deposited. But both Hinayana and Mahayana believe that the sanctity of any object was to a great extent generated by the faith and worship bestowed upon it. A well-known story may illustrate this. An old woman in China heard that a friend of hers was going on a trade journey to India, and she asked him to bring her back one of the Buddha's teeth. The trader went to India, but forgot all about the old woman's request, which he remembered only when he was nearly back home again. He saw a dead dog lying by the wayside, took out one of the teeth and gave it to the old woman as his present from India. The old woman was overjoyed, built a shrine for the tooth, and she and her friends worshipped it daily. After a time the tooth became radiant, and emitted a strange light. Even after the merchant had explained that it was only a dog's tooth, the halo round the tooth persisted, so strong was the faith and devotion of this old woman.

It would, incidentally, never have occurred to the Buddhists that they could in any way please the Buddha by worshipping his relics. The Gods of Olympus insisted on their hecatombs, and Jehovah on being treated with respect. The Buddha, however, does not desire to be worshipped, *in the same way as an extinct fire does not require or desire any fuel.* The purpose of worship consisted in promoting in the worshipper a mental disposition favourable to spiritual progress. For " *Faith is the seed, Faith is the wealth here best for man.*"

3. We now must say a few words about the *Magical* functions of Buddhism. It is not quite easy for us at present to see the magical convictions of our forefathers

in the light in which they did. A complete historical revolution separates the reader, and to some extent also the historian, from the ideas about magic which have dominated human thought for at least twenty thousand, and for perhaps two hundred thousand years. Urbanisation and the startling practical success of scientific methods in industry and medicine have destroyed the belief in magic among most educated people. Science in every way appears to us as much more plausible because it is so much more successful than magic. Wherever the practical results of magic can be accurately assessed and compared with those of science—be it in raising crops or cattle, in warfare, in fighting disease, in chemistry or even in weather making—magic seems to compare most unfavourably with science. To the educated public, for which this book is intended, the value of magic seems to be once and for all symbolised in the efforts of the Burmese peasants, who in 1930 " *advanced upon machine guns chanting formulas. With amulets in their hands, they ran upon regular troops. They pointed their fingers at aeroplanes and expected to see them fall.*" (M. Collis, *Trials in Burma*, 209). To us it seems just ludicrous to believe that one could be made invulnerable to bullets by the use of pills and oils, or by chanted formulas and letters tattooed on the body.

This contempt for magic may act as a serious obstacle to our historical understanding of the past. In order to live, in order to keep its feet on the earth, a religion must to some extent serve the material preoccupations of the average man. It must be able to insert itself into the rhythm of communal life which in the past was everywhere permeated and dominated by magic. Then, as now, the average man was deeply absorbed in the problems of everyday life which concerned his crops or cattle, and the cycle of birth, marriage, and death in the family. To some extent he expected from a religion the peace of mind which results from a firm faith and a pure life, and which is the reward of a life of renunciation. But with a strange absence of logical consistency, he also expected that same religion, which was based on the renunciation of all things of the world, to provide him with that control over the unseen magical forces all around him, which would guarantee or at least assist the secure possession of the things of the world.

Like all the other religions of the past, Buddhism provided magical protection and magical power. The success of crops depended, in popular belief, to a great extent on the ceremonies which Buddhist priests performed ; and one assumed that some evil force would destroy the crops if those ceremonies were omitted. The fertility of the soil and the health of the community depended on the monks. At the same time the private desires of individuals were not neglected. In Mahayana countries the Bodhisattvas were believed to be concerned also with the earthly fortunes of the faithful. They might deliver from fire and water, protect ships and cattle, or give children. The Scriptures of the later Tantric school give detailed advice on how one can, by propitiation of the unseen powers, fulfil all one's desires. It is a testimony to the all-embracing compassion of the Buddhist religion that it considers really everything which man can desire— from full enlightenment to the gift of eloquence and the seduction of a particular woman who has taken one's fancy. In countries like China and Japan, Buddhism acquired a great deal of social stability by acquiring a kind of monopoly in everything connected with death. In China, death and funerals are the prerogatives of Buddhist priests who, however, would never think of officiating at a marriage. In Japan, Buddhism found it easy to fuse with the native Shinto system of magic, with its reverence for the ancestors.

We shall hear more about the magical side of Buddhism (Chapter VIII). This is an historical work, and it is sufficient for me to stress the importance of magic in the actual practice of historical Buddhism. Any attempt to make these beliefs plausible would consume too much space. Readers who regard magic, miracles and the occult as so much superannuated superstition, must, however, be warned against assuming that the more enlightened Buddhists participated in magical practices as a kind of time-serving gesture, and as a materially necessary con-

cession to beliefs which they did not share. Protestant
readers, in particular, are faced here with the same difficulty
which confronts them in the life of the Catholic church,
where the belief in the occult, in magic, and in miracles
has always been shared by all, from the most intellectual
to the least instructed. In Buddhism we have, for instance,
the example of Hiuen Tsiang, one of the master-minds of
Chinese Buddhism. Superbly educated, widely travelled,
deeply versed in philosophy, he nevertheless found himself
continually confronted by miraculous events on his journey
in India. Historically, the display of supernatural powers
and the working of miracles were among the most potent
causes of the conversion of tribes and individuals to
Buddhism. To a Buddhist, however refined and intellectual
he may be, the impossibility of miracles is not obvious.
He does not see why the spiritual must be necessarily
impotent in the material world. As a matter of fact, he
would be inclined to think that a belief in miracles is
indispensable to the survival of any spiritual life. In Europe,
from the 18th century onwards, the conviction that
spiritual forces can act effectively on material events has
given way to a belief in the inexorable rule of natural law.
The result has been that the experience of the spiritual
has become more and more inaccessible to modern society.
No known religion has become mature without embracing
both the spiritual and the magical. If it rejects the spiritual,
religion becomes a mere weapon to dominate the world,
unable to reform or even restrain the men who dominate
it. Such was the case in Nazism and in modern Japan.
If, however, religion rejects the magical side of life, it
cuts itself off from the living forces of the world to such
an extent that it cannot even bring the spiritual side of
man to maturity.

It has, therefore, been essential to Buddhism to combine
lofty metaphysics with an adherence to the most commonly
accepted superstitions of mankind. Even in a Scripture as
exalted and other-worldly as the Prajñāpāramitā, the
traces of this synthesis are clearly visible. The chief
message of the Prajñāpāramitā books is that perfect wisdom
can be attained only by the complete and total extinction

of all self-interest, and only in an emptiness in which everything that we see around us has disappeared like an insignificant dream. But side by side with this extreme spiritual teaching, we find the same perfection of wisdom recommended as a sort of magical talisman or lucky amulet ; and the tangible and visible advantages which perfect wisdom confers in this very life here and now are set out in loving detail. The perfection of wisdom protects from the attacks of others, from illness, from violent death and from all ' worldly ills.' Beneficial deities will guard the believer, and the evil spirits will have no chance against him. *" When one bears this perfection of wisdom in mind and goes into battle, one will not lose one's life therein. Swords and sticks will be unable to touch the body of the believer."* Among all the paradoxes with which the history of Buddhism presents us, this combination of spiritual negation of self-interest with magical subservience to self-interest is perhaps one of the most striking. Illogical though it may seem, a great deal of the actual life of the Buddhist religion has been due to it.

The Influence of the Laity

We have just considered the services—spiritual, mythological and magical—which the Samgha rendered to the laity. Our account of popular Buddhism would be incomplete without a sketch of the effect which Asoka's patronage (c. 250 B.C.) seems to have had on the attitude of the monks to the laity.

Originally, the monks seem to have given very little scope to the laity. There were, of course, discourses and advice on spiritual problems. There was some outlet for devotional needs by worship of caityas and stupas, and by pilgrimage to the holy places. There was almost no ritual or ceremony in which laymen could participate. Contact with the magical properties of the relics of the Buddha and of his foremost disciples gave a sense of strength to laymen, for whom the relic worship was reserved, since for the monks it was held to be a waste of time and effort. For the rest, the Buddhists worshipped the Hindu deities like everybody else, and used the spells of the Hindu environment to further their aims. Since on the whole the average man finds it easier to worship his gods than to do their will, the monks continually remind the laymen that the Buddha is best honoured not by worship, but by doing the duties enjoined. The minimum duties of a householder are summed up in what was traditionally known as *The Three Treasures*, or *Jewels*, and the observance of the five Precepts. The formula of the Three Jewels, which has been recited for more than 2,500 years, runs like this :

> " *To the Buddha for refuge I go.*
> *To the Dharma for refuge I go.*
> *To the Samgha for refuge I go.*
> *For the second time to the Buddha for refuge I go.*
> *For the second time to the Dharma for refuge I go.*
> *For the second time to the Samgha for refuge I go.*
> *For the third time to the Buddha for refuge I go.*
> *For the third time to the Dharma for refuge I go.*
> *For the third time to the Samgha for refuge I go.*"

As for the five commandments, the accepted formula is :

1. *To abstain from taking life.*
2. *To abstain from taking what is not given.*
3. *To abstain from going wrong about sensuous pleasures.*
4. *To abstain from false speech.*
5. *To abstain from intoxicants as tending to cloud the mind.*

These commandments are capable of much interpretation, but their essential meaning is perfectly clear.

The patronage of Asoka seems to have brought about a considerable change in the attitude to the laity. Some sections of the order appear from then onwards to have made a greater bid for popularity. We must particularly mention the sect of the *Mahasanghikas* who from the beginning of their separate existence had tried to make the order of monks more comprehensive by relaxing the Vinaya rules which, by their very strictness, excluded many potential members. Engaged as they were for about a century in combating the somewhat stiff exclusiveness of some of the other sects, they strove, after Asoka, to find a bigger place for the laity; and the other sects collaborated more or less wholeheartedly in the new approach. As a result, Buddhism became more of an all-round religion than it had been before. The Buddha became a kind of God, the highest God of all. The adoration of the Buddha was rendered more concrete by the representation of the Buddha in human form, which developed one or two centuries after Asoka. The teaching, instead of being chiefly concerned with Nirvana, ' Dharmas,' ' Concentrations,' and similar subjects, unattractive to laymen, lays greater stress on the doctrines of Karma and Rebirth, which seem to concern the average man much more closely. A large popular literature for the edification of the laity was produced. This literature consists of stories of the former lives of the Buddha, which are preserved for us either as *Jatakas* (Birth stories), or as *Avadanas* (see p.32). In many temples sculptures illustrated those stories. This new literature contains nothing about the monks and their life in the monasteries. It has little to do with the fundamental teachings of Buddhism. It is concerned just with the general moral virtues, and the inexorable law of Karma, according to which we reap as we sow, however many lives it may take for the reward or the punishment to come to fruition. We have here to do with a new gospel—a gospel for the busy householder—which strives to stimulate his imagination and devotion and to bind him in loyalty to the Buddhist order.

This concern for the needs of the laity gained in momentum as time went on, and it resulted in the development of the Mahayana (see Chapter V). It is here sufficient to give some of the reasons why the patronage of Asoka should have created a kind of crisis in the order. The royal patronage had been lavish but short-lived. It had meant that a part of the crown revenue was used for the upkeep of the monks. Many persons would have joined the order without any real vocation just because it offered a fairly easy life. Much of the primitive simplicity of monastic life had gone. The monks lived no longer content with any old rags for their dress, but had come to rely on gifts of robes. Many of them would no longer beg for food, but have regular meals cooked in their monasteries. As the Scriptures were written down, the monks would become accustomed to the accessories of learning, and learning proved itself here as detrimental to the vows of poverty as in the case of the early Dominicans and Franciscans. In all these ways the monks had given hostages to fortune and become more dependent on outside support than ever before.

At the same time, it must be remembered that a certain aloofness from mundane matters as a result of Buddhist practices may easily militate against the survival of the religion. It is, indeed, remarkable how closely interwoven the monastic community was with the life of the clans in Magadha in the first decades of Buddhist history. This intimate contact with the villagers would in many cases have been dissolved when the Royal Treasury took over the responsibility for the upkeep of monks. When Asoka's support was withdrawn, a great need arose to strengthen the bonds of the monks with the outside world, and to win the goodwill of the householders. The Mahayana, with its greater solicitude for the salvation of the many, had its origin in these circumstances ; and it was a successful way of meeting the crisis.

IV

THE OLD WISDOM SCHOOL

Sects

IN ca 480 B.C., when the Buddha died, a number of Buddhist monastic communities seem to have been in existence in the North-East of India. The loss of the Buddha's physical presence and of his guidance were felt as a severe blow. No successor was appointed. In the words of the Scriptures, only the Buddha's doctrine (Dharma) remained to guide his community. This doctrine did not, of course, exist in a written form. For four centuries the Scriptures were not written down, and only existed in the memory of the monks. Like the Brahmins, the Buddhists had a strong aversion to writing down religious knowledge. In ancient times we find such an attitude as far West as Gaul, where, according to Julius Caesar (De Bello Gall : VI, 14) the Druids " *did not think it proper to commit these utterances (on philosophy) to writing. I believe they have adopted the practice for two reasons— they do not wish the rule (discipline) to become common property, nor those who learn the rule to rely on writing and so neglect the cultivation of the memory ; and, in fact, it does usually happen that the assistance of writing tends to relax the diligence of the student and the action of the memory.*" It is incidentally due to this aversion to written records that our knowledge of the early history of Buddhism is so scrappy and unsatisfactory.

It is, however, obvious that during those centuries, when the sacred texts were kept alive by being recited or chanted communally, a great variety of traditions was bound to develop in different localities, particularly as the religion spread. It is commonly believed that immediately after the decease of the Buddha a council of 500 Arhats rehearsed the Scriptures as Ananda remembered them. But even at that time there was another monk, who said that the sayings of the Lord as he remembered them were quite different, and he was allowed to go in peace.

Of the schools and sects which developed as a result of differences in Scriptural tradition, in the philosophical interpretation of the Scriptures and in local customs (see pp. 79–81), we must first of all consider those sects which we can group together as *The Old Wisdom School*.

Sariputra

It has often been observed that it is not the founder himself, but one of his followers who shapes the policy of religious and monastic movements in the first generation of their existence. The specific shape of the organisation of the Franciscan Order owed more to Elias of Cortona than to Saint Francis himself, that of the Jesuit Order to Laynez than to Saint Ignatius of Loyola. As Saint Paul stands to Jesus, as Abu Bekr to Mohammed, as Xenocrates to Plato, as Stalin to Lenin, so does Sariputra stand to the Buddha.

It is easy to see why a comparatively subordinate follower should exert a more decisive influence than the founder himself. The founder would be, of course, the living source of the life-giving inspiration which initiates the movement, but a great deal of his teachings and insight would be beyond the range of more ordinary people. With less genius the successor produces a kind of portable edition of the Gospel which accords more with the needs of the average man and his capacity for comprehension. Robin's remark covers all the cases referred to above when he says about Xenocrates, Plato's successor, that he " enclosed Plato's living thought in the rigid framework of a bookish doctrine, mechanised in response to the daily needs of teaching." It is true that Sariputra died 6 months before the Buddha, and therefore could not take over the organization after his death. The influence Sariputra exerted was due to the shape which he gave to the teaching, and which determined not only the training of the monks for a long time, but also decided which aspects of the Buddha's doctrine should be emphasised, and which should be relegated into the background.

As a matter of fact, Sariputra's version and understanding of the Buddha's doctrine dominated the Buddhist community for about fifteen to twenty generations. He dominated it in the sense that one section of the community adopted his interpretation, and that another section formed their opinions in conscious and direct opposition to it.

Sariputra, 'The Son of Sari,' was born in Magadha of a Brahmin family. He early took up the religious life under Sañjaya, a thorough-going sceptic. Within a fortnight of entering the Buddhist order he attained full enlightenment, and from then onwards until his death spent his time teaching and instructing the younger monks. His was a predominantly analytical intellect. He liked to arrange knowledge so that it could be easily learned and remembered, studied and taught, and there is a certain soberness and dryness about him.

To the Theravadins and Sarvastivadins, Sariputra appeared as a kind of second founder of the religion. Just as the Buddha is the King of Dharma, so Sariputra is its Field Marshal. He excelled all other disciples in 'Wisdom' and learning. "*If we except the Saviour of the world, no one possesses even one-sixteenth part of Sariputra's Wisdom.*" We must bear in mind that the word 'Wisdom' here is taken in a quite special sense, as a kind of methodical contemplation based on the rules of the Abhidharma (see p. 105 sq.).

There were, however, other currents in the Order. Many monks may not have found the Abhidharma very much to their liking. In their memory, other disciples stood out as more important than Sariputra,—for instance, Mahamogallana, who excelled in psychic power, or Ananda, the Buddha's personal attendant for 20 years—the most lovable of the great disciples, but, to the orthodox Abhidharmists, a constant object of adverse comment and a kind of scapegoat for all the misfortunes which befell the Church. Among the opponents of Sariputra's interpretation the Sautrantikas were the most influential group.

About four hundred years after the death of the Buddha, the literature of the Mahayana (see Chapter V) began to develop. Sariputra's name continued to represent a programme. In works like the Prajñāpāramitā-Sutras, the Lotus of the Good Law, and the Avatamsaka-Sutra, Sariputra perpetually occurs as the representative of an inferior kind of wisdom, who has still a great deal to learn, and as a person of slow and dull intellect, who was unable to understand the real teaching of the Buddha—so that for his sake the Buddha taught an inferior form of his doctrine, known as the Hinayana.

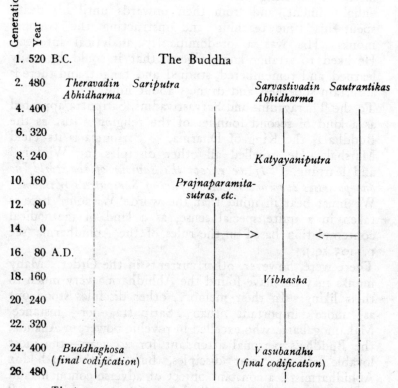

The two arrows indicate that the thought of the Mahayana and of the Sautrantikas was developed as a reaction to the Abhidharma of the Sarvastivadins.

Before I set out the main tenets of the school which derives from Sariputra, I must say a few words in explanation of the term *Old Wisdom School,* by which I refer to it throughout this book. It is called *Wisdom* School because 'Wisdom' is in the Scriptures of Sariputra's School held to be the highest of the five cardinal virtues, which are Faith, Vigour, Mindfulness, Concentration, and Wisdom. Among these the development of Wisdom alone can assure final salvation. Sariputra's School is called *Old* as distinct from the *New* Wisdom School which developed in reaction to it after about 100 B.C. (see Chapter V).

Arhats

There is no better way of understanding the spirit of the Old Wisdom School than by considering the type of man which it wished to produce, and the idea of perfection which it set up for the emulation of its disciples. The ideal man, the saint or sage at the highest stage of development is called an 'Arhat.' The Buddhists themselves derived the word 'Arhat' from the two words 'Ari,' which means 'enemy,' and 'han,' which means 'to kill,' so that an Arhat would be 'A slayer of the foe,' the foe being the passions. Modern scholars prefer to derive the word from 'Arhati,' 'to be worthy of,' and meaning 'deserving, worthy,' i.e. of worship and gifts. It appears that originally, at the rise of Buddhism, the term 'Arhat' was applied popularly to all ascetics. As a technical term in Buddhism, however, it is restricted to the perfect saints who are fully and finally emancipated. The Buddha himself is habitually called an Arhat.

Through Buddhist art many idealised portraits of Arhats have come down to us. An Arhat is normally depicted as dignified, bald, and with a certain severity. The Scriptures of the Old Wisdom School define or describe an Arhat by a standard formula, which is repeated very frequently. An Arhat is a person *in whom the ' outflows '* (i.e. sense desire, becoming, ignorance, wrong views) *have dried up, who has greatly lived, who has done what had to be done, who has shed the burden, who has won his aim, who is no longer bound to ' becoming,' who is set free, having rightly come to know*. He has shed all attachment to I and mine, is secluded, zealous, and earnest, inwardly free, fully controlled, master of himself, self-restrained, dispassionate and austere.

The *Avadana Sataka* (II, 348) gives a slightly fuller description of an Arhat : "*He exerted himself, he strove and struggled, and thus he realised that this circle of 'Birth-and-Death,' with its 'Five Constituents' (Skandhas) is in constant flux. He rejected all the conditions of existence which are brought about by a compound of conditions, since it is their nature to decay and crumble away, to change and to be destroyed. He abandoned all the 'defilements' and won Arhatship. On becoming an Arhat, he lost all his attachment to the 'Triple World'* (i.e. the world of sense desire, the world of form, the formless world). *Gold and a clod of earth were the same to him. The sky and the palm of his hand were to his mind the same. He remained cool (in danger) like the fragrant sandalwood to the axe which cuts it down. By his Gnosis he had torn the 'eggshell of ignorance.' He had obtained Gnosis, the 'Super-knowledges'* [1] *and the 'Powers of analytical Insight.' He became averse to worldly gain and honour, and he became worthy of being honoured, saluted and revered by the Devas (gods), including Indra, Vishnu and Krishna.*"

Except for the Buddhas, no being could be as perfect as an Arhat. It was logical to assume that a Buddha would possess a number of additional perfections as compared with an Arhat (Dial. II, 1–3, III, 6). In the early days, however, little attention was paid to that question, which seemed to be devoid of any practical importance. It was only after three or four centuries, when the Arhat ideal lost its hold over a section of the Buddhist community (see p. 114 sq.), that the question of the difference between Arhats and Buddhas began to exercise the curiosity of Buddhist thinkers.

---

[1] i.e. the heavenly eye; the heavenly ear; the cognition of others' thoughts; the ability to recollect former lives ; wonder-working powers ; the knowledge that his 'outflows' are dried up.

Mystics of all ages have never tired of mapping out the steps of the spiritual ladder. Before a man could become an Arhat a number of recognised stages had to be passed through. It is not necessary here to give all the details, but some understanding of the turning point in a man's career is essential for all that follows. All people are said to belong to one of two classes : they are either *ordinary people* or they are *saints*. The saints are called *Aryas*.

In Sanskrit *Aryan* means 'noble,' 'right' or 'good.' The ordinary, common people live entirely in the world of their senses and the spiritual world beyond is to them either a matter of indifference, or of mere vague and impotent longing. The supra-sensory world of abiding reality is known in Buddhist theory either by the name of *Nirvana*—which is the final and ultimate state of quietude—or as the *Path*. The Path is the same as Nirvana, considered as it manifests itself to us during certain stages of our spiritual progress. As a result of the spiritual practices which will be described soon, we reach, in the course of time, an experience which transforms us from 'common people' into 'Saints.' It is technically known as the *Entrance into the stream*. To some extent it corresponds to what Christians call 'conversion.' On that occasion, the vision of the *Supra-mundane Path* bursts in upon us, and in the words of Buddhaghosa we see the 'Path' as we see the bright full moon through a rent in the clouds—the clouds symbolising our sensory attachments. Once the stream is won a long struggle is still ahead. It sometimes takes many lives to wear down our attachments to sensory objects and the love of ourselves. But the corner has been turned.

Practices

In Buddhism the meditational practices are the well from which springs all that is alive in it. The historical development of Buddhism is essentially an elaboration of ever new means of salvation. It is, however, not so easy to give an intelligible account of these practices, because they are all of them methods which have the renunciation of the world as their aim, and most people to-day are not really interested in such an aim. It is only at two points that these methods hit the ken of the average man—at the beginning and at the end. The starting-point of all Buddhist endeavours is discontent with the world as it is found ; many people feel such discontent fairly often, although they rarely know what to do with it. At the end the Buddhist struggles bring forth the fruit of even-mindedness which everybody would very much like to have, if he only knew how to get it. But in between the beginning and the end of the way there is a great deal of toil which people usually prefer to avoid.

It is in the nature of things that intimate knowledge of the Path is given only to those who walk on it. Nevertheless, we shall now try to explain the methods which were used by the Old Wisdom School to train Arhats. These methods traditionally fall under three headings, namely, *Moral Discipline*, *Trance*, and *Wisdom*. We are fortunate in possessing an excellent text-book dealing with these practices in Buddhaghosa's *Visuddhimagga*, which has been translated, though very imperfectly, as *The Path of Purity*.

Moral Discipline

We spoke above about the monastic side of Buddhist discipline (see Chapter II). The Buddhists believe that knowledge or insight is not mastered when we know about it as verbal expression, but only when we have impressed it upon our reluctant body. Little is gained by having an abstract conviction of the unimportance of sensory pleasures, or of the inherent repulsiveness and unloveliness of that which excites it, if this conviction of one's tongue and brain is contradicted by one's muscles, or one's glands, or one's skin. These parts of one's body act as the embodiments of desires which have become almost automatic. If we are greedy for food, look at all the girls we meet in the street and become miserable when we are cold, hungry and uncomfortable, then our intellectual convictions about the unimportance of worldly things possess only a fraction of our personality and are refuted in action by the remainder of it. This is well illustrated by the Hindu story about the teacher who asks his disciple what he values most of all. The disciple dutifully replies : " Brahma, or the supreme Spirit." The teacher thereupon takes his disciple to a pond, ducks his head under the water for two minutes, and then asks his disciple what he desired most at the end of these two minutes. The disciple could not help replying that it was air he desired most of all, and that the supreme Spirit appeared curiously irrelevant at that moment. While we are in the frame of mind of that disciple, what use is the Holy Doctrine to us ?

A mindful and disciplined attitude to the body is the very basis of Buddhist training. The step that frees us more decisively than any other from the illusions of individuality is the rejection of our self-infatuated and narcissistic attachment to the body. The physical body has always stood in the very centre of attention : " *Within this very body, mortal as it is and only six feet in length, I do declare to you are the world and the origin of the world, and the ceasing of the world, and likewise the Path that leads to the cessation thereof.*"

The human mind is wont to operate through contrasts. When we look at Buddhist works of art, either sculptures or paintings, we find that the human form is treated with great sensuousness in Amaravati and Ajanta, and that it is idealised into an ethereal refinement in the art of China and Tibet. A great deal of the training of the monk, however, consisted in the exact opposite. Again and again he is taught to view this material body as repulsive, disgusting and most offensive : " *And further the disciple contemplates this body, from the sole of the foot upwards, and from the top of the hair downwards, with a skin stretched over it, and filled with manifold impurities. There are in this body :*

> *hairs of the head, hairs of the body, nails, teeth, skin ;*
> *muscles, sinews, bones, marrow, kidneys ;*
> *heart, liver, serous membranes, spleen, lungs ;*
> *intestines, mesentery, stomach, excrement, brain ;*
> *bile, digestive juices, pus, blood, grease, fat ;*
> *tears, sweat, spittle, snot, fluid of the joints, urine.*"

When such a vision or image of the " thirty-two parts of the body " is superimposed on the sight of an attractive woman, it is sure to have some disintegrating effect on any sexual passions there may be. In addition, the Buddhists, like the Jains, are taught to concentrate their attention on the " *Nine Apertures,*" from which filthy and repulsive substances flow unceasingly—the two eyes, the two ears, the two nostrils, the mouth, the urethra, and the anus. Not content with this, the monk is urged to visit cemeteries or burial grounds in order to see what his body is really like in the varying stages of decomposition. In all this, Buddhist practice goes deliberately against the habits of civilised society which taboos the very aspects of life which the Buddhist dwells upon. The aim of civilised society is the very opposite to that of the Dharma, and its average member is put off by any consideration which might endanger his somewhat precarious joy of life.

Like so many Christians the Buddhist is not supposed to take pride in his body, but to feel shame and disgust towards it. We must never forget that in this system of thought it was due to an act of will on our part that we joined ourselves to such a body, because it is such an admirable tool for preferences and desires. When we see how precarious our body is, how exposed to all sorts of dangers and frailties, how repulsive in its essential function, then we should feel shame and horror at the conditions in which our divine Self has landed itself— precariously placed between the two skins which, as we would say in modern jargon, have developed from the ectoderm and the entoderm respectively. Certainly in such conditions our Self is not at its best. Certainly it cannot be free and at its ease in such conditions which are created by greed, and which induce more greed. In this respect the Buddhist Tradition agrees with the well-known poem by Andrew Marvell, when he says :

> " *Oh who shall from its dungeon raise*
> *This soul enslaved so many ways*
> *With bonds of bone, that fettered stands*
> *In feet and manacled in hands ;*
> *Here blinded with an eye, and there*
> *Deaf with the drumming of an ear !* "

It is nice to find words with which to convince others

of the emptiness of all conditioned things. It is held to be
more essential to teach one's own body this lesson. The
sense organs are singled out for special attention, and they
are subjected to rigid control. The technical term is
" *indriya-gutti*," literally " *guarding the sense organs*."
When a monk walks along he should look straight ahead
in front of him, and not look at everything right and left
the whole time.

> " *Let not the eye wander like forest ape*
> *Or trembling wood-deer, or affrighted child.*
> *The eyes should be cast downward, they should look*
> *The distance of a yoke, he shall not serve*
> *His thoughts dominion, like a restless ape.*"

Then there is what is called " *guarding the doors of the
senses*." We may distinguish two components in sensory
experience. The one is the mere sensory apprehension
of a stimulus, the other is our volitional reaction to it.
The contact of our sense organs, with their specific stimuli
is an " *occasion*" for, to use the Buddhist formula,
" *covetous, sad, evil and unwholesome states to flow in over
us, so long as we dwell unrestrained*" with regard to the sense
organs. We must therefore learn to check our insatiable
desire for sights, sounds, etc., which really estrange us
from ourselves ; we must learn to prevent our mind or
thoughts or heart from becoming entranced with the
objects which our senses meet. We must learn to examine
each stimulus as it enters the citadel of our mind so that
our unwholesome passions should not cluster round it
and be fortified by finding again and again a new centre.
Anyone who has tried to carry out the Buddha's instructions
for guarding his senses knows what an enormous degree of
violence he must inflict on his mind, even to keep it still
for one or two minutes. How can we find out what is the
true nature of our mind if we cannot protect it from
perpetual invasion by what is external to it and view it
as it is in its own pure self ?

Trance

The second group of Buddhist methods is traditionally
referred to as *Concentration*. The Sanscrit word is

Samādhi, a word which etymologically corresponds to the Greek " synthesis." To " concentrate " consists in narrowing the field of attention in a manner and for a time determined by the will. The result is that the mind becomes steady, like the flame of an oil lamp in the absence of the wind. Emotionally speaking, concentration results in a state of quiet calm, because one has withdrawn for the time being from everything which can cause turmoil. Three kinds of practices are traditionally comprised under " Concentration " :

  1. *The* 8 *Dhyanas.*
  2. *The* 4 *Unlimited.*
  3. *Occult Powers.*

These three items were the germ of much that unfolded itself in the later development of Buddhism. The practice of the Dhyanas became of decisive importance in the Yogacara system ; the Unlimited were one of the seeds of the early Mahayana ; and the Occult Powers were destined to become the core of the Tantra. We now have to explain each of these items one by one.

1. *The Dhyānas*, in Pali *Jhānas*, are means for transcending the impact of sensory stimuli and our normal reactions to it. One begins the exercise by concentrating on a sense stimulus—such as a circle made of light red sand, or a circle made of blue flowers, or a bowl of water, or an image of the Buddha. The first stage of trance is achieved when one can suppress for the time being one's unwholesome tendencies—i.e. sense-desire, ill-will, sloth and torpor, excitedness and perplexity. One learns to become detached from them and is able to direct all one's thoughts unto the chosen object. At the second stage one goes beyond the thoughts which went towards and round the object. One ceases to be discursive and adopts a more unified, peaceful and assured attitude of confidence, which the texts call *Faith*. This attitude of groping or stretching oneself out towards something which one does not know discursively, but which one knows would be more satisfying than anything known discursively, results in elation and rapturous delight. In a manner of speaking, this elation is still a blot and a pollution, and in its turn it has to be

overcome. This task is achieved in the next two stages, so that in the fourth Dhyana one ceases to be conscious of ease and dis-ease, well-fare and ill-fare, elation and dejection, promotion or hindrance as applied to oneself. Personal preferences have become so uninteresting as to be imperceptible. What remains is a condition of limpid, translucent and alert receptiveness *in utter purity of mindfulness and evenmindedness.* Above this, there are four " formless " dhyānas, which represent stages of overcoming the vestiges of the object. As long as we suck ourselves on to any object, however refined, we cannot drop into Nirvana. One first sees everything as *boundless space,* then as *unlimited consciousness,* then as *emptiness,* then by giving up even the act which grasped the nothingness, one reaches a station where there is *neither perception nor non-perception.* Consciousness and self-consciousness are here at the very margin of disappearance.

Above this there is the *cessation of perception and feelings,* where one is said to *touch Nirvana with one's body.* Outwardly this state appears as one of coma. Motion, speech and thought are absent. Only life and warmth remain. Even the unconscious impulses are said to be *asleep.* Inwardly it seems to correspond to what other mystical traditions knew as the ineffable awareness of *Naked Contemplation,* a naked intent stretching into Reality, the union of nothing with nothing, or of the One with the One, a dwelling in the *Divine Abyss,* or the *Desert of the Godhead.*

According to the doctrine of the orthodox, these states, however exalted they may be, do not guarantee final salvation. That requires the complete obliteration of the individual self, whereas these ecstatic experiences cannot achieve more than a temporary self-extinction. The mind becomes progressively more simple, more renounced, more calm, but it is only for the duration of the Dhyana that this self is forgotten. Wisdom alone can enter the *Great Emptiness.* It alone can enter the Nirvana which permanently and for all time replaces the impact of sensory stimuli as the force which directs our mind, as long as there is a mind to direct.

2. The *Unlimited* (*Apramāna*) are methods of cultivating the emotions. They proceed by four stages : *Friendliness* (Mettā), *Compassion*, *Sympathetic Joy*, and *Evenmindedness*. The essential purpose of these exercises consists in reducing the boundary lines between oneself and other people— be they very dear, indifferent, or hostile. One attempts to feel equally friendly towards oneself, friends, strangers, and enemies. *Friendliness* is regarded as a virtue. It is defined as an attitude in which one wishes well to others, desires to promote their welfare and tries to discover behind an often unpleasing or forbidding exterior the lovable sides of their nature. It is not the place here to expound technical details of these meditations. Their spirit may become evident from this short passage from the Mettā Sutta :

" *May all beings be happy and at their ease ! May they be joyous and live in safety ! All beings, whether weak or strong—omitting none—in high, middle, or low realms of existence, small or great, visible or invisible, near or far away, born or to be born—may all beings be happy and at their ease ! Let none deceive another, or despise any being in any state ; let none by anger or ill-will wish harm to another ! Even as a mother watches over and protects her child, her only child, so with a boundless mind should one cherish all living beings, radiating friendliness over the entire world, above, below, and all around without limit ; so let him cultivate a boundless goodwill towards the entire world, uncramped, free from ill-will or enmity.*"

Next in order is *Compassion*, far more difficult to develop. It is an attitude in which one concentrates on the sufferings of others, suffers with them and desires to remove that suffering. Thirdly, after having learned to call forth compassion at will, one should practise *Sympathetic Joy*. Here one concentrates on the prosperous condition of others, is glad about it, and enters into joyous sympathy with their happiness. Last of all is *Evenmindedness*, to which we may, according to tradition, successfully aspire only after we have repeatedly attained the third dhyana with regard to the first three emotional states. It is, therefore, but rarely attained and we need only mention it here.

One is not only told to develop these emotional attitudes, but to make them *Unlimited* in the sense that one should learn to treat all people alike, and to steadily diminish one's personal preferences and antipathies. Anyone who has tried to carry out Buddhaghosa's prescriptions for doing these exercises, will have noticed that, in our normal state of scatter-brainedness, we are unable to get very far with them. It is assumed that the mind must acquire the refinement and detachment which only the practice of the dhyanas can give it, to carry the *Unlimited* forward to anything like a successful conclusion.

3. There is so much that is eminently rational in Buddhism that the importance of the occult in it has often been underestimated, especially by modern European authors. Such a view ignores two decisive factors, the historical circumstances in which the Buddhist religion has developed, and the laws of the spiritual life. It also makes nonsense of the later stages of Buddhist thought which appear as a degeneration, as a fall from the original heights. Buddhism has had its life among populations who believed as sincerely in magic as modern town-dwellers believe in Science. The relics of the Buddha were prized for their magical potency. The heavens, the rivers, the forests with their trees, the wells, almost the whole of Nature was filled with spirits. Thaumaturgical miracle-working is a common-place of Indian life, and it was regularly used by all religious bodies for the conversion of outsiders. Throughout the Buddhist world, representations of miracles are favourite subjects of art. Even if the occult had not formed a part of the Holy Doctrine itself, it would have been impressed upon the church by its social environment.

There is, however, an additional point. Experience in all countries of the earth has shown that one cannot possibly cultivate a spiritual life without at the same time calling forth psychic powers and sharpening one's psychic senses. This fact can arouse astonishment only where spiritual practices are virtually unknown. As a result of practising the trances the Buddha and his disciples came into the possession of all kinds of miraculous or magical powers

called *Riddhi*, or *Iddhi*. Some of these are what we now
call *psychic*—clairvoyance, clairaudience, recollection of
former births, and knowledge of the thoughts of others.
Others were more physical. The disciples could "*pass at
will through wall or fence or hill as if through air, pass in
and out of the solid earth, walk on the water's surface, or
glide through the air.*" By magical action, they could
prolong life in this body. Or they could project or conjure
up a double of themselves, and make it endure. They
could give their body the form of a boy, of a snake, etc.
The Christian Gospels have to some extent been influenced
by Buddhist doctrines, which were known in Alexandria
and other parts of the Mediterranean world. The miraculous side of Buddhism in particular seems to have
appealed to the early Christians. Saint Peter, walking
on the water, trod in the footsteps of many Buddhist
Saints. One of the favourite miracles of the Buddhists
was the *Twin Miracle*. Fire streamed forth from the
upper part of the body of the Tathagata, and "*from his
lower body proceeds a torrent of water.*" In John VII, 38,
we find the curious statement : "*He that believes in me
as the Scripture has said, out of his belly shall flow rivers of
living water.*" As a third example, we may mention that
the Tathagata could, if he should so wish, remain for
the aeon just as the Christ "*abideth for the aeon.*"
Although psychic abilities are inseparable from a certain
stage of spiritual development, they are not in all cases
beneficial to the character or the spirituality of the person
in whom they manifest themselves. There is much danger
in psychic manifestations : conceit may be further increased;
one may search for the power and lose the kingdom and the
glory ; one may expose oneself to contact with forces
which demoralise. On the whole, the attitude of the
Buddhist Church during the first millennium of its existence
seems to have been that the occult and the psychic are
allright as long as one does not take too much notice of
them, and exhibits them as a kind of cheap stunt to the
populace. One day the Buddha came across an ascetic
who sat by the bank of a river, and who had practised
austerities for 25 years. The Buddha asked him what he

had got out of all his labour. The ascetic proudly replied that now at last he could cross the river by walking on the water. The Buddha tried to point out that this was little gain for so much labour, since for one penny the ferry would take him across.

Wisdom

Wisdom is the highest virtue of all. It is usual to translate the Sanscrit term *Pra-jñā (Pali : Paññā)* by 'wisdom,' and that is not positively inaccurate. When we are dealing with the Buddhist tradition, however, we must always bear in mind that there Wisdom is taken in a special sense that is truly unique in the history of human thought. 'Wisdom' is understood by Buddhists as the *methodical contemplation of 'Dharmas.'* This is clearly shown by Buddhaghosa's formal and academic definition of the term : "*Wisdom has the characteristic of penetrating into dharmas as they are themselves. It has the function of destroying the darkness of delusion which covers the own-being of dharmas. It has the manifestation of not being deluded. Because of the statement : 'He who is concentrated knows, sees what really is,' concentration is its proximate cause.*"

The methods by which Wisdom should be developed have been set out in the *Abhidharma* books. These books are obviously later than the other parts of the Canon (see p. 32). Some schools, like the Sautrantikas, insisted that they were not the authentic Buddha word, and should therefore be rejected. The meaning of the word *Abhi-dharma* is not quite certain. Abhi-dharma may mean *Further* dharma, or *Supreme* dharma. It is difficult to know at what time the Abhidharma books were composed. One does not, perhaps, go far wrong when assigning them to the first two centuries after the death of the Buddha.

Two recensions of the Abhidharma books have come down to us : a set of seven in Pali and another set of seven, preserved in Chinese, but originally composed in Sanskrit. The Pali texts represent the tradition of the Theravadins, the Sanskrit texts that of the Sarvastivadins. About seven centuries after the original composition of the Abhidharma books, the teachings of both Abhidharma traditions were finally codified, probably between 400 and 450 A.D. This work was carried out for the Theravadins in Ceylon by Buddha-ghosa, and for the Sarvastivadins by Vasabandhu in the North of India. After 450 A.D. there has been little, if any, further development in the Abhidharma doctrines.

It must be admitted that the style of the Abhidharma books is extremely dry and unattractive. The treatment of the various topics resembles that which one would expect in a treatise on accountancy, or a manual of engineering, or a handbook of physics. Allurements of style are not altogether absent from Buddhist literature when it was destined for propaganda and attempted to win the consent of the unconverted, or to edify the sentiments of the faithful. The Abhidharma books, however, were meant for the very core of the Buddhist elite, and it was assumed that the Wisdom acquired from their perusal would be a sufficient reward and incentive of study.

The chief purpose of Buddhism is the extinction of separate individuality, which is brought about when we cease to *identify* anything with ourselves. From long habit it has become quite natural to us to think of our own experiences in the terms of ' I ' and ' mine.' Even when we are convinced that strictly speaking such words are too nebulous to be tenable and that their unthinking use leads to unhappiness in our daily lives, even then do we go on using them. The reasons for this are manifold. One of them is that we see no alternative way of explaining our experiences to ourselves except by way of statements which include such words as " I " and " Mine." It is the great merit of the Abhidharma that it has attempted to construct an alternative method of accounting for our experiences, a method in which the " I " and " Mine " are completely omitted, and in which all the agents invoked are impersonal dharmas. The Abhidharma is the oldest recorded psychology, and it is, I think, still sound for the purpose for which it was designed.

What then is our individuality in terms of *Dharmas ?* A person with all his possible belongings, can, according to Buddhist tradition, be analysed into five *Heaps*, technically called *Skandhas*. Anything a person may think of as his own, anything he may appropriate or lean on, must fall within those five groups. It must be either :

1. *Material.*
   (*Our physical body and material possessions*)
2. *A feeling.*
3. *A perception.*
4. *An impulse.*
5. *An act of consciousness.*

The false belief in individuality or personality is said to arise from the invention of a " Self " over and above those five heaps. In the form of a diagram :

REALITY   FICTION

FORM
(=*matter*)
FEELING
(*pleasant, unpleasant, neutral*)
PERCEPTIONS
(*sight, etc.*)
IMPULSES
(*greed, hate, faith, wisdom, etc.*)
CONSCIOUSNESS

       ⟶   " SELF "

The insertion of a fictitious self into the actuality of our experience can be recognised wherever I assume that anything is mine, or that I am anything, or that anything is myself. In order to make this teaching slightly more tangible, I will return to our example of the toothache (p. 18). Normally, one simply says " *I have a toothache.*" To Sariputra this would have appeared as a very unscientific way of speaking. Neither *I*, nor *have*, nor *toothache* are counted among the ultimate facts of existence (dharmas). In the Abhidharma personal expressions are replaced by impersonal ones. Impersonally, in terms of ultimate events, this experience is divided up into :

1. This here is the *form*, i.e. the tooth as matter ;
2. There is a painful *feeling ;*
3. There is a sight-, touch-, and pain- *perception* of the tooth ;

4. There is by way of *volitional reactions* : resentment at pain, fear of possible consequences for future well-being, greed for physical well-being, etc.

5. There is *consciousness*,—an awareness of all this.

The ' I ' of commonsense parlance has disappeared : it forms no part of this analysis. It is not one of the ultimate events. One might reply, of course : an imagined ' I ' is a part of the actual experience. In that case, it would be booked either under the skandha of consciousness (corresponding to the Self as the subject), or as one of the fifty-four items included among the skandha of volitional reactions which is called a *wrong belief in self*.

This analysis is offered as an example of Abhidharma teaching, and it is not claimed that by itself it will appreciably reduce the woes we may feel about aching teeth. The analysis can be applied to any item of our experience whatsoever. The Abhidharma books supply us with a list of between 79 and 174 factors which they claim as *Ultimates*, and as more real than the *things* of the common-sense world which can be analysed into them. At the same time, they give us some rules for combining those factors in the form of a classified list of the possible relations between *Ultimates*. The five skandhas are merely the first five of those factors. The reader should remember that in order to make this method work, a great deal of technical knowledge about the contents of the Abhidharma text-books must be combined with great mental discipline and prolonged perseverance in strenuous introspection. Otherwise, neither skill in the meditation nor benefit from it can be expected.

The central idea, however, is clear. Experiences should be analysed into an interplay of impersonal forces. When one has shown up the ultimate events behind the surface appearance of any datum that may present itself inside or outside our so-called personality, then, if we can believe the Abhidharma, one has accounted for it as it really is, or one has seen it as Wisdom sees it. The Western mind must, however, beware of assuming that the dharma theory is offered as a metaphysical explanation of the world, to be discussed and argued about. It is, on the contrary, presented as a practical method of destroying, through meditation, those aspects of the commonsense world which tie down our spirit. Its value is meant to be therapeutical, not theoretical. Properly applied, the method must have a tremendous power to disintegrate unwholesome experience. The meditation on dharmas by itself alone can obviously not uproot all the evil in our hearts. It is not a panacea, a cure-all, but just one of the medicines in the chest of the *Great Physician*. It is, however, bound to contribute to our mental health to the extent that, when it is repeated often enough, it may set up the habit of viewing all things impersonally. The burden of the world should be correspondingly diminished. Sri Aurobindo, in his *Bases of Yoga* has well set out the effect which meditation on dharmas may have on our perspective :

"*In the calm mind, it is the substance of the mental being that is still, so still that nothing disturbs it. If thoughts or activities come, they do not arise at all out of the mind, but they come from outside and cross the mind as a flight of birds crosses the sky in a windless air. It passes, disturbs nothing, leaving no trace. Even if a thousand images, or the most violent events pass across it, the calm stillness remains as if the very texture of the mind were a substance of eternal and indestructible peace. A mind that has achieved this calmness can begin to act, even intensely and powerfully, but it will keep its fundamental stillness— originating nothing from itself, but receiving from Above and giving it a mental form without adding anything of its own, calmly, dispassionately, though with the joy of the Truth and the happy power and light of its passage.*"

We saw that our mental ill-health goes back to the habit of identifying ourselves with what we are not. Our personality appropriates all sorts of pieces of the Universe in things one can see or touch. In these *belongings* our true self gets estranged from itself, and for each and every attachment which we may form we pay the penalty of a corresponding fear, of which we are more or less aware. The Buddha teaches that we can get well—that we can escape this terrible round of Birth-and-Death only by getting rid of these accretions.

To some extent the hold which belongings have upon us is weakened by the practice of sound rules of moral conduct. The Buddhist is advised to possess as little as possible, to give up home and family, to cherish poverty rather than wealth, to prefer giving to getting, etc. In addition, the experience of trance works in the same direction. Although the state of trance itself is comparatively shortlived, nevertheless the memory of it must continue to shake the belief in the ultimate reality of the sensory world. It is the inevitable result of the habitual practice of trance that the things of our common-sense world appear delusive, deceptive, remote and dreamlike, and that they are deprived of the character of solidity and reliability which is usually attributed to them. It is, however, believed that morality and trance cannot by themselves completely uproot and destroy the foundation of our belief in individuality. According to the doctrine of the Old Wisdom School, wisdom alone is able to chase the illusion of individuality from our thoughts where it has persisted from age-old habit. Not action, not trance, but only thought can kill the illusion which resides in thought.

If all our sufferings are attributed to the fact that we identify ourselves with spurious belongings which are not really our own, we imply that we would be really much better off without those belongings. This simple and perfectly obvious inference can also be stated in a more metaphysical way by saying that what we really are is identical with the Absolute. It is assumed first of all that there is an ultimate reality, and secondly that there is a point in ourselves at which we touc thhat ultimate reality. The ultimate reality, also called Dharma by the Buddhists, or Nirvana, is defined as that which stands completely outside the sensory world of illusion and ignorance, a world inextricably interwoven with craving and greed. To get somehow to that ultimate reality is the supremely worthwhile goal of the Buddhist life. The Buddhist idea of ultimate reality is very much akin to the philosophical notion of the 'Absolute,' and not easily distinguished from the notion of God among the more mystical theologians, like Dionysius Areopagita and Eckart. Nirvana is said to be *absolutely* good, and the Dharma *absolutely* true in the sense that they are good and true unquestionably, without any argument, and in all circumstances.

These convictions form the basis of a great deal of Buddhist meditation and contemplation. One distinguishes an unconditional world from the world of conditioned things. We suffer because we identify ourselves with conditioned things, and act as if what happens to them happened to us. By persistent meditation and mortification, we must reject and renounce everything but the highest, which is the Unconditioned alone. In other words, we de-identify ourselves from all conditioned things. The assumption is that if and when we manage to do so habitually and completely, our individual self becomes extinct, and Nirvana automatically takes its place. This approach requires, of course, that we should take a very exalted view of ourselves. In a sense we should be ashamed that our actual being falls short of the Unconditioned. It also involves a high degree of audacity because we must be willing to throw away everything we value in the conviction that it hinders us from regaining our original unconditioned nature. As Buddhaghosa puts it : " *The monk reviews all his conditioned experiences as perilous, he is repelled by them, he frets against them, he takes no delight in them. Just as a golden swan which delights in a fair lake at the foot of Mount Splendid Spur in the Himalayas is loath to dwell in a filthy muddy puddle at the gate of an outcast village, so the Yogin does not delight in complex and conditioned things, but only in the tranquil path.*" Our ability to recollect the godlike stature we had before we fell into this world is regarded as one of the first steps which lead on to the path of perfect wisdom.

By its very definition, the Absolute has no relation to anything. At the same time the idea of salvation implies that there is some kind of contact or fusion between the Unconditioned and the Conditioned. This idea is logically untenable, and when they thought about it, the Buddhists discovered a great number of paradoxes and contradictions (see Chapter V).   If the Absolute as such has no relation to this world, it is neither correct to say that it is transcendent nor that it is immanent.   The Ch'an school of Buddhists made this fact into a basis for meditation, by asking the disciple to answer the question : " *Is the Buddha-nature in this dog ?* "   The Buddha nature is, of course, the Unconditioned, and the dog is taken as a not particularly exalted example of a conditioned object. The correct answer to this question is ' *Nyes,*' i.e. ' *Either yes and no,*' or ' *Neither yes and no.*'

As far as the Absolute itself is concerned, nothing can be said about it at all, nor can anything be done about it. Any exertion put forward in favour of the Unconditioned, results only in useless toil.   Any idea we form of the Absolute is ipso facto false.   Nevertheless, during a considerable part of the way to salvation, some idea of the Absolute is valuable when used as a form or standard by which one measures the value and width of our experiences.   This ' Absolute,' which forms the object of a provisional and ultimately untrue thought, is then, in religious practice, seen side by side with the conditioned world, considered to be either inside it or outside it.   It is characteristic of the Old Wisdom School that it everywhere stresses the transcendence of the Absolute, its complete difference from anything which we do or can experience in or around us.   Later Buddhists, of the Mahayana, corrected this somewhat one-sided emphasis, by making more of the immanence of the Unconditioned.   The Old Wisdom School approaches ultimate reality by the Via Negativa, which in India was expounded by the great Yajñavalka in the Upanishads (c. 600 B.C.), and which Dionysius Areopagita later on introduced into the West.   We must, however, never lose sight of the fact that, ultimately, Nirvana is unthinkable and incomprehensible.   It is only as a therapeutically valuable, though basically false, concept that, during certain phases of our spiritual progress, it can be of use to our thoughts, and enter into the practice of contemplation.

In actual practice, this conviction of the transcendence of

the Unconditioned meant that it was approached as the total negation of the things of this world as we know them. I must refer the reader to the text-books on Buddhist meditation for the actual details, but a general outline of this approach cannot be omitted here : Assuming that we are displeased with the world as it appears to us, we ask what it is that displeases us. Three *marks* are said to sum up all the irksome features of this world : *Impermanence*, *Suffering* and *Not-self*. Everything here is *impermanent*, everchanging, doomed to destruction, quite unreliable, crumbling away, however much we may try to hold it. As for the mark of *suffering*, I must refer to the discussion of the first Truth in Chapter I. It is a fundamental thesis of Buddhism that there is nothing which is not either directly experienced as ill, or in some way bound up with ill—past or future, one's own or another's. Finally, everything is *Not-self*, for we never possess it quite surely, we never control it completely, and we do not really possess the possessor, nor control the controller. It is not asserted that this analysis of worldly experience is self-evident. On the contrary, the Buddhists repeat again and again that it can be accepted only after strenuous and prolonged exercise in methodical contemplation. Our normal inclinations induce us to dwell on the relative permanence of things, on what happiness there is in the world, and on the power, however slight, which we exert over our circumstances and ourselves. Only those people would be naturally inclined to agree with the Buddhist analysis who are extremely sensitive to pain and suffering, and possess a considerable capacity for renunciation. In order to do full justice to the Buddhist point of view, and to see the world as they did, we must, however, be willing to go through the prescribed meditations, which alone are said to foster and mature the conviction that this world is completely and utterly worthless. In this argument we must take the meditations and their result for granted.

So we would have on the one hand Ultimate Reality, which at a certain stage of the Path would appear as the unceasing, undisturbed, self-controlled bliss of peace. On the other hand we have conditioned events, which would all turn out to be *impermanent, bound up with suffering, and not our own*. As we repeat the comparison between the two, we end up by becoming thoroughly disgusted with anything that may have those three marks. None of it can give our Self the security it looks for. None of it can dispel our anxiety. The revulsion from all conditioned things is supposed to open our eyes more and more to the true nature of the Unconditioned. The Self becomes extinct and the Absolute remains. All the ideas about the Absolute which form the basis of meditation turn out to be a provisional framework which is discarded once the house is completed.

Decline

The Buddhists who dwell so constantly on the impermanence of all things in this world could not expect their own institutions to be an exception to the general rule. Like everything else, so the Law must decay—at least in so far as it has gained a precarious foothold in this world. In its full vigour and purity, it remains only for a short time ; then follows a long period of decay, and finally total disappearance, until a new revelation takes place. Accounts vary as regards the exact duration of the Law. At first, one spoke of a period of 500 years. Later on, that was extended to 1,000, 1,500 or 2,500 years. The Scriptures composed between 200 B.C. and 400 A.D. contain, in the form of *prophecies*, many descriptions of the stages of the decline of the Good Law. According to one account, preserved in Pali, the monks are capable of attaining to the Path, and of becoming Arhats only during the first period. From then onward the full fruit of the holy life is no longer attainable. Purity of conduct persists into the second period, a learned knowledge of the Scriptures into the third, but in the fourth only the outward symbols, like the uniform of the clergy, remain ; in the fifth the relics alone are left, and the religion disappears from the earth. Another sutra predicts that in the first 500 years after the Nirvana, the monks and other faithful will be strong in attaining union with Dharma ; in the second 500 years they will be strong in meditation ; in the third 500 years they will be strong in erudition ; in the fourth 500 years they will be strong in founding monasteries ; and in the last 500 years they will be strong in fighting and reproving. The pure Law will then become invisible. In China, it became usual to distinguish three periods. First, 500 years during which the Law was correctly practised and its fruits realised. Then 1,000 years of *counterfeit* Law, followed by a final period of 1,000 or 3,000 years in which the Law just decays. Through all the differences in the accounts we notice that there was a strong conviction that after 500 years some crisis would arise, some decisive change for the worse would take place.

The whole of later Buddhism proceeds under the shadow of this sense of decline. The literature bears witness to it everywhere. About 400 A.D., when Buddhism was outwardly still very vigorous in India, Vasubandhu concludes his famous *Treasure of the Abhidharma* with the melancholy observation that " *the religion of the Sage is at its last breath ; this is an age in which the vices are powerful ; those who want to be delivered must be diligent.*"
Centuries later, about 1,200 A.D., Ho-nen in Japan justifies his abrogation of the old Buddhist practices by the assertion that his age was too far away from the Buddha, that times had become so degenerate that nobody could any longer properly understand the depth of Buddhist wisdom, and a simple act of faith in the Buddha was all that people were still capable of. In the 19th century again, Sri Weligama of Ceylon assured Sir Edwin Arnold that men had fallen from the old wisdom, and that to-day nobody was so advanced as the Sages of the past.

Unfavourable historical conditions were only in part to blame for the sense of despondency which came over the Order as the beginning of our era approached. The difficulty went much deeper than that. The very methods which the Old Wisdom School had advocated began, about 300 years after the Buddha's Nirvana, to lose much of their efficacy. In the beginning of the Order, we hear of many who became Arhats, some of them with astonishing ease. Fewer and fewer cases are recorded in later writings. In the end, as shown by the *prophecies* quoted above, the conviction spread that the time for Arhats was over. The cream had been taken off the milk. The scholars ousted the saints, and erudition took the place of attainment. One of the Scriptures of the Sarvastivadins relates the terrible and sad story of the death of the last Arhat by the hands of one of the scholars. The story well illustrates the mood of the times.

The community reacted in two ways to this failure. One section turned away from the interpretation which Sariputra had given to the original doctrine, and built a new Gospel (Chapters V—IX). Another section remained faithful to the old views, but effected one or two minor adjustments. Owing to the decline in their vigour, which they interpreted as a decline in faith, the members of the conservative section began to change over from an oral to a written tradition. In Ceylon the Pali Scriptures were first committed to writing in the first century B.C. Another change was the lowering of the goal. In the first centuries many of the monks had aspired directly for Nirvana. Only the laity and the less ambitious monks were content with the hope of winning a better rebirth. But from ca 200 B.C. onward, almost everybody felt that conditions were too unfavourable for winning enlightenment in this life. It is natural that about this time a tradition about the coming Buddha, *Maitreya*, came to the fore. Maitreya (from maitri) personifies *friendliness*. His legend was to some extent stimulated by Persian eschatology, but it met the needs of the new situation. The Theravadins, it is true, accepted it without much enthusiasm, and Metteya never held a great place among them. But for the Sarvastivadins, and the followers of the Great Vehicle, it assumed an increasing importance. According to Buddhist cosmology, the earth goes through periodic cycles. In some of the cycles it improves, it others it degenerates. The average age of man is an index of the quality of the period in which he lives. It may vary between 10 years and many hundreds of thousands of years. At the time of Shakyamuni, the average life-span was 100 years. After him, the world becomes more depraved, and the life of man shortens. The peak of sin and misery will be reached when the average length of life has fallen to 10 years. The Dharma of Shakyamuni will then be completely forgotten. But after that the upward swing begins again. When the life of man reaches 80,000 years, Maitreya, at present in the Heaven of the *Satisfied Gods (Tushita)*, will appear on the earth, which will then be in a particularly fruitful and exuberant state. It will be bigger than it is now. A fertile golden sand will cover its surface. Everywhere there will be trees and flowers, pure lakes and jewel heaps. All men will be moral and decent, prosperous and joyous. The population will be very dense, and the fields will yield sevenfold. Those people who at present do meritorious deeds, make images of the Buddha, build Stupas, offer gifts, will be reborn as men in the time of Maitreya, and will obtain Nirvana through the influence of his teaching, which will be identical with that of the Buddha Shakyamuni. In this way, salvation became a hope of the remote future not only for the laity, but for the monks as well.

In the first period of its decline, the Old Wisdom School still gave evidence of a vigorous intellectual life. Between 100 B.C. and 400 A.D. the monks codified the doctrine, and composed many commentaries and treatises on Abhidharma. After that time they were content to defend the gains of the past. During the last 1,500 years, the Old Wisdom School has been dying slowly, like a magnificent old tree, one branch breaking off after the other, until the trunk alone remains. Between 1,000 and 1,200 Buddhism disappeared from India, through the combined effects of its own weaknesses, a revived Hinduism and Mohammedan persecution. The Sarvastivadins had possessed outposts in Central Asia and in Sumatra, but those also were lost at about 800, when the Tantric Vajrayana replaced the Hinayana in Sumatra, and about 900, when Islam conquered Central Asia. The Theravadins on the other hand, have continued to exist in Ceylon, Burma and Siam. Buddhism was brought by Asoka to Ceylon about 250 B.C. In the Middle Ages the Mahayana had many adherents there. At the present time the

Theravadin school has ousted all the others. Buddhism
had been introduced into Burma in the 5th century, in
the form of the Mahayana, but from 1,050 onwards, the
Theravadins have dominated the intellectual and social
life of the country. Similarly in Siam, Hinayana and
Mahayana co-existed at first, but after 1,150 the
Theravadins became more and more preponderant, with
Pali as the sacred language.

V

THE MAHAYANA AND THE NEW WISDOM SCHOOL

The Mahasanghikas

IN the early history of the Order, divergencies were chiefly due to geographical causes. The Dharma had begun in Magadha, and from there it spread to the West and to the South. About 100 to 200 years after the Nirvana some separation and rivalry seems to have developed between East and West. About the time of Asoka the dissensions in the Order seem to have led to the first schism. The *Sthavira-vada* seceded from the Mahasanghikas, or vice versa. The Sthavira-vada were the conservatives who *followed the doctrine of the Elders*, while the more democratic *Maha-sanghikas*, the *Great-Assemblists* stood for the *Great Assembly*, which included monks of lesser attainments and householders, in contrast to the exclusive and aristocratic *Assembly of the Arhats*.

It is not easy to get at the true facts about this schism. The writings of one of the parties concerned, i.e. of the Mahasanghikas, have nearly all been lost. A great deal of sectarian pride and spite enter into all the accounts which we possess. All that seems certain is that this split occurred about the time of Asoka, and that it was connected with the *Five points* of a monk called Mahadeva. This Mahadeva succeeded in arousing the indignation of his opponents, who described him as the son of a merchant who committed incest with his mother, poisoned his father, and then killed his mother and several Arhats. Having done all this, he felt remorse, left family life, ordained himself—quite irregularly—and then tried to fasten his *Five points* on the Order. Two of these points are directed against the Arhats, and imputed to them some deficiency, both moral and intellectual. The one claimed that the

Arhats could still have seminal emissions at night. This seemed to suggest that their passions were not quite exhausted, because they could be tempted and remained open to the molestations of Mara. In addition to a residue of passion, they also had some remainder of ignorance in them. They were not fully omniscient, and so there was still something which obstructed their thoughts. This second point became very important for the development of the ideal of *omniscience* in the Mahayana (see pp. 137 sq.). Mahadeva's five points were only the occasion for the separate emergence of the Mahasanghikas. In spite of what their opponents say about them, we have no reason to believe that their doctrines were any less old than those which we have described in Chapter IV. If we do not speak about them here in greater detail it is because we have very little to go by.

The Mahasanghikas became the starting point of the development of the Mahayana by their more liberal attitude, and by some of their special theories. In every way, the Mahasanghikas were more liberal than their opponents. They were less strict in interpreting the disciplinary rules, less exclusive with regard to householders, they looked more kindly on the spiritual possibilities of women and of the less gifted monks, and were more willing to consider as authentic those additions to the Scriptures which were composed at a later date. Among them, several of the distinctive features of the Bodhisattva ideal of the Mahayana were worked out for the first time, and in addition, some of their tenets had the historically very important effect of cutting the Buddhist tradition loose from the historical Buddha, making exclusive adherence to his sayings no longer imperative. " *With one single sound the Buddha has expounded all his doctrines.*" " *He understands all things in one moment.*" " *The form-body of the Tathagata is boundless ; so is his power, and the length of his life.*" " *The Buddha is never tired of enlightening sentient beings and of awakening pure faith in them.*" " *The Buddha neither sleeps nor dreams.*" " *The Buddha is always in trance.*" Such sayings do not fit at all the man Gautama who lived in Magadha many years ago. By placing all the emphasis on the supernatural, or supramundane, qualities of the Buddha, in which he differed from all other men, they led the believer away from the fortuitous historical circumstances of his appearance. Some Mahasanghikas even went so far as to maintain that Shakyamuni had been no more than a *magical creation* who, on behalf of the Supramundane Buddha, had preached the Dharma. If the Buddha existed only about 500 B.C., then he could teach only at that time, and the body of his teachings would be completed at his death. If, however, the true Buddha exists at all times, then there is no reason why he should not at all times find instruments to do his teaching. A free and unfettered development of the doctrine was thus assured, and innovations, even if untraceable in the existing body of Scriptures, could be justified as revelations of the real principle of Buddhahood.

Hinayana and Mahayana

From the Mahasanghikas developed a new gospel. Its adherents first called it the Bodhisattva-career (Bodhisattva-yana), and, later on, the *Mahā-yāna*, the *Great Career*, or the Great Vehicle. By contrast, the followers of the Old Wisdom School were occasionally referred to as Hīna-yāna, or the *Lesser*, the *Inferior*, the *Low Vehicle*. The Mahayana seemed *great* for many reasons—chiefly because of the all-embracing nature of the sympathy, and emptiness which it taught, and because of the greatness of the goal it advocated, which was no other than Buddha-hood itself.

In its original meaning, Hinayana is a term of abuse, and the Mahayanists used it but rarely. They usually referred to their opponents as *The Disciples and Pratyekabuddhas*. At present, when its original connotation is but dimly felt, the term *Hinayana* can be used for purposes of description, just as in art history words like *Baroque* or *Rococo* are nowadays descriptive terms, although originally they expressed a disapproval of the art in question.

We do not have any clear idea about the numerical proportions between Hinayanists and Mahayanists in India at different times. It seems probable that the Mahayanists began to outnumber the Hinayanists only from ca 800 A.D. onwards, when Buddhism definitely declined in India. When the Buddhist faith spread to China, Japan and Tibet, the Great Vehicle ousted, and almost completely obliterated the Hinayana, which is now preserved in Ceylon, Burma, Cambodia and Siam only.

Mahayanists and Hinayanists lived together in the same monasteries, and for a very long time they adhered to the same Vinaya rules. As I-tsing (ca 700) reports :

> "*The adherents of the Mahayana and Hinayana both practise the same Vinaya, recognise the same five categories of faults, are attached to the same four truths. Those who worship the Bodhisattvas and who read the Mahayana sutras get the name of Mahayanists ; those who do not are Hinayanists.*"

How did Mahayanists and Hinayanists define their relations to each other ? Hinayana literature simply ignores the Mahayana innovators. Rarely, if ever, are Mahayana authors or doctrines named in controversy. Nevertheless, a certain amount of Mahayana teaching was tacitly absorbed.

The Mahayana, in its turn, seems never to have reached a definite conclusion about its relation to the Hinayana. In the first centuries, up to about 400 A.D., we hear a great deal about the *Disciples and Pratyekabuddhas.* After that time, they are more and more lost sight of, as the Mahayana becomes more and more independent in doctrine, terminology and mythology. In their views on the relative value of the two ' vehicles,' the Mahayanists were actuated by two conflicting sets of emotions. Sectarian bias, together with concern for self-justification and desire for superiority, struggled with tolerance, loving kindness and modesty. This conflict led to all kinds of contradictory statements, which were never really resolved.

At some times the *Buddha-vehicle* is said to exclude the vehicle of the Disciples, while at other times it is said to be identical with it. Occasionally, the Hinayanists are treated with the utmost contempt, threatened with hell fire, and described as " chaff," or worse. On other occasions,

one adopts a more broad-minded attitude. One would
" *break faith with the Tathagata* " if one were to " *show
contempt to those who walk in the way of the Disciples or the
Pratyekabuddhas, saying, 'We are more distinguished than
they.'* "

The Sarvastivadins had recognised three different *Families*
(*Gotra*), or ways to salvation : There are the *Disciples*,
who attain Nirvana through Arhatship. There is the
Pratyekabuddha, who is " *one enlightened by himself, i.e.
one who has attained full enlightenment, but who dies without
proclaiming the truth to the world.*" There are the *Supreme
Buddhas*, who win perfect enlightenment, and teach the
Dharma to others. Each individual, by his past, by
character and temperament, belongs to one of those three
groups, and he must use the means which suit his make-up.
Some Mahayanists agreed to leave it at that. Others,
however, insisted that there is but one way to final salvation
—the Buddha-vehicle, or the Great Vehicle, while the
other vehicles do not get very far. The *Lotus*, for instance,
says : " *All Disciples fancy they have attained Nirvana.
But the Jina instructs them, and says : ' This is a temporary
repose, no final rest.' It is a device of the Buddha when he
taught this method. There is no real Nirvana without
omniscience. Strive to reach this !* " The Arhats are told
that, contrary to their belief, they had not " *accomplished
their tasks,*" they had not "*finished what they had to do.*"
They had to strive on, until they gained the Buddha-
knowledge.

The hesitations of the Mahayanists concerning the relative
value of the two *vehicles* seem to indicate that a sense of
sectarian superiority cannot be organically incorporated
into the Buddhist doctrine.

Literary Development

Between 100 B.C. and 200 A.D. the Mahayana burst out
into a profusion of Sutras. If one wants to catch its spirit,
one will find it expressed with particular force in the
Lotus of the Good Law, and in the *Exposition of Vimalakirti*,
both of which are available in English translations. The

core of the new doctrine is set forth in the voluminous Sutras dealing with *Perfection of Wisdom*. The sanskrit word is *pra-JNĀ-pāram-itā*, literally *wisdom-gone-beyond*, or, as we might say, *Transcendental Wisdom*. Buddhists at all times have compared this world of suffering, of birth-and-death, with a river in full spate. On the hither shore we are erring about, tormented by all kinds of unease and distress. On the yonder shore, lies the *Beyond*, the Paradise, Nirvana, where all ills have, together with separate individuality, come to an end. These writings on Prajñaparamita are very elusive, and not easily understood. Whereas the original Buddhism came from Northern India, from the region between Nepal and the Ganges, the Prajñaparamita originated in South-Eastern India, in the Deccan, between the Godavari River and the Kistna River, near Amaravati and Nagarjunikonda.

The doctrine of the Mahayana sutras, and of the Prajñaparamita in particular, was developed in a systematic and philosophical form by the *Madhyamikas*. *Madhyama* means *middle*, and the *Madhyamikas* are those who take the *Middle Way*, between affirming and denying. The school was founded, probably about 150 A.D., by Nagarjuna and Aryadeva. Nagarjuna was one of the most subtle dialecticians of all times. Of Brahmin family, he came from Berar in South India, and was active in Nagarjunikonda near Amaravati, and in Northern India. His name is explained by the legend that he was born under an Arjuna tree, and that Nagas, i.e. *serpent-kings*, or *dragons*, had instructed him in secret lore in the Dragons' Palace under the sea. His theory is called Sūnya-vāda, or *emptiness-doctrine*. He supplemented with a logical apparatus the views expounded in the Sutras on perfect wisdom, which he is said to have rescued from the Nether world of the Nagas. While Shakyamuni, so the story goes, taught to men the doctrine of the *Disciples*, in heaven he taught at the same time a deeper doctrine, which was first preserved by the *Dragons*, and then brought to earth by Nagarjuna.

The Madhyamika school flourished in India for well over 800 years. About 450 A.D. it split into two sub-divisions :

one side, the *Prasangikas*, interpreted Nagarjuna's doctrine as a universal scepticism, and claimed that their argument-ations had the exclusive purpose of refuting the opinions of others ; the other side, the *Svatantrikas*, maintained that argument could also establish some positive truths. To-gether with Buddhism the Madhyamikas disappeared from India after 1,000 A.D. Their leading ideas have survived up to the present day in the Vedanta system of Hinduism into which they were incorporated by Gaudapada and Sankara, its founders.

Translations of the Prajnaparamita-sutras have exerted a profound influence in China from 180 A.D. onwards. The Madhyamikas existed for a few centuries, from 400, or 600 to 900, as a separate school called San loen t'sung. In 625 the school came to Japan, as Sanron, but it has been extinct there for a long time. Adapted to the Chinese and Japanese outlook on life, the doctrine lives on as Ch'an or Zen.

The ideal Man of the Mahayana, a Bodhisattva

The two key words which occur on almost each page of the Mahayana writings are the words Bodhisattva and emptiness. What then is first of all a Bodhi-sattva ? A Buddha is one who is enlightened. A Bodhi-sattva is literally an *Enlightenment-being*. He is a Buddha-to-be, one who wishes to become a Buddha, that is to say, an Enlightened One. So far for the literal meaning.

It would be a mistake to assume that the conception of a Bodhisattva was a creation of the Mahayana. For all Buddhists each Buddha had been, for a long period before his enlightenment, a Bodhisattva. The Sarvastivadins, in particular, had given much thought to the career of a Bodhisattva. The *Abhidharmakosa* gives a fine description of the mentality of a Bodhisattva :

" But why do the Bodhisattvas, once they have taken the vow to obtain the supreme enlightenment, take such a long time to obtain it ?

Because the supreme enlightenment is very difficult to obtain : one needs a vast accumulation of knowledge and merit, innumerable heroic deeds in the course of three immeasurable kalpas.

One could understand that the Bodhisattva seeks for this enlightenment, which is so difficult to obtain, if this enlightenment were his only means of arriving at deliverance. But this is not the case. Why then do they undertake such infinite labour?

For the good of others, because they want to become capable of pulling others out of this great flood of suffering. But what personal benefit do they find in the benefit of others? The benefit of others is their own benefit, because they desire it.

Who could believe that?

It is true that men devoid of pity and who think only of themselves, find it hard to believe in the altruism of the Bodhisattva. But compassionate men do so easily. Do we not see that certain people, confirmed in the absence of pity, find pleasure in the suffering of others, even when it is not useful to them? As well one must admit that the Bodhisattvas, confirmed in pity, find pleasure in doing good to others without any egoistic preoccupation. Do we not see that certain people, ignorant of the true nature of the conditioned Dharmas which constitute their so-called 'Self,' attach themselves to these Dharmas by force of habit— however completely these Dharmas may be devoid of personality—and suffer a thousand pains because of this attachment? Likewise, one must admit that the Bodhisattvas, by the force of habit, detach themselves from the Dharmas which constitute their so-called 'Self,' do no longer consider these Dharmas as 'I' or 'mine,' growing in pitying solicitude for others, and are ready to suffer a thousand pains for this solicitude."

This is the idea of the Mahayana, fully formed within the Hinayana schools. The innovation of the Mahayana is that it elaborated this idea into an ideal valid for all. It compared the Arhat unfavourably with the Bodhisattva, and it claimed that all should emulate the Bodhisattvas, and not the Arhats.

As to the Arhat, the Mahayanists maintained that he had not completely shaken off all attachment to 'I' and 'mine.' He set out to obtain Nirvana for himself, and he won

Nirvana for himself, but others were left out of it. In this way, the Arhat could be said to make a difference between himself and others, and thereby to retain, by implication, some notion of himself as different from others—thus showing his inability to realise the truth of *Not-Self* to the full. Two passages from the Prajñaparamita put this criticism rather forcibly : The first contrasts the career of a Bodhisattva with the Hinayana career of a disciple, who aims at Arhatship, and of a Pratyekabuddha, who wins a fuller enlightenment, but, solitary like a rhinoceros, does not preach the doctrine to others.

> "*How do the persons belonging to the Vehicle of the Disciples and Pratyekabuddhas train themselves? They think : 'One single self we will tame, one single self we will pacify, one single self we will lead into Nirvana.' Then they undertake exercises which bring about wholesome roots for the sake of taming themselves, pacifying themselves, nirvanising themselves. Certainly, the Bodhisattva should not train himself like that. He should undertake exercises for bringing about wholesome roots with the idea : 'My self I will place in Suchness (=Nirvana), and, for the sake of helping all the world, I will also place all beings in Suchness, the immeasurable world of beings I will lead to Nirvana.'* "

In Tibetan, Bodhisattva is translated as *Heroic Being*. The Christians also canonise only those saints who have exhibited virtues *in gradu heroico*. The heroic quality of the Bodhisattva is brought out by the Prajñaparamita in another place by way of a parable :

Suppose a hero, endowed with great accomplishments, had gone out with his mother, father, sons and daughters. By some set of circumstances, they would get into a huge wild forest. The foolish among them would be greatly frightened. The hero would, however, fearlessly say to them : "Do not be afraid! I will speedily take you out of this great and terrible jungle, and bring you to safety." Since he is fearless, vigorous, exceedingly tender, compassionate, courageous and resourceful, it does not occur to him to take himself alone out of the jungle, leaving his relatives behind. Against the Arhat it is claimed that we

must take the whole of the creation with us to enlightenment, that we cannot just abandon it to its fate, as all
beings are as near to us as our relatives are.

What a man should do is to make no discrimination between
himself and others, and to wait until he had helped everybody into Nirvana before losing himself into it. The
Mahayanists thus claimed that the Arhat had not aimed
high enough. The ideal man, the aim of the Buddhist
effort, was, according to them, not the rather self-centred,
cold and narrow-minded Arhat, but the all-compassionate
Bodhisattva, who abandoned the world, but not the
beings in it. Whereas wisdom had been taught as the
highest, and compassion as a subsidiary virtue, compassion
now came to rank as equal with wisdom. While the wisdom
of the Arhat had been fruitful in setting free in himself
what there was to be set free, it was rather sterile in ways
and means of helping ordinary people. The Bodhisattva
would be a man who does not only set himself free, but
who is also skilful in devising means for bringing out and
maturing the latent seeds of enlightenment in others.
As again the *Prajñaparamita* puts it :

" *Doers of what is hard are the Bodhisattvas, the great
beings who have set out to win supreme enlightenment. They
do not wish to attain their own private Nirvana. On the
contrary, they have surveyed the highly painful world of
being, and yet, desirous to win supreme enlightenment, they
do not tremble at birth-and-death. They have set out for
the benefit of the world, for the ease of the world, out of
pity for the world. They have resolved: 'We will become a
shelter for the world, a refuge for the world, the world's
place of rest, the final relief of the world, islands of the
world, lights of the world, leaders of the world, the world's
means of salvation.' "*

The ideal of the Bodhisattva was partly due to social
pressure on the Order (cf. p. 85 sq.), but to a great extent
it was inherent in the practice of the *Unlimited*, which
had trained the monks not to discriminate between themselves and others. As we saw, Buddhism has at its disposal
two methods by which it reduces the sense of separateness
on the part of individuals. The one is the culture of the

social emotions, or sentiments, such as friendliness and compassion. The other consists in acquiring the habit of regarding whatever one thinks, feels or does as an inter-play of impersonal forces—called Dharmas—weaning oneself slowly from such ideas as ' I ' or ' mine ' or ' self.' There is a logical contradiction between the method of wisdom, which sees no persons at all, but only Dharmas, and the method of the Unlimited which cultivates relations to people as persons. The meditation on Dharmas dissolves other people, as well as oneself, into a conglomeration of impersonal and instantaneous dharmas. It reduces our manhood into five heaps, or pieces, plus a label. If there is nothing in the world except bundles of Dharmas—as cold and as impersonal as atoms—instantaneously perishing all the time, there is nothing which friendliness and compassion could work on. One cannot wish well to a Dharma which is gone by the time one has come to wish it well, nor can one pity a Dharma—say a ' mind-object,' or a ' sight-organ,' or a ' sound-consciousness.' In those Buddhist circles where the method of Dharmas was prac-tised to a greater extent than the Unlimited, it led to a certain dryness of mind, to aloofness, and to lack of human warmth. The true task of the Buddhist is to carry on with both contradictory methods at the same time. As the method of Dharmas leads to boundless contraction of the self—because everything is emptied out of it—so the method of the Unlimited leads to a boundless expansion of the self—because one identifies oneself with more and more living beings. As the method of wisdom explodes the idea that there are any persons at all in the world, so the method of the Unlimited increases the awareness of the personal problems of more and more persons.

How then does the Mahayana resolve this contradiction ? The Buddhist philosophers differ from philosophers bred in the Aristotelean tradition in that they are not frightened but delighted by a contradiction. They deal with this, as with other contradictions, by merely stating it in an uncompromising form, and then they leave it at that. Here is a very famous passage from the *Diamond Sutra* to illustrate this point :

*" Here, O Subhuti, a Bodhisattva should think thus :
" As many beings as there are in the universe of beings—
be they egg-born, or born from a womb, or moisture-born,
or miraculously born ; be they with form, or without ; be
they with perception, without perception, or with neither
perception nor no-perception—as far as any conceivable
universe of beings is conceived ; all these should be led
by me into Nirvana, into that realm of Nirvana which
leaves nothing behind. And yet, although innumerable
beings have thus been led to Nirvana, no being at all has
been led to Nirvana. And why ? If in a Bodhisattva
the perception of a ' being ' should take place, he would
not be called an 'enlightenment-being ' (=bodhi-sattva)."*

A Bodhisattva is a being compounded of the two contradictory forces of wisdom and compassion. In his
wisdom, he sees no persons; in his compassion he is resolved
to save them. His ability to combine these contradictory
attitudes is the source of his greatness, and of his ability
to save himself and others.

Emptiness

Two things, the Sutra tells us, are most needful to the
Bodhisattva, and to his practice of wisdom : *" Never to
abandon all beings and to see into the truth that all things
are empty."* We must now make an effort to understand
this all-important idea of *Emptiness*.

Here again the sanskrit root helps. It shows how easily
the word *empty* could become a synonym for *Not-Self*.
What we call *emptiness* in English is *śūnyatā* in sanskrit.
The sanskrit word *śūnya* is derived from the root *SVI*, to
swell. *Śūnya* means literally : *relating to the swollen*.
In the remote past, our ancestors, with a fine instinct for
the dialectical nature of reality, frequently used the same
verbal root to denote the two opposite aspects of a situation.
They were as distinctly aware of the unity of opposites,
as of their opposition. Thus the root SVI, Greek KY,
seems to have expressed the idea that something which
looks ' swollen ' from the outside is ' hollow ' inside. This
is easily shown by the facts of comparative philology.
You have the meaning *swollen* in such words as Latin

cumulus (pile, heap) and caulis (stalk). You have the meaning *hollow*, from the same root, in Greek koilos, Latin cavus. Thus our personality is *swollen* in so far as constituted by the five skandhas, but it is also *hollow* inside, because devoid of a central self. Furthermore ' swollen ' may mean ' filled with something foreign.' When a woman is ' swollen ' in pregnancy—and here again the Greeks use the same root in *kyo*—she is full of a foreign body, of something not herself. Similarly in this view, the personality contains nothing that really belongs to it. It is swollen with foreign matter. Like the child the foreign body must be expelled.

It is a great pity that these connotations of the word *sūnyatā* are lost when we speak of *emptiness*. The door is opened to innumerable misunderstandings. Particularly to the uninitiated, this emptiness will appear as a mere nothingness, just as Nirvana did.[1]

Although in Buddhist art *emptiness* is usually symbolised by an empty circle, one must not regard the Buddhist emptiness as a mere nought, or a blank. It is a term for the absence of self, or for self-effacement. In Buddhist thought some ideas belong together which we do not usually associate. I set them out here in a diagram :

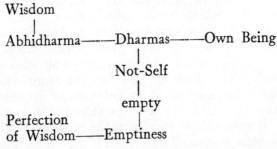

```
Wisdom
  |
Abhidharma——Dharmas——Own Being
                |
             Not-Self
                |
              empty
                |
Perfection      |
of Wisdom——Emptiness
```

[1] It is one of the ironies of history that Buddhism, this most uncommercial and even anticommercial system, should have been responsible for the elaboration of a tool without which modern commercialism could scarcely have been developed. Without the invention of a zero, or nought, our shopkeepers, bankers and statisticians would still be hampered right and left by the clumsiness of the abacus. The little circle which we know as zero, was known to the Arabs about 950 A.D. as shifr, empty. This became cifra in Latin, when about 1150 the nought came to Europe. In English we had originally ' cypher ' as the name for zero, and cypher is nothing but the sanskrit word sunya.

Bodhidharma, an Indian or Persian, who went to China about 500 A.D. expressed the meaning of the term concisely when he said : "*All things are empty, and there is nothing desirable or to be sought after.*"

Used as technical terms, the words *empty* and *emptiness* express in Buddhist tradition the complete negation of this world by the exercise of wisdom. The central idea is the complete denial and renunciation of, the complete withdrawal and liberation from the world around us, in all its aspects and along its entire breadth.

The Abhidharmists knew the term *empty*, but used it very sparingly. In the Pali Canon it occurs only on a few occasions. The New Wisdom School treats the term as the sesame which opens all doors, and Nagarjuna worked out its epistemological implications. *Emptiness* here means the identity of yes and no. In this system of thought the gentle art of undoing with one hand what one has done with the other is considered as the very quintessence of fruitful living. The Buddhist sage is depicted as a kind of faithful Penelope, patiently waiting for the coming of the Ulysses of enlightenment. He should really never commit himself to either ' yes ' or ' no ' on anything. But, if he once says ' yes,' he must also say ' no.' And when he says ' no,' he must also say ' yes,' to the same.

Emptiness is that which stands right in the middle between affirmation and negation, existence and non-existence, eternity and annihilation. The germ of this idea is found in an early saying, which the scriptures of all schools have transmitted. The Buddha says to Katyayana that the world usually bases its views on two things, existence and non-existence. ' It is,' is one extreme ; ' it is not ' is another. Between those two limits the world is imprisoned. The holy men transcend this limitation. Avoiding both extremes, the Tathagata teaches a Dharma in the middle between them, where alone the truth can be found. This Dharma is now called *emptiness*. The Absolute is emptiness and all things also are empty. In their emptiness Nirvana and this world coincide, they are no longer different but the same.

The Anatta doctrine openly disagrees with commonsense.

The doctors of the Old Wisdom School had admitted the conflict as irreducible by distinguishing two kinds of truth : *Ultimate* truth consists of statements about *dharmas*, *conventional* truth speaks of *persons* and *things*. The *ultimate* events of this school have very much the same function as atoms, cells and similar entities, also normally ignored in daily life, to which the propositions of modern science properly refer. The New Wisdom School takes the concept of *Ultimate Truth* a step further. It is now found exclusively in relation to the one ultimate reality, which is the Absolute in its emptiness. *Ultimate* truth means no longer *scientific* but *mystical* truth. It is obvious that in this sense anything we may say is ultimately untrue. Emptiness cannot be the object of a definite belief. We cannot get at it, and even if we could, we would not recognise it, since it has no distinctive marks. All doctrines, even the Four Holy Truths, are ultimately false, evidence of ignorance. Theories cover up the Ineffable Light of the One, and they are only conventionally true, in the sense that they conform to peoples' varying capacities for understanding spiritual experiences. In accordance with the inclinations and gifts of beings the teaching can, and must, be varied indefinitely.

The doctrine of emptiness is frequently expressed by way of simile. The Old Wisdom School had already compared this world around us to a mass of foam, a bubble, a mirage, a dream, a magical show. The similes had the purpose of bringing home the insight that the world is relatively unimportant, worthless, deceptive and unsubstantial. Poets in the West have often used the same similes with a similar intention :

> " *But what are men who grasp at praise sublime*
> *But bubbles on the rapid stream of time,*
> *That rise and fall and swell and are no more*
> *Born and forgot, ten thousand in an hour.*"

Or, the more famous :

> " *The world is but a fleeting show*
> *For man's illusion given ;*
> *The smiles of joy, the tears of woe,*
> *Deceitful shine, deceitful flow—*
> *There's nothing true but Heaven.*"

When the New Wisdom School, in its turn, compares all Dharmas to a dream, an echo, a reflected image, a mirage, or a magical show, it does so in a more technical sense. The Absolute alone is not dependent on anything else; it is ultimately real. Any relative thing is functionally dependent on other things, and can exist, and be conceived, only in and through its relations with other things. By itself it is nothing, it has no separate inward reality. " *A borrowed sum is not one's own capital*," as Candrakirti puts it. But if each and every thing is " *devoid of an own-being*," and does not really exist, like " *the daughter of a barren virgin carved in stone*," how is it that we can see, hear and feel the things around us which are really just emptiness ? The similes of a dream, etc., are intended to answer that question. One sees a magical show, or a mirage, one hears an echo, one dreams a dream, and yet we all know that the magical appearance is merely deceptive (see p. 172), that there is no real water in the mirage, that the echo does not come from a man's voice and that an echo is not someone speaking, and that the objects one loved, hated and feared in one's dream did not really exist.

Many misunderstandings of the Madhyamika conception of emptiness would have been avoided if full weight had been given to the terms which are used as synonymous with it. One of the most frequent synonyms is *Non-duality*. In the perfect gnosis, all dualities are abolished, the object does not differ from the subject, Nirvana is not distinguished from the world, existence is no longer something apart from non-existence. Discrimination and multiplicity are the hall-marks of ignorance. From another point of view emptiness is called *Suchness*, because one takes reality such as it is, without superimposing any ideas upon it.

The statements which the Mahayana philosophers make about true knowledge cease to be paradoxical and absurd when one realises that they attempt to describe the Universe as it appears on the level of complete self-extinction, or from the point of view of the Absolute. If it is a meaningful and rational undertaking to describe this world as it appears to God, then the sutras of the Mahayana are full of meaning and rationality. Master Eckhart and Hegel attempted a similar task. Their writings also suggest that God's meaning is not always easily understood.

Salvation

Salvation, as the New Wisdom School understands it, can be summed up in three negations—*Non-attainment, Non-assertion, Non-relying*—and one positive attribute—*Omniscience*. A profusion of argument is expended on showing that Nirvana cannot be attained, that salvation cannot really take place and that the long and laborious struggle of the Bodhisattva really leads nowhere at all—" *In emptiness there are neither attainment nor non-attainment.*" The Unconditioned is by definition devoid of any relation to anything else, or, as the Sutras put it, it is absolutely isolated and solitary. It is therefore impossible for a person to enter into any kind of relation with it, much less to possess or gain it. Further, one could never know that one had attained Nirvana. Emptiness has no properties, no marks, it has nothing by which it could be recognised, and so we can never know whether we have it or not.

Non-attainment amounts really to self-extinction, or forgetting oneself in complete self-surrender. It is characteristic of the highest virtues of all, that one cannot be aware of them without losing them. It is so with simplicity and humility. One cannot deliberately acquire an unstudied simplicity, nor can one reflect on one's humility without pandering to pride. One cannot say that one has gained Nirvana without making a distinction between oneself and Nirvana, between one's former state and one's present state, between Nirvana and its opposite. And all these distinctions are signs of that very ignorance which excludes one from the other shore.

It is really a danger inherent in the very use of language that any statement which one makes looks like the assertion of something. In a system in which *Non-assertion* is one of the marks of salvation, one must always remember that it is not put forward as a positive theory or as a metaphysical system. "*This sublime doctrine is not a cockpit for logicians.*" The doctrine of emptiness is not taught to support one theory against others, but to get rid of theories altogether. It would therefore be quite unjust to the intentions of the New Wisdom School if one were to regard emptiness as a kind of Absolute behind the conditioned world, as a kind of basis for it, as a kind of anchor for us. This is certainly not so—"*Nirvana is not in the least distinct from birth-and-death.*" It is not a separate reality at all. It would be equally fallacious to describe it as a metaphysical Monism directed against the pluralism of the Sarvastivadins. It is true that the Madhyamika doctrine is often so represented in textbooks of philosophy. It would, however, be against the spirit of a doctrine which avoids falling into dualism, to posit a One as against a Many. The mind of Nagarjuna was more subtle than such philosophisings. Emptiness is the non-difference between yes and no, and the truth escapes us when we say ' it is,' and when we say ' it is not '; but it lies somewhere between these two. The man who *dwells in emptiness* has neither a positive nor a negative attitude to anything. Nagarjuna's doctrine is not a metaphysical one at all, but it describes a practical attitude of non-assertion which alone can assure lasting peace. Nothing is more alien to the mentality of the sage than to fight or contend for or against anything. This peacefulness of the true sage is the germ of the Madhyamika dialectics. It is clearly expressed already in Scriptures much older than Nagarjuna. It is found clearly and unmistakably in the very ancient *Sutta Nipata* (verses 796–803). And in the *Samyutta Nikaya*, the Buddha states: "*I do not fight with the world, but the world fights with me, for one who knows about dharma never fights with the world. And what the learned in the world regard as non-existent, that also I teach as non-existent. And what the learned in the world regard as existent, that also I regard as existent.*" The purpose of Nagarjuna's dialectics was not to come to any definite conclusion at all, but to destroy all opinions and to reduce all positive beliefs to absurdity.

The New Testament tells us concisely in one short sentence

that " *the son of man has not where he can rest his head.*"
Through an almost infinite variety of expressions, the
New Wisdom School preaches the gospel of *Non-relying*.
The clue to the doctrine lies in the importance of anxiety
in our lives (see p. 22). This anxiety forces us to hold
perpetually on to something which is different from us.
We cling to one person after another, and nothing terrifies
us so much as to be quite solitary, by ourselves, without
even the thought of something to flee into. In order to
be saved, we must reject all these supports one by one, and
learn to view without trembling the emptiness of our
soul, as it is naked by itself. When we are thus without
any stable support, without any hope of one, then we are
said " *to rely on nothing but perfect wisdom,* "or on *emptiness,*
which is the same thing.

From a positive point of view, salvation is described as
Omniscience. This ambition to become omniscient appears
rather curious to us and requires some words of explanation.
It is a result of a double development, which, on the one
side, make the final Nirvana of Buddha-hood into the goal
after which the believer should strive, and which, on the
other side, stressed omniscience as the essential attribute
of a Buddha. The first is, as we saw, implied in the
Bodhisattva ideal. In what sense, then, is the Buddha
held to be omniscient ? The Mahayanists claim that the
Buddha was omniscient in the strictest sense of the term.
With unimpeded cognition, he knew correctly all the
aspects of existence, in all its details. Finite minds could,
of course, not hope to understand the workings of an
infinite intellect. The Buddha's thoughts would really
be quite different from ours qualitatively. They would
be ' absolute ' thoughts, thoughts of an Absolute by an
Absolute. When properly considered, the thought of the
Buddha would really not be a thought at all, because an
unconditioned thought cannot be included in the skandha
of consciousness, and because it is not separated from its
object, but identical with it. In any case, Omniscience
could not be attributed to the Buddha in so far as he
was a human being, or even in so far as he was in his
' glorified body,' but it would be essentially bound up

with the Buddha as a pure spiritual principle, with the *Dharma-body* of the Buddha. Not all Buddhists seem to have believed that strict Omniscience on the part of the Buddha would be necessary to invest his religion with the required authority. If he knew everything that was essential to salvation, that would be sufficient to make him into a trustworthy guide. In some passages of the Pali Scriptures, as a matter of fact, the Buddha expressly disclaims any other kind of Omniscience. The Mahayana, on the other hand, explains that while primarily the Omniscience of the Buddha consists in his acquaintance with the means of attaining heaven and liberation, he also comprehends all things without exception, including such unnecessary pieces of information as the number of insects in the world. If the Buddha were deficient in this respect, he would be hampered by things outside the range of his knowledge and he would fall short of identity with the Absolute.

Leaving aside the philosophical implications of this problem, the search after Omniscience is, from a practical point of view, identical with the search after self-extinction, and therefore it is salutary to hold it up as a goal of the spiritual life. If we take ourselves in our natural condition, we probably have to agree that we have no particular desire to become totally omniscient. To the average seeker after Dharma, all-knowledge is certainly not one of the fruits, it is not the reward he really seeks. The state of being which one often expects from the pursuit of the Dharma, would be marked, I think, by three chief properties : (1) Protection from physical pain ; (2) Deliverance from fear, anxiety and apprehension by the removal of all attachment to self, and of its consequences, such as death ; (3) Finally, there would be some hope of becoming the centre or abode of a calm, pure strength which would overcome and dispel the world. Our historical documents suggest that in the ancient Buddhist order in India, these were the motives which inspired the efforts of a considerable section of the community of monks. Before their minds was an ideal state of *Unconcernedness*, almost like the Stoic ideal of *apatheia*. It is against them that the

Mahayana's stress on Omniscience is directed. If you are all the time dominated by a desire to escape from the evils of the world, your idea of self-extinction may very well come to resemble a perpetual dreamless sleep. The Buddha, however, is one who is awake all the time, and in Sanskrit the root BUDH denotes both *to wake up* and *to know*. That is one of the reasons why the Mahayana stressed Omniscience as a goal for all.

In addition, the virtue of Omniscience lies precisely in that *I* have not the slightest desire for it. Not one of our instincts impels us to seek all-knowledge. As a goal it is quite alien to our natural constitution. We are obviously faced with a contradiction : My goal as a follower of the Path, must be attractive to me, because otherwise *I* would not try to reach it. It must, however, also be unattractive to me, because otherwise *I* would try to reach it. But the goal is where my present I, and all that it values and understands, has ceased to be, and cannot enter at all. It is clearly ridiculous for me, or for anyone else, seriously to pretend that they want to know every detail of the entire universe. Compared with the vast universe, the whole of mankind is less than a small spot of fungus on a pebble in the Atlantic Ocean as compared with the Atlantic Ocean itself. How much less am I. Omniscience and I can never be brought together. But when I am no longer I, anything may happen.

It is not easy, it is against our nature, to accept this contradiction, and to remain contented with it. To persons constituted as we are, it is tempting to conceive of our goal as something to be got hold of—like a butterfly caught in a net, or like an interest-bearing bank account. We like an emancipation which, in the words of Eckhart, we can *wrap into a blanket, and put underneath a bench*. To correct the error of trying to approach the goal as a thing out there, one may say that the goal is nothing at all, i.e. emptiness, or the identity of yes and no. Or, alternatively, one may say that it is all things, not the sum of all things, but a totality of all things which both includes and excludes each individual thing. Clearly unthinkable, but in all-knowledge an object identical with its subject. To do all things, not conscious of doing anything. To think all things, and not be conscious of any thing. To strive for all things, and be content never to get to them. That is the miracle we must perform to be rid of ourselves. *" One who does not train himself to get hold of all-knowledge, he trains himself in all-knowledge, he will go forth into all-knowledge."*

Parallels

The ideas of the Prajñaparamita and of the Madhyamikas are apt to appear strange to Europeans, as standing completely outside the stream of our own philosophical tradition. It may therefore be useful to remind the reader that we have here not a peculiarly Indian phenomenon, but that the Mediterranean world knows, or knew, a number of similar developments.

The a-theoretical attitude of the Madhyamikas had, for instance, a striking parallel in the so-called Greek *Sceptics*. The founder of this school is Pyrrhon of Elis (c. 330 B.C.). Except for the stress on Omniscience, his view of life corresponds in all its details closely to that of the Madhyamikas. Pyrrhon had no positive doctrines. To be his disciple meant *to lead a kind of life similar to that of Pyrrhon.* " He wanted to reveal to men the secret of happiness, by showing them that ' salvation ' can be found only in the peace of a thought which is indifferent, a sensibility which is extinct, a will which is obedient; and further, that this quest requires an effort which is, on the part of the individual, an effort to die to himself." (L. Robin, *Pyrrhon et le scepticisme grec*, 1944, p. 24.)

Freedom from passion is the great aim of life, and even-mindedness is the attitude one must strive to cultivate. All external things are *the same*, there *is no difference between them*, and the sage does not distinguish between them. To gain this state of indifference one must sacrifice all natural instincts. All theoretical views are equally unfounded and one must completely abstain from forming propositions and from passing judgments. There is, in Pyrrhon's philosophy, the same distinction between

conventional truth, the *appearances* (phainomena) on the one side, and the *ultimate truth* (adēla) on the other. The ultimate truth is completely hidden. " *I do not know that honey is sweet, but I agree that it* appears *to me so.*"
Pyrrhon's inhibition of all theoretical judgment is technically called *epokhe*. Its meaning is very clearly explained by Aristocles of Messene, under three headings : 1. What is the inner nature (=own-being, svabhāva in Sanskrit) of things ? It can be characterised only by negations, because all things are equally *in-different, im-ponderable, un-decided*. They are all equal and none weighs more than another. One cannot say of any thing that it is *more this than it is not this*. One might equally well *affirm that it is and is not, or deny that it is or is not*. 2. What is our situation with regard to them ? We should not trust more in one than in another. We should not incline towards them. We should not be agitated by them. 3. How should we conduct ourselves towards them ? The wisest attitude is a speechless silence, imperturbability, and indifference. *Non-action* is the only action possible.
From this parallel, one can incidentally draw a conclusion as regards the date of the appearance of the Madhyamika views in India itself. This conclusion sounds rather extravagant, but I think it has sufficient plausibility to be mentioned here. It is a fact that Pyrrhon founded his school immediately on his return from Asia, which, together with his teacher, Anaxarchos, he had visited in the train of Alexander's army. It has further been asserted by Robin, and other authorities, that the sceptic philosophy was something quite new to Greece, and that none of the preceding indigenous Greek developments led up to it. One can therefore infer with some probability that Pyrrhon acquired his views in India or Iran. If he did not acquire them in Iran, the tenets of the Madhyamikas would have been present in India already by about 350 B.C. They were, of course, not necessarily transmitted to Pyrrhon by Buddhist monks. It is perhaps more probable that he was in contact with the Digambara Jains, who, in the Greek accounts, occur under the name ' gymnosophists,' *the naked ascetics*. The Jains and Buddhists lived in close

contact with each other, and the doctrine of each shows the influence of the other. It is, for instance, curious that the Jains have a list of twenty-four successive Tirthankaras (saviours), and that ancient Hinayana Buddhism knows a list of twenty-four predecessors of Shakyamuni. I believe that the Mahayana doctrine of Omniscience has also been profoundly influenced by the Jain views on that subject. As a matter of fact, a typical Jain doctrine is recorded among the sayings of Pyrrhon. He gave as his reason for writing no books that he was *resolved to exert no pressure on anybody's mind.* The Jains, before him, had drawn, from their injunction of 'inoffensiveness,' the logical conclusion that one must not do violence to anyone by imposing one's views upon him. However that may be, if it is granted that Pyrrhon owed his basic ideas to his conversion by Indians, and if his philosophy is very similar to that of the Madhyamikas, then the Madhyamika doctrines, which are known to us only from writings certainly not older than about 100 B.C., must go back in their essentials to ca 350 B.C., i.e. to within 150 years after the Buddha's Nirvana.

Whatever the merits of this argument, the extraordinary fact remains that during the same period, i.e. from ca 200 B.C. onward—two distinct civilisations, one in the Mediterranean, the other in India, constructed out of their own cultural antecedents, a closely analogous set of ideas concerning Wisdom, each one independently, as it seems. In the Eastern Mediterranean we have the Wisdom books of the Old Testament, nearly contemporaneous with the Prajñaparamita in its first form. Later on, under the influence of Alexandria, the Gnostics and Neoplatonists developed a literature which assigned a central position to *Wisdom* (Sophia) and which, from Philon to Proclus, reveals a profusion of verbal coincidences with the Prajñaparamita texts. Among the Christians, this tradition was continued by Origenes and Dionysius Areopagita ; among others, the magnificent church of Hagia Sophia is an eloquent witness to the importance of wisdom in the Eastern branch of the Christian church. Numerous are the parallels, or coincidences, between the treatment of Chochma and Sophia, on the one hand, and the Buddhist texts dealing with perfect wisdom on the other hand. To explain these coincidences by ' borrowing ' does not get us very far. We do not ' explain ' Lloyd George's social legislation by saying that he ' borrowed ' it from Germany. A real explanation would have to go into the *motive* of the borrower. Mere borrowing also would not explain the fact that both in Buddhism and Judaism the conception of wisdom, as it evolved after 200 B.C., grew quite naturally out of the preceding tradition, and is in no conflict with any of their basic concepts. To note only one difference : Sophia plays a definite role at the creation of the world, while the Prajñaparamita has no cosmic functions, and remains unburdened by the genesis of this universe. The iconographies of Sophia and Prajñaparamita also seem to have evolved independently. I was, however, interested to come across a Byzantine miniature of the 10th century (Vat. Palat. gr. 381 fol. 2) which is said to go back to an Alexandrian model. There, the right hand of Sophia makes the gesture of teaching, while the left arm holds a book. This is not unlike some Indian statues of the Prajñaparamita. In all this we may have parallel developments, under the influence of local conditions, from a general widely diffused pattern of human culture. Or, of course, there may be some hidden rhythm in history which activates certain archetypes— as Jung would call them—at certain periods in widely distant places.

VI

THE BUDDHISM OF FAITH AND DEVOTION

The Reception of Bhakti

THE New Wisdom School was the movement of an elite which from compassion regarded the interests of the common people as their own. It could therefore not content itself with formulating the highly abstract metaphysics described in the last chapter. In order to fulfil its mission, it had to supplement its metaphysical doctrines with a mythological system.

The Bodhisattva was committed to *Skill in means*. He could not possibly confine his activities on behalf of the salvation of others to the advice to meditate on emptiness. Otherwise the majority of the people would be left out, by their lack of metaphysical inclinations, their preoccupation with earning a living, and their deep-rooted attachment to property, family and home. Since, however, the layman also is involved in suffering, and, as originally divine, endowed with spiritual longings and potentialities, the word of the Buddha is addressed to him as well.

Incapable of wisdom, he must use Faith. The way of transcendental wisdom is supplemented by that of Faith, or *Bhakti*. Nagarjuna distinguishes the easy way of Faith from the hard and difficult way of Wisdom. Both lead to the same goal, just as one can travel to the same town either by water, or on land. Some prefer the method of zealous vigour, of austerities, and of meditation. Others can, by the easy practice of the *helpful means* of Faith, simply by thinking of the Buddha while invoking his names, rapidly attain to a state *from which there is no falling back*, i.e. from which they go on to full enlightenment, in the certainty of reaching it.

Faith, a rather subordinate virtue in the Hinayana, now

comes to rank equal with wisdom itself. Its power to save is much greater than the old schools assumed. The increasing degeneration of mankind had to be recognised. The *hard* way of self-trained, vigorous wisdom was no longer feasible for many, if not for the majority, even among the monks. Under these circumstances, the *easy* way of Faith was the only one of which people were still capable.

From ca 400 B.C. onward a movement of Bhakti had gathered momentum in India, and about the beginning of our era it had gained great strength. Bhakti means the loving personal devotion to adored deities conceived in human form. About the time of the Christian era the bhaktic tendencies of the Indian masses, which had influenced Buddhism for a long time, invaded it in full force. The metaphysics of the New Wisdom School was sufficiently elastic to absorb the trend towards Bhakti, and to provide it with a philosophical foundation. The 'result of the organic fusion between the ' new wisdom ' Buddhism and the bhaktic movement is what we shall call the *Buddhism of Faith*.

The Mahayana had insisted on the universality of salvation as against a Hinayana that seemed incomplete not least because it had concentrated on the elite, and had few effective means of helping the less endowed to salvation. The Mahayanist takes his duty towards his less developed fellow-beings most seriously. He must make the Dharma, if not intelligible, then at least accessible to them. The inner logic of perfect wisdom leads to its negation in faith. If Nirvana and the world are identical, if everything is the same as everything else, then there is no real difference between the enlightened and the unenlightened, between the wise and the fools, between purity and impurity, and everyone must have the same opportunity for salvation. If the Buddha's compassion is unlimited, he must save also the fools. If the Buddha-nature is equally present in all, then all are equally near Buddhahood. The Mahayana *Buddhism of Faith* draws the practical conclusions. It evolves methods which remove the difference between poor and rich, between ignorant and learned, between sinners and saints, between the pure and the impure. Since all have the same claim to salvation, it must be made equally accessible to all.

Literary History

The literature of this school combines the terms, phrases and ideas of the New Wisdom School with devotion to personal saviours. It began in India about the beginning of our era. Four hundred or five hundred years later it was more and more submerged by Tantric ideas. To an increasing extent, it became preoccupied with the provision of 'spells' by which one could approach deities, and induce them to do one's will (see p. 182 sq.).

One of the first Buddhas to become an object of Bhakti was Akshobhya (*The Imperturbable*), who rules in the East, in the Buddha-land of Abhirati. He is mentioned in quite a number of early Mahayana Sutras. His worship must have been fairly widespread, but only fragments of his legend have survived. The cult of Amitabha shows strong Iranian influence, and began about the same time. Amitabha is the Buddha of Infinite (amita) Light (ābhā) and his kingdom is in the West. He is also known as Amitayus, because his life-span (āyuh) is infinite (amita). A great number of texts are devoted to Amitabha. The best known among them is the *Sukhavati-vyuha*, *The Array of the Happy Land*, which describes his Paradise, its origin and structure. In addition, Bhaishajyaguru, the Buddha of healing, enjoyed a great popularity. In China and Japan Amitabha has been much more popular than any other Buddha. In India he seems never to have occupied such an overtowering position, although Huei-je, a Chinese pilgrim, who visited India between 702 and 719, reports that everyone spoke to him about Amitabha and his Paradise

Other texts, again, dealt with the Bodhisattvas. Like the Buddhas, they are very numerous, and we can only mention a few. Among the creations of the mythological imagination of the Buddhism of Faith, Avalokitesvara is easily the most outstanding. By the power of his magic, and by his infinite

care and skill he *affords safety to those who are anxious.*
The word Avalokitesvara is a compound of the word
ishvara (Lord, Sovereign), and of *avalokita*, which means
he who looks down with compassion, i.e. on beings suffering
in this world. Avalokitesvara personifies compassion. The
texts and the images suggest that in India one may distinguish three stages in his development. At first, he is
a member of a Trinity, consisting of Amitāyus,
Avalokitesvara and Mahāsthāmaprāpta (i.e. " *The one who
has attained great strength* "). This Trinity has many
counterparts in Iranean religion, i.e. in the Mithras cult
and in Zervanism, a Persian religion which recognised
Infinite Time (Zervan Akarana=Amita-āyus) as the
fundamental principle. Assimilated by Buddhism,
Avalokitesvara becomes a great Bodhisattva, so great that
he is nearly as perfect as a Buddha. He possesses a great
miraculous power to help in all kinds of dangers and
difficulties. In the second stage, Avalokitesvara acquires
a number of cosmic functions and features. He " *holds
the world in his hand,*" he is immensely big—" 800,000
myriads of miles* "—," *each of the pores of his skin conceals
a world system.*" He is the Lord and Sovereign of the
world. From his eyes come the sun and the moon, from
his mouth the winds, from his feet the earth. In all these
respects Avalokitesvara resembles the Hindu God, Brahma.
Finally, in the third stage, at a time when the magical
elements of Buddhism come to the fore, he becomes a
great magician who owes his power to his mantras, and
he adopts many of the characteristics of Shiva. This is
the Tantric Avalokitesvara. In some ways Mañjusrī
was Avalokitesvara's equal in popularity. He personifies
wisdom. A number of Sutras were composed in his honour,
some before 250 A.D. Many other Bodhisattvas, like
Kshitigarbha, and Samantabhadra, could be enumerated,
but for the details we must refer the reader to Ch. Eliot's
book on *Japanese Buddhism.*

The Agent of Salvation

To judge from the Scriptures of the Old Wisdom School,

self-reliance seems to have been one of the outstanding
traits of its adherents. It was taken for granted that one
could only save oneself by one's own personal effort and
that ' none could be saved by another.'   Three new
ideas helped to undermine, in the Buddhism of Faith, such
an attitude of exclusive self-reliance.   They were the
doctrine of the *Transfer of Merit*, the notion that the
Buddha nature is present *in all of us*, and the invention of
a large number of *Saviours*.

The belief that merit can be transferred from one person
to another runs counter to the *Law of Karma*, as it had been
understood in the old order.   The original belief seems
to have been that each one of us has his own series of
karma, that the punishment for his misdeeds must be
suffered by him, and that the rewards for his good deeds
are enjoyed only by him.   This excessive individualism
was not essential to the karma doctrine, and just as
historically the notion of collective responsibility preceded
that of individual responsibility, so, in the Vedas, it had
been assumed that the members of a family or clan all
share one common karma.   The individualistic interpretation of the law of karma throws each individual on
his own resources, and seems to deny any solidarity between
the different persons as regards the more essential things
of life, i.e. as regards merit and demerit. We hear of a
Brahmin who objected to the Buddha's teaching on the
count that, when carried into practice, it created merit
only in one single person.   The Buddha replied that
the actions of the saints affected usually a multitude of
people whom they inspired with their example, but there
is no sign that any Buddhist Scripture before 200 B.C.
definitely teaches the transfer of merit from one person
to another.

Merit is that quality in us which ensures future benefits
to us, be they material or spiritual.   It is not difficult to
perceive that to desire merit, to hoard, store, and accumulate
merit, does, however meritorious it may be, imply a considerable degree of self-seeking.   It has always been the
tactics of the Buddhists to weaken the possessive instincts
of the spiritually less-endowed members of the community

by withdrawing them from such objects as wealth and family, and directing them instead towards one aim and object, i.e. the acquisition of merit. But that, of course, is good enough only on a fairly low spiritual level. At higher stages one will have to turn also against this form of possessiveness, one will have to be willing to give up one's store of merit for the sake of the happiness of others. The Mahayana drew this conclusion and expected its followers to endow other beings with their own merit, or, as the Scriptures put it, ' *to turn over, or dedicate, their merit to the enlightenment of all beings.*'   " *Through the merit derived from all my good deeds I wish to appease the suffering of all creatures, to be the medicine, the physician, and the nurse of the sick as long as there is sickness. Through rains of food and drink I wish to extinguish the fire of hunger and thirst.   I wish to be an inexhaustible treasure to the poor, a servant who furnishes them with all they lack.   My life, and all my re-births, all my possessions, all the merit that I have acquired or will acquire, all that I abandon without hope of any gain for myself in order that the salvation of all beings might be promoted.*"

This is the intention.   It is carried out by the great Bodhisattvas in the last stages of their spiritual progress, and it is embodied in their *vows*.   A portion of their immeasurable merit is transferred to the believer, if asked for in faith.

Secondly, the emphasis on the identity of the Buddha with this world had accustomed the Mahayanists to the idea that the Buddha nature dwells in every part of the universe, and therefore in the heart of each one of us.

' *The Lord Buddha on his lion-throne*
    Dwells in each particle of sand and stone.'

If one assumes that by our own efforts we ourselves strive for salvation, which part of ourselves is it then that seeks Nirvana ?   Is it our individual self, or perhaps our ' higher self,' our ' Buddha-self,' which does the seeking ?   The Mahayana came to the conclusion that it is really the Buddha in us who does the seeking and that it is the Buddha nature in us which seeks Buddha-hood.

Thirdly, the Buddha had been a teacher and not a saviour.

In the Buddhism of Faith the higher Bodhisattvas developed into the saviours of the faithful. Once a Bodhisattva had saturated himself with the perfection of wisdom, and annihilated himself by a thorough understanding of emptiness, his being underwent a complete transformation. All self-interest and attachment are then abolished. A Bodhisattva could, on principle, extinguish himself at this point, but compassion prevented him. He would continue to act, but his activity would be perfectly pure. A true king, he enjoys sovereignty over the world. A Bodhisattva at this stage acquired all kinds of unearthly and supernatural qualities. He could be miraculously reborn at will wherever, and in whatever shape, he desired; he possessed an unlimited power of transformation, etc. The New Wisdom School had conceived of the possibility of such supernatural beings. The Buddhism of Faith conceived of them as concrete individuals, and furnished them with names, legends, and a definite and tangible individuality.

Akshobhya and Amitabha, Avalokitesvara and Manjusri, all the celestial Buddhas and Bodhisattvas of this school are, however, obviously productions of the mind, and without historical or factual basis. It is not easy to understand that the Mahayanists could admit this, as they did, and yet deny that these new saviours were mere creatures, nay figments, of the imagination, subjective and arbitrary inventions. It is impossible to explain their attitude by the absence of an historical sense generally found among Hindus, since we know that the Indian Buddhists of the Hinayana used to argue that they could not believe in the celestial Buddhas and Bodhisattvas of the Mahayana because there was no evidence of their actual existence.

It seems to me that we have here a philosophical difference which corresponds to the age-old cleavage between " Nominalism " and " Realism." To the Nominalist only the individual has real existence, to the Realist the universal. Similarly, in religion, one type of mind requires an actual historical fact to base its belief on, while another regards the productions of the creative mythological imagination as in no way inferior to the products of human history. Many Christians set much store by the assertion that

Jesus Christ was an historical person. To the mythological school, the question of historical existence seems to be quite irrelevant. Such a mentality considers only Christ as religiously and spiritually significant, and not the man Jesus. In early Christian history, the Mahayanist attitude was represented by some Gnostic sects, who claimed that the Christ descended on the man Jesus at baptism and left him again on the Cross, at the point where Jesus said, " *My God, my God, why hast Thou forsaken me ?* " Philosophers distinguish between *what* a person is and the fact *that* he is. In the traditional conception of the Christ there is not one single element which is not pre-Christian, which is not shared by other religious systems, which does not recur in the legends about the Messiah, about Osiris, about Herakles, and many others. The mythological school regards the mythological concept as the essential thing. Whether it is embodied, or not, in a person in history appears as a quite incidental and trivial detail. The names of Amitabha, etc., may be invented, but the reality behind them, the Absolute, is there all the time.

In China, this attitude of the Mahayana came up against the keen and accurate historical sense of the Chinese literary tradition, and we find an inclination to seek for an historical nucleus of the celestial Bodhisattvas. One said, for instance, of Mañjushri, that he was originally a Chinese prince, who lived in the first century, at Wu-t'ai-shan, the Mountain of the Five Peaks (Pañcashirsha), at the time of the Emperor Ming-ti. Thus located in time and space he was satisfactorily accounted for. Similarly, the Green Tara was traced back to a Chinese princess. The Tibetan king, Song Tsen Gampo (d. 650) had two wives, one Chinese and one Nepalese. They were identified with two goddesses, the White Tara and the Green Tara. To the Indian mind this was an ordinary case of incarnation of a pre-existing spiritual force. Some Chinese reversed the process. To their instinctive Euhemerism it appeared that the princesses were ' deified ' as the two Taras, that the Goddess Tara was an apotheosis of the historical persons, who, far from being the embodiment of an idea, were its real starting point. In the large cosmic perspective of the early Mahayana this insistence on the puny data of human history would have appeared quite incomprehensible.

The Aims of the Faithful

What, then, did the faithful expect of the Buddhas and Bodhisattvas ? In the Buddhism of Faith the saviours have, in the main, four functions :

1. They promote the virtues of the faithful, help to remove greed, hate and delusion, and protect from ghosts and men who may maliciously try to interfere with spiritual practices.

2. In addition, they bestow material benefits. Since the Buddhas and Bodhisattvas are all-merciful, it was natural, and, in some ways, logical to assume that they should concern themselves with the actual wishes of their adherents, protect their earthly fortunes and ward off disasters. Avalokitesvara, for instance, protects caravans from robbers, sailors from ship wreck, criminals from execution. By his help women obtain the children they desire. If one but thinks of Avalokitesvara, fire ceases to burn, swords fall to pieces, enemies become kind-hearted, bonds are loosened, spells *revert to whence they came*, beasts flee, and snakes lose their poison. This aspect of the Buddhism of Faith stands in logical contradiction to the emphasis on the need for renunciation which pervades the Buddhist doctrine. As a magical doctrine, Buddhism promises to remove evils physically, as a spiritual doctrine it aims at purging the mind of a wrong attitude to them. We have stated before (p. 83) that what is contradictory in thought may well co-exist in life.

3. The Buddhas and Bodhisattvas become an object of the desire to *love*. Now the word *love* is extremely ambiguous, and harbours a great multiplicity of meanings. In this context, *love* in the sense of *Bhakti* means a personal relationship with a person whom one not only cherishes and adores, but whom one wishes to see, wishes to be with, whom one does not want to let go, whom one wants to persist. The orthodox view which the " *Wise* " had formed

of the Buddha had made him quite unsuitable as an object of such love. He was said to be *extinct*, and, after his Nirvana, to have gone to nowhere at all. He was really lost to the world, quite isolated from it. Only his Dharma, an impersonal entity, remained. This theory had, from the very start, proved emotionally quite unsatisfactory to those whose religion meant *love*. Ananda, among the immediate disciples of the Buddha the chief representative of bhaktic mentality, a man who *loved* the Lord as a person, could not resign himself to his loss. He formed the quite heretical opinion that, when he entered Nirvana, the Buddha had gone up to the Heavens of Brahma, just as at birth he had come down from the Tushita Heavens.

As time went on, the bhaktic trend grew in India. Buddhism was not exempt from it. Increasingly the faithful wished to " *dwell in the sight of the Buddha*," or to " *see the Tathagatas*." In spite of official discouragement, they wished to believe that the Lord Buddha was not really extinct, but that somewhere he was present and in existence. Wisdom and devotion were in open conflict. Wisdom consisted in giving up all supports whatsoever. Devotion was unhappy without some persisting person as its support. The Mahasanghikas came to the rescue of the devotional needs of the laity by fostering the belief that the Buddha, as a supramundane being (see p. 121) had not quite passed away, but persisted after his Nirvana in some form or other. The Mahayana greatly developed this idea, and filled the entire universe to the utmost limits of space with Buddhas and Bodhisattvas who were alive and thus could be loved and treasured.

4. Finally, the Buddhas and Bodhisattvas provided favourable conditions for the attainment of enlightenment in a future life. In this respect the Mahayana merely continued the line of its predecessors. The majority of the faithful had obviously never expected to obtain the highest goal of Nirvana in this very life. Instead, they could only hope to gain access to a plane of the universe which offered fewer obstacles to the attainment of full enlightenment than the world of men. Rebirth in the heavens was to them the immediate reward of a holy life, and of the act

of taking refuge in the Three Treasures. There, among the Gods, the virtuous might "*finally pass away*" (parinibbayati), "*not to return from that world*" All the Mahayana did was to replace the heavens of the old Hindu Gods by the heavens of the Buddhas and Bodhisattvas, and to increase the opportunities of the average man by multiplying the Paradises in which he could be reborn. Even within the Hinayana, the Paradise of Maitreya (see p. 116) had become increasingly popular as a place of future rebirth. Maitreya, the next Buddha, at present reigns and preaches in the *Tushita Heavens*, which, inhabited by the *Satisfied Gods*, are the regular abode of a future Buddha of this world system in his last existence but one. The pious aspired, after death, to go to Maitreya's kingdom and to stay there until they would be with him in his final life on earth.

Looking out on the starry sky in its immensity, the Mahayana perceived such paradises everywhere. Just as the Buddha Shakyamuni appeared in this world system, so other world systems have their Buddhas also. In assigning different Buddhas to different world systems, the Mahayana was not original. The Mahasanghikas and Sautrantikas had already done so. The originality of the Mahayana consisted in the development of the notion of a *Buddha-field* (*buddha-kshetra*), or *Buddha-land*, and in the distinction they made between *pure* and *impure* Buddha-fields.

Each Buddha has a certain limited field of influence, in which, with a "*deep, sublime and wonderful voice*," he teaches the Dharma to creatures, and thereby helps them to win enlightenment. A Buddha-field is a kind of *kingdom of God*, a mystical universe, inhabited by the Buddha and by the beings whom he *rules* and *matures*. According to Buddhaghosa, a Buddha has a twofold relation to his universe: (1) In his omniscience he knows the entire universe, which is a *field of his knowledge*. (2) By his sovereignty he exercises authority and influence over a certain range of world systems. The first relation is clearly developed in earlier Hinayana literature. The second idea—that of a spatially limited magical influence of the Buddha, of his sovereignty over a particular area (as distinct from his supreme eminence in it)—is almost completely absent from earlier Hinayana literature, and was adopted by Buddhaghosa from the Mahayana.

But this is not all. Many Buddha-fields are identical with the natural and *impure* world systems which are inhabited by creatures in all the six states of existence (see p. 50 sq.). Other Buddha-fields again, like that of the Buddha Amitabha, for instance, are " *Pure Lands.*" Some Buddhas create realms which are not natural, but ideal, or transcendent in the sense that they stand outside the " *triple world* " of sense-desire, form and formlessness ; devoid of women, animals, ghosts and the damned ; inhabited only by Bodhisattvas of great spiritual perfection, either Gods or men, " *pure in body, voice and mind,*" come into being by apparitional birth. There one sees the radiant body of the Buddha, listens to his preaching, and undergoes further and further purification until Buddahood is reached by all. This " *paradise* " is often described with much sensory imagery. It is bright, made of lapis lazuli, free from stones and gravel, holes and steep precipices, gutters and sewers. It is even, lovely, calming and beautiful to behold, adorned with jewel trees that are fastened in a checker-board marked off with gold threads, covered with flowers etc. " *Beings who are born in that land will never suffer untimely death, will be abundantly rich, doers of good, truthful and sincere, tender in talk. Their families and relatives will never be scattered. They will be skilful in reconciling quarrels, ever benefiting others when speaking. They will never be envious or angry, but ever maintain right principles.*"

All this is straightforward popular religion. It is, however, characteristic of Buddhism that great efforts are made to integrate these popular conceptions with the basic ideas of the New Wisdom School. It would go against the spirit of the doctrine of universal emptiness if one would have those paradises as a kind of crude actuality out there in space. As a matter of fact, they are really produced by the minds of the Bodhisattvas. To quote the Avatamsaka :

" The Buddha-lands as innumerable as particles of

dust are raised from one thought cherished in the
mind of the Bodhisattva of mercy,
Who, practising meritorious deeds in numberless kalpas
has led all beings to the truth.
All the Buddha-lands rise from one's own mind and
have infinite forms,
Sometimes pure, sometimes defiled, they are in various
cycles of enjoyment or suffering."

The Buddha-field is the result of a Bodhisattva's altruism,
which does not aim at isolation from the evil-doers, but
at their conversion. The " *Ratnamegha* " is instructive
on this point : " *If the Bodhisattva learns of peoples' grasping
greed and violence, he must not say, 'Away with these people
so grasping and violent,' and on that account be depressed
and turn back on them. He makes a vow to have a very pure
Field in which the very name of such persons shall not be
heard. But if the Bodhisattva turns his face away from the
welfare of all creatures, his field is not pure and his work
is not accomplished.*"

Few of us would at present believe that one can create
a world by merely wishing to. The creative power of
ethically relevant actions is as axiomatic to the Buddhists,
as it is strange to us. The environment in which beings
have to live is to a great extent, especially in regard to its
pleasantness or unpleasantness, determined by their deeds
(karma). The various hells, for instance, are *produced* by
the deeds of the creatures who are reborn there. We have
waterless deserts in our world because of our small merit.
The world of things (bhajana-loka) is really nothing more
than a kind of reflex of peoples' deeds. An environment
can exist only as long as there are persons whose karma
compels them to perceive it. In the same spirit one now
claims that the merit of a Bodhisattva may be great enough
to create a Pure Land not only for himself, but also for
others to whom he transfers it.

As a popular religion, the Buddhism of Faith teaches a
multiplicity of Buddha-fields. As an off-shoot of Wisdom-
Buddhism, it knows that this multiplicity is only pro-
visionally true. Ultimately all fields are one field, and
one field is all fields. Ultimately, the natural and the

ideal Buddha-fields are one and the same. The Buddha is omnipresent, and *this* world is essentially the ideal world, if one will only recognise it as such. " *Here in this very chamber*," says **Vimalakirti**, " *all the magnificent heavenly palaces and all the Pure Lands of all the Buddhas are manifested*." This world of ours seems quite impure, replete with all kinds of woes and sorrows, wretched and full of terrors. To those, however, who have a true faith, this same world appears with all the features of a Pure Land, " *made of lapis lazuli, forming a level plain, forming a checkerboard of eight compartments with gold threads, set off with jewel trees*." It is again Vimalakirti who brings out the paradoxical character of this teaching, when he says : " *Beings, because of their sins, cannot see the pureness of this Buddha-land of ours. Really this land of ours is ever pure. The impurities are in your own mind. I tell you, Sariputra, the Bodhisattva, pure in his firm mind, looks upon all things impartially with the wisdom of a Buddha, and therefore this Buddha-land is to him pure without blemish. This world of ours is ever pure as this. And yet, to save beings of inferior capacities is this wicked and impure world shown.*"

Methods

The goal having been thus defined, we can proceed to enumerate the five methods by which one hopes to gain rebirth in one of the " *Lands of the Blessed* " :

1. One should lead a pure life, and cultivate the desire to become like the Buddhas.

2. As the Mahayana developed, more and more stress was laid upon worship of the Buddhas as a means of accumulating merit. *Worship* comprises such acts as praising the Buddha's virtues, doing homage to his beauty, delighting in the thought of him, requesting to be reborn one day as a perfect Buddha (pranidhana), and the giving of gifts to the Buddha. The latter is a particular source of merit. The merit to be obtained from a gift is the greater the more exalted its recipient. Some individuals and groups, especially the Saints and the Samgha, were from early on

regarded as the world's ' *peerless field of merit.*' In the Mahayana, the Buddha became increasingly the supreme ' *field of merit.*'

3. One should think of the Buddha while repeatedly pronouncing his name. Since the name contains the power of the Buddhas and Bodhisattvas, its invocation is an act of the highest virtue. Innumerable formulas of invocation were elaborated. The most famous of all is " Homage to the Buddha Amitabha ! " Om Namo Amitabhāya Buddhāya in Sanskrit, Om O-mi-to-fo in Chinese, Namo Amida Butsu in Japanese. While on the one hand the professionals surpassed themselves in the number of their repetitions of the holy name, it was conceded to the laymen that " *one single act of devotion,*" " *one single thought of the Buddha,*" " *for one single moment* " will effect his salvation.

4. One should believe firmly that one's chosen Buddha or Bodhisattva has made a " vow " to save all, and that therefore he is both willing and able to save you, and to take you to his paradise. A firm belief is recognised by three features : It must be sincere ; one must be deeply convinced of one's own wretchedness and the power of the Buddha's vow ; one must ' transfer,' or deflect, one's merits to the Paradise, and form a vow to be reborn therein. The collaboration of compassion on the part of the Buddha, and of faith on ours brings about the desired rebirth.

5. One should concentrate in one's meditations on the perfection of a Buddha-land, and one should train the visual imagination to see the Buddhas and Bodhisattvas, and the senses of sound, sight and smell to perceive the sensory beauty of the Buddha-lands.

These are the five methods. Some authorities assume that it is the faith which saves, others that it is the repetition of the holy name. There was much controversy on the first and the fifth of the above methods since, according to some, they savoured too much of self-reliance. In general, the Buddhism of Faith in India was disinclined to disregard the moral worth of the worshipper. Gross sinners, and " *those who calumniate the holy Dharma,*" cannot be saved by faith alone. How can they claim to love the Buddha with all their heart if they offend against his moral teachings, if they refuse to do his will ? It was left to the later developments of Amidism in Japan to proclaim a kind of totalitarianism of Faith, in which faith becomes all-powerful, regardless of moral conduct (see Chapter IX).

Self-extinction and Faith

The specific features of the Buddhist schools which developed after the first 500 years are partly due to social pressure, and partly to the latent implications of the problem of self-extinction. The Mahayana, by adopting the ideal of a Bodhisattva, tries, as we saw (p. 125 sq.), to drive out the last residue of self-seeking. The bhaktic trend eliminates, in faith, all reliance on *self-power*, all reliance on one's own ability to plan and control one's own life and salvation. As soon as we judge it by the standard of self-extinction, the " *Buddhism of Faith* " is in the direct line of Buddhist orthodoxy. Surrender in faith involves a high degree of extinction of separate selfhood, partly because one does not rely on oneself, or one's own power, partly because one sees the futility of all conscious and personal efforts and allows oneself to be ' carried ' to salvation, and partly because one does not claim any special privileges, as due to superior merit or wisdom. Elementary modesty lets us perceive that any merit we may claim compares as nothing with that of the Buddhas and Bodhisattvas, and with the power of their help. Pride has always been a sin to which the more advanced Buddhists were particularly prone. Now they were taught humbly to accept gifts from another, whom they could only perceive in faith. All pride in our intellect, all pride in the purity of our heart, sets up a self against others. If the intellect is seen as futile, the heart as corrupt, that self is deflated. The grace of the Absolute alone can carry us across, and our own personal schemes and endeavours are quite trivial. For it must never be forgotten that that which is represented to the relatively ignorant in the form of a personal saviour and of a paradise is exactly the same thing as that which is taught to the

relatively learned as the Absolute itself. Following out
the logic of the Buddhist dialectics, Buddhist perfection
is found only in its extinction, and it is manifested only
where it becomes quite indiscernible. The distinctive
Buddhist life must go so that Buddhism may be fulfilled.
A sincere heart and belief, unaware of the merit of its
sincerity, is all that is needed. The Buddha's demand
that, in order to be saved, one should learn to do nothing
in particular, is fulfilled in this way as perfectly as in
any other.

VII

THE YOGACARINS

Wisdom and Trance

DURING the first centuries of our era a new school, known as the *Yogacarins*, began to grow up. After 500 A.D. it came to dominate the thought of the Mahayana more and more. The theories of this school are very complex, and do not easily lend themselves to popular exposition. They presuppose a greater familiarity with the methods and effects of trance (samādhi) than most of us possess nowadays.

The initial impulse of Buddhism contained all the later systems of thought in its system of practices (pp. 95, 100). The various practices were grouped under the three headings of *Morality, Trance* and *Wisdom* (pp. 96–114). The theoretical developments discussed in Chapters IV–VI were inaugurated by specialists in Wisdom, and the methods of the Abhidharma were the real driving force behind the theoretical work. But what about morality and trance ? Morality does not enter into the controversies at all until quite late, when the Left Tantra repudiates it (pp. 195 sq.). As for the special approach and the experiences of those who concentrated on the practice of ecstatic meditation, the theoretical formulations of the doctrine had not taken them sufficiently into account. It was the function and purpose of the Yogacarins to give due emphasis to the outlook on the world revealed by withdrawal into trance. *Trance* would suit better the temperament of some monks, *Wisdom* that of others. In the Samyutta Nikaya (II, 115), the difference of the two roads is exemplified by the persons of Musīla and Nārada. The *Bhagavat Gita* devotes a great deal of its space to contrasting the two under the names of Samkhya and Yoga. The " *men of wisdom* " are

chiefly intellectual, the "*men of trance*" chiefly meditative
and ascetic. The former are "*devoted to Dharma*," the
latter just "*muse*" (jhāyin). The Wise are led to *insight*,
while trance leads to *calm*. The Wise pay little attention
to magic, the others a great deal. According to the orthodox
doctrine, only both *wings* together could carry one to
enlightenment. The Sarvastivadins always emphasised the
primacy of wisdom, understood as the contemplation of
Dharmas. In the case of some of them, like for instance
Harivarman, the ecstatic practices of trance have quite
faded into the background. Again, among the Madhyamikas all the attention is given to *Wisdom*, here understood
as a refined dialectics which kills all thought. The
Yogacarins represented a reaction against such over-
emphasis on *thought-processes* with its consequent neglect
of the practice of Trance.

What then was the distinctive doctrine of the Yogacarins ?
They taught that the Absolute is Thought. Not that this
theory, as such, is really new. It had been clearly stated
in the Scriptures of all schools, and we must try to understand why it had been neglected for so long, and for what
reasons the Yogacarins developed it now.

In the Pali Scriptures the Buddha states expressly that
the well-directed mind is like the pellucid water of a clear
pool, free from any scum on the surface. "*Self-luminous
through and through (pabhassara) is that thought, but usually
it is defiled by adventitious taints which come from without.*"
In other words, when the mind is face to face with the
Truth, a self-luminous *spark* of thought is revealed at
the inner core of ourselves and, by analogy, of all reality.
The teachers of the old wisdom school, without expressly
denying the statement, had made little of it. The
Abhidharma wholly dominated their theorizings, and the
Abhidharma considered reality as composed of a succession
of dharmas, or momentary events. We see the world as
it truly is when we see that "*there are dharmas only*"
(*dhamma-matta*), to quote Buddhaghosa's short formula.
The formula of the Yogacarins, "*Thought-only*" (citta-
mātra) derives a great deal of its meaning from its contrast
to the traditional Abhidharma.

In the Prajñaparamita, again, *emptiness* is the ultimate fact of life. To describe that emptiness as *Thought*, as the Yogacarins did, seemed to the Madhyamikas to fulfil no useful purpose whatever. Not that the Prajnaparamita Sutras ignore the tradition about a self-luminous thought at the centre of everything. The fact that it is " *Thought* " does not interest them at all, however. All that concerns them is the dialectical nature of the thought of the absolute, or of an absolute thought (see p. 112 sq.), which is self-contradictory, and identical with its own negation. Of course, thought " *in its essential original nature*," when free from all greed, hate and delusion, is " *a state of transparent luminosity*," and on that level it constitutes " *the essential being of all dharmas*." But, as the Sutra continues, that thought " *is really no thought*," and it neither exists, nor does it not exist. The preoccupation with wisdom, understood as the dialectical dissolution of everything, determines in this case clearly the approach to the problem.

Nor did the career of an absolute " *self-luminous thought* " end here. Chinese Buddhists, with their insistence on passivity and Non-action took up the saying of the Prajnaparamita, and claimed that salvation consisted in attaining to a state of " *No-thought*." They rejected all mental activity, and argued that only stupid people practise virtues and meditate. Their thesis that " *one should not think of anything* " found little favour with their Indian brethren of the Madhyamika school.

The Yogacarins, in their turn, gave quite a different meaning to the old saying. What seemed important to them was the statement that the Absolute is " *Thought*," in the sense that it is to be sought not in any object at all, but in the pure subject which is free from all objects. Before we go on with the explanation of this somewhat cryptic doctrine, we must, first of all, give a sketch of the history of the school.

Literary History

A trend in the direction of the Yogacara school started

about 150 A.D. with the *Sandhinirmocana Sutra*. Between
150 and 400 we have several other literary documents
which teach " *Thought-only*." The *Lankavatara Sutra*,
the *Avatamsaka*, and the *Abhisamayalankara* occupy a
position midway between Madhyamikas and Yogacaras.
The " *Abhisamayalankara* " is an influential commentary
on the Prajñaparamita which has guided its exegesis from
ca 350 A.D. onward, and which is still the basis of the
explanation of the Prajñaparamita in the monasteries of
Tibet and Mongolia. The Avatamsaka takes up the teaching
of the *sameness* of everything (see p. 134), and interprets
it as the interpenetration of every element in the world
with everything else. The one eternal principle of the
universe, which is the *serenity of Mind*, is reflected in the
cosmos, its presence charges everything with spiritual
significance, its mysteries can be beheld everywhere, and
by means of any object one may generate all virtues
and fathom the secrets of the entire universe. The
Avatamsaka Sutra was the basic text of a school which
became powerful in China as the Hua-yen-tsung, in Japan
as the Kegon-shu. Fa-tsang (+ 712) was its greatest
theoretician. The school did a great deal to refine the
attitude to nature in the Far East, and it has inspired
many artists in China and Japan. In India it represents
an important link between the Yogacarins and the Tantra.
The *Yogacara school* was founded about 400 A.D. by the
two brothers, Asanga and Vasubandhu, natives of North-
West India. Some scholars place Asanga as early as 320 A.D.
Asanga and Vasubandhu systematised the theory of
Mind-only, and in addition elaborated three further doctrines, concerning the *store-consciousness*, the three kinds
of *own-being*, and the three *bodies* of the Buddha. The
school evolved an extremely complicated scholastic system,
and was not entirely free from speculative exuberance.
From the ranks of the Yogacara school came the men who
developed a Buddhist version of the science of Logic.
Buddhist Logic was founded by Dignaga, ca 440 A.D.,
and a great deal was written in India on the subject up
to about 1,100 A.D. Interest in logic was stimulated by
its great value for propaganda. During the Indian Middle

Ages, rulers were in the habit of arranging tournaments in which ascetics of different schools, before huge audiences, were pitted against each other in debate. Victory in debate carried with it enhanced prestige and increased patronage. A training in logic gave the Buddhists an advantage over their rivals, and the Hindu sects were soon compelled to elaborate logical systems of their own. Dignaga's logic had an important indirect consequence. Wherever the Yogacarins were influential, interest was deflected from the traditional Abhidharma to the new logic, and so, without being expressly repudiated, the Abhidharma was increasingly neglected. The tradition of Yogacara logic is still active in Tibet. In China we have a fairly extensive, and in Japan, up to the 15th century, a vast literature connected with Indian logical texts.

Together with Buddhism, the Yogacara school disappeared from India about 1,100 A.D. It was brought to China by several teachers. Among them were two first-class intellects, Paramartha (500–569), who came from Ujjayini (Ogein) in East India in 546 A.D., and Hiuen-tsiang, the great pilgrim (ca 650) Hiuen-tsiang's school is known as Weih-shih.

Hiuen-tsiang summed up his teachings in the Ch'eng-wei-shih-lun, *The treatise on the achievement (of the insight that everything is) ' nothing but idea,'* which is still the classical text book of the school in the Far East. The work is an abstract of ten Indian commentaries to Vasubandhu's *Thirty Stanzas*. Hiuen-tsiang relied chiefly on Dharmapala, abbot of Nalanda, rather neglecting the other nine. A great and influential exponent of the Weih-shih school was Hiuen-tsiang's disciple K'uei-chi (632–685). He wrote a great number of commentaries, and also an *Encyclopedia of the doctrines of the Great Vehicle*. The Weih-shih school soon fell apart into a Northern and a Southern branch. In addition to Paramartha's school and the Weih-shih some other versions of the Yogacara tradition were current in China, where long scholastic disputes on the intricacies of the doctrine marked its history. In 653, and again in 712, the school was brought to Japan, as the *Hosso* (=Chinese : *fa tsiang tsong*, ' *mark of dharma* ') sect. In the Tempyo period it flourished greatly through the exertions of the Sojo Gien (+ 728). It survives even now as one of the smaller Japanese sects, with forty-four temples and monasteries, and seven hundred priests.

" *Mind-only* "

Mind, Thought and Consciousness are used as interchange-able terms in Buddhist philosophy. In describing Nirvana by positive terms—calling it *Mind-only*, or *Thought-only*, or *Consciousness-only*—the Yogacarins seem to deviate from the Buddhist tradition which has always preferred negative names for the Absolute. The word *Nirvana* itself means to *be blown out*, and where other traditions speak of *eternal life*, Buddhism speaks of *the Deathless*. It wishes jealously to guard the transcendence of the Absolute, and to avoid the danger of misconceptions which arise if the same name which applies to something found in this world is also given to what is absolutely different from the world—as when Christians call God a *person*. Why then should the Yogacarins choose *Consciousness* among all the constituents of the world, and designate the Absolute by it ?

They intended to point to a spot in the world, to a dimension of self-awareness, where we are most likely to find it. In all our experience, an object stands out against a subject. The subject is identified by the Abhidharma with the skandha of Consciousness, defined by *Awareness* as its essential mark. Just as the blade of a knife cannot cut itself, so we cannot experience consciousness directly, as an object in front of us. For as soon as we turn to the subject, it becomes an object and ceases to be the subject. Introspection can thus never hope to meet the subject face to face. The final subject—which might be at the end of the infinite regress—is completely beyond our experience, it is not really of this world, it is transcendental. To try to get to it would be to attempt the impossible. This is exactly what the Yogacarins set themselves out to do.

By ruthless withdrawal from each and every object, in the introversion of trance, one could hope to move towards such a result. In any condition in which my personality might normally find itself, the subject is always associated with some object. If, on the other hand, there is, in the absence of an object standing up against the subject, no such admixture of any relation to an object, then I could be said to have realised my *inmost self* in its purity. Salvation could then be said to consist in a revulsion from all objective and external accretions to that inmost self itself, which is realised when it can stand alone, without an object or the thought of one. " *There is no grasping where there is nothing to be grasped.*"

We can now see more clearly the link between this line of reasoning, and the experience of ecstatic trance. The wisdom schools had annihilated the objects around us by a ruthless *analysis* which found but countless momentary Dharmas, too impersonal or fragile to bear much attachment, and by a ruthless *dissociation*, which cuts off identification with all objects in turn by the thought, " *I am not this, this is not mine, this is not myself.*" The ruthless *introversion* of ecstatic meditation also removes the object, but by withdrawing from it. The experience of it gave their special tone to the Yogacara theories. We remember (pp. 100-101) that the stages of *Dhyana* proceed by the successive withdrawal from all external stimuli or objects, which impinge less and less on the mind, until the six organs of sense are *in repose ;* in the highest trance there is no external object left at all. The Yogin seeks for happiness and fulfilment not in outer things, but in the quiet calm of the pure inwardness of his own thought. The wisdom schools had always maintained that we are troubled because we falsely identify with our true self something we find in our empirical self. The Yogacarins now define the true self as the ultimate subject. Then, as a natural consequence, the root of all evil must lie in our proclivity to see anything as separated from, or as external to, that inmost self, in the way of an object. In reality all things and thoughts are but *Mind-only*. The basis of all our illusions consists in that we regard the objectifications of our own mind as a world independent of that mind, which is really its source and substance. As a philosophical doctrine, this is very similar to the Idealism of Berkeley. Bishop Berkeley said that "*some truths are so near and obvious to the mind that a man need only open his eyes to see them. Such I take this important one to be, viz. that all the choir of heaven and furniture of the earth— in a word, all those bodies which compose the mighty frame of the world—have not any subsistence without a mind.*" The external world is really Mind itself. The multiplicity of external objects is "*mere representation,*" "*nothing but ideas.*" "*Just as in a mirage there is no real water, and yet the notion of real water is produced, so there is no object, but the notion of an object is engendered.*" The highest insight is reached when everything appears as sheer hallucination. The Yogacarins based this conviction not merely on a number of logical arguments which proved the impossibility of an external object, but on the living experience of ecstatic meditation. In the higher stages of trance the Yogin was accustomed to meet with vivid visual images without a corresponding external stimulus. In the course of his exercises he saw directly before him such objects as a blue circle, or a skeleton, which were mere hallucinatory ideas, or, as interpreted by Asanga, mere thought. The world is like a dream. A dream is merely an awareness of ideas ; the corresponding objects are not really there. Just as one perceives the lack of objectivity in the dream pictures after one has woken up, so the lack of objectivity in the perceptions of waking life is perceived by those who have been awakened by the knowledge of true reality.

"*Store-consciousness*"

The Yogacara concept of a "*Store-consciousness*" (*ālaya-vijñāna*) is of interest less for its actual value, than for the motive behind it. Asanga postulated an overpersonal consciousness which is the foundation of all acts of thought. The impressions of the whole of past experience are *stored* up in it, all deeds and their fruits. It is not an individual soul, bound to a psycho-physical organism, but it is the objective fact which in our ignorance and self-love we mistake for an individual soul, or self. As worked out by the Yogacarins, the concept of a Store-consciousness is far from intelligible, and it has led to little more than ardent discussions.

That such a concept, unsatisfactory as it is, should have been worked out at all, indicates an important difficulty in the Buddhist system of thought. The Anatta-doctrine had claimed that there was in fact no individual self, or permanent ego, which could account for the self-contained unity of an individual. What appears as an individual is really a series of momentary Dharmas which continuously succeed each other. But there remained the relative unity of each series, and its distinction from the others. There remained the observation of commonsense that I remember my own inner experiences so much better than those of others, which, in fact, I do not remember at all. There remained the teaching of karma, according to which I experience the fruit of my deeds, and am not punished or rewarded for the deeds of another. There remained the observation that some of my own past experiences are, as it were, *stored up* for a time in a kind of *unconscious*, and influence my actions at a later date. The illusion of individuality may indeed be due to craving, but it is strongly fortified by ordinary observation. One could, of course, brush all this aside, and refer the enquirer to the state of Nirvana in which all these observations would appear in quite a different light.

To all those who have not gone so far, the belief in individuality must, however, seem so plausible that they would expect it to have some kind of objective foundation somewhere. Here was the weak spot in the Buddhist armour, and the problem has harassed the Buddhist theoreticians throughout their history. The heresy of a belief in a self invaded even the ranks of the Order. The followers of one of the eighteen traditional sects—the Sammitiyas—were known as *Pudgala-vadins*, "*Upholders of the belief in a person.*" They attempted to retain some form of belief in a self, or a soul, without quite doing so. They spoke of an indefinable principle called the *pudgala*, the person, who is neither different nor not different from the five Skandhas. It persists through the several lives of a being until he reaches Nirvana. It has a sort of middle position between our true and our empirical self. On the one hand it accounts for our sense of personal identity (like the " empirical self "), and on the other it lasts into Nirvana (like the " true self "). Among all controversial issues, this one was considered as the most critical of all. Throughout the centuries the orthodox never wearied of piling argument upon argument to defeat this admission of a *Self* by the Pudgalavadins. But the more tenaciously and persistently one tries to keep something out of one's mind, or out of a system of thought, the more surely it will come in. The orthodox, in the end, were forced to admit the notion of a permanent ego, not openly, but in various disguises, hidden in particularly obscure and abstruse concepts, like the *Subconscious Life-continuum* (*bhavanga*) of the Theravadins, the *continued existence of a very subtle Consciousness* of the Sautrantikas, the *Root-Consciousness* of the Mahasanghikas, etc. The *Store-Consciousness* of the Yogacarins is conceived in the same spirit. As soon as the advice to disregard the individual self had hardened into the proposition that " *there is no self,*" such concessions to commonsense became quite inevitable.

Once the Yogacarins had given way to the desire to probe into the origins of our illusions, they found themselves carried into an ocean of boundless speculation. Beginning with the Store-Consciousness, they set themselves the task of deducing the actual world from it, and to trace the exact process of evolution by which the ultimate subject became estranged from itself and unfolded itself into an objective world. In doing so, they built up an extremely involved and complicated system of speculative metaphysics which has no direct bearing on the practice of emancipation. They departed from the theoretical simplicity of the past, which was more concerned with undoing illusions than with explaining them. The bulk of Yogacara philosophy, though occasioned by the difficulties inherent in the Anatta-doctrine, represents really an invasion of Buddhism by the Samkhya system of Hindu philosophy which, at about the time of Asanga, was used by Patanjali (ca 450 A.D.) for his theoretical exposition of the Yoga methods still current in India. A complete change had taken place in the mental climate of India between the time of the Abhidharma, and the centuries which saw the growth of the Yogacarins. In the old times the monks were very little concerned with the universe in general. Mental states and psychological methods were all that mattered if one wanted to know oneself. Now, however, when no longer individual but universal salvation is sought after, mental states are considered in their relation to the evolution of the cosmos to which more and more attention is directed. This shift in emphasis began with the Yogacaras, and became more and more marked in the Tantric developments to which we will turn soon.

Further Doctrines

Apart from their identification of Nirvana with Thought, and their speculations about the store-consciousness, the Yogacarins are remembered for the final systematic form they gave to two old ideas, the one ontological, the other Buddhological.

As to the first, they distinguished three kinds of *Own-being*. It is sufficient to mention this doctrine in passing. It means that anything can be viewed from three angles : First, as commonsense sees it, in its *imagined* appearance as an object, where a thing is simply itself, and distinct from others. Secondly, in its *dependent* aspect. One views, more scientifically, events in so far as they are conditioned by one another. Finally, there is a side to everything where it is fully and perfectly real. It then no longer stands out as an object, and it is intuited by Yoga. All things are then one Suchness, Mind-only, undifferentiated, both transcendental and immanent in everything.

The doctrine of the *Three Bodies* of the Buddha must be mentioned because it is the final result of many centuries of thought about the three aspects of the Buddha which we have described above (pp. 34–38). The three bodies are the *Dharmabody*, the *Enjoyment-body*, and the *apparitional body*. The Dharmabody is the Buddha as the Absolute. In his Dharmabody alone is the Buddha truly himself. It is one and single, the other two bodies emanate from it and are supported by it. The Enjoyment-body of the Buddha is his manifestation to the Bodhisattvas in different pure Buddha-fields. In different *assemblies* a different enjoyment-body is seen and heard. This body bears the thirty-two marks, and many miraculous manifestations issue from it. It is *mind-made*, and comes into being without the ordinary processes of procreation and birth. The apparitional body, finally, is a person who is a fictitious magical creation which goes through the motions of descending from heaven, leaving home, practising austerities, winning enlightenment, gathering and teaching disciples, and dying on earth, in order to aid and mature beings of little insight. The Buddha's humanity, always more or less unimportant, has now become a mere figment or phantom. In the Hinayana, already, the Buddha was credited with the miraculous power of conjuring up an appearance of himself, a "*nimitta-Buddha*," which preached elsewhere, while he went begging. The Hindu Gods also had such powers. So we read in the Digha Nikaya that Brahma Sahampati, when he appears in the assembly of the "*Gods of the Thirty-three*," manifests himself in a material body. "*For his shape, as it naturally is, is unbearable to the sight of those Gods.*" This idea is now used in the Mahayana to define the relation of the historical Buddha to the One Eternal Buddha. The One Buddha, the Dharmabody, has existed at all times, but on various occasions it has projected into this world phantom bodies of *Buddhas* to do its work.

The magical connotations of such ideas have been of great historical importance. The world itself, in which the *Buddha-frames* appear, is no more than a magical show (māyā). When teaching the world as a magical illusion, the Buddhists do not mean to say that it is just non-existent. It is tangibly and visually real, but it is deceptive, because one mistakes it for what it is not. It is not genuine, and as a magical trick it should not be treated too seriously. In this practical sense, the things of the world had been called Maya from the beginning of Buddhist history. Now the application of the term is extended. As the Buddha had said to the juggler Bhadra in the "*Ratnakuta*": "*The enjoyments of all beings and their possessions are conjured up by the Maya of their deeds ; this Order of monks by the Maya of the Dharma ; I myself by the Maya of wisdom ; and everything in general by the Maya of the complexity of conditions.*" The world, in other words, is a kind of phantasmagoria, in which magically created beings are saved from a magically created suffering by a magically created saviour, who shows them the unsubstantiality of all that comes into being. It is no wonder that the conviction began to spread that magical methods alone could deal effectively with such a universe. This conviction found shape in the Tantra to which we must now turn.

VIII

THE TANTRA, OR MAGICAL BUDDHISM

The Problem of the Tantra

A S distinct from modern Europeans, Asiatics were quite familiar with the magical feats of conjurers, jugglers, etc., who formed a regular part of their daily lives. At this point I think, a concrete example will be helpful to show how the average Hindu, Arab, or Chinese viewed these things. In the 14th century Ibn Batuta, an Arab traveller, visited the Viceroy of Hang-chau fu. A juggler " *took a wooden ball, with several holes in it, through which long ropes were passed, and, laying hold of one of these, slung it into the air. It went so high that we lost sight of it altogether. There now remained only a little of the end of a thong in the conjurer's hand, and he desired one of the boys who assisted him to lay hold of it and to mount. He did so climbing by the rope, and we lost sight of him also! The conjurer then called to him three times, but getting no answer, he snatched up a knife as if in a great rage, laid hold of the thong, and disappeared also! Bye and bye he threw down one of the boy's hands, then a foot, then the other hand, and the other foot, then the trunk and last of all the head! Then he came down himself, all puffing and panting, and with his clothes all bloody, kissed the ground before the Amir, and said something to him in Chinese. The Amir gave some order in reply, and our friend then took the lad's limbs, laid them together in their places, and gave a kick, when, presto! there was the boy, who got up and stood before us! All this astonished me beyond measure. The Kazi Afkharuddin was next to me, and quoth he, ' Wallah! 'tis my opinion there has been neither going up nor coming down, neither marring nor mending; 'tis all hocus pocus.*"
According to the Prajñaparamita, the whole process of

salvation is of the same nature as this conjuring trick. Witness this dialogue between the Lord Buddha and Subhuti. "LORD: '*Just as if, Subhuti, a clever magician, or magician's apprentice, would conjure up at the cross roads a great crowd of people ; and, after he had conjured them up, he would make that great crowd of people vanish again. What do you think, Subhuti, has there anyone been killed by anyone, or murdered, or destroyed, or made to vanish?* SUBHUTI : '*No, indeed, Lord!*' LORD: '*Even so a Bodhisattva, a great being, leads innumerable and incalculable beings to Nirvana, and yet there is not any being that has been led to Nirvana, nor anyone who has led one. If a Bodhisattva hears this, and does not tremble, is not frightened, nor terrified, then he is to be known as ' armed with the great armour.*'' "

The Buddhist Tantra draws the practical consequences. It is the logical outcome of the developments which preceded it, and the difficulties which it has presented to many scholars are of their own making. Of course, if one makes up one's mind that " original " Buddhism was a perfectly rational religion, after the heart of the ' Ethical Society,' without any touch of the super-natural or mysterious, then the Tantra will become an almost incomprehensible ' degeneration ' of that presumed original Buddhism. In actual fact, Buddhism has always been closely associated with what to rationalists would appear as superstitions (see pp. 81–85). The reality of extraordinary psychic, nay of wonderworking powers, was never questioned (pp. 103–105). The cultivation of such powers was, for those suited to it, part of the program of salvation, although for others a dubious blessing. The existence of many kinds of disembodied spirits and the reality of magical forces were taken for granted, and the belief in them formed part of the current cosmology.

Europeans who write about the Tantra are often beside themselves with emotion. Their revulsion is partly intellectual, because they believe to have outgrown the magical beliefs of our forefathers. In addition, the Tantra is apt to provoke their moral indignation. It seems to them that in the history of Buddhism an abstract metaphysics of great sublimity has slowly given way to a preoccupation with personal deities and with witchcraft, with the mumbo jumbo of magical ritual and all manner of superstitions. Deliberate immorality seems to replace the lofty austerity of the past. The former disinterested non-attachment to the world seems supplanted by a desire to coerce it to fit in with the basest desires, and resignation to circumstances by a wish to gain power over them. Where poverty had been a prime condition of spiritual growth, one now thinks of propitiating Kuvera and Jambhala, Gods of wealth. And so on.

This hostile attitude does little justice to the Tantra. It is true the Tantra proclaims that it has two aims— success (siddhi) in winning full enlightenment in this life, and success in gaining health, wealth and power. But this illogical combination of worldly and other worldly aims is as old as Buddhism itself, and it has been one of the main pillars of its strength (see pp .86 sq). The immorality is, as we shall see, not an immorality of men of the world, but of saints. The claim that charms and magical ritual are the surest way to full enlightenment is, indeed, new in its emphasis, but a long historical development has steadily led up to it. Far from being a nightmare of a few deluded perverts of doubtful respectability, the Tantra was, and is, an inevitable phase of Buddhist history.

History of the Tantra

It is impossible at present to indicate the exact time when Tantric practices were first thought of. The Tantrists are habitually inclined to secrecy. Occult and esoteric views must have circulated in small circles of initiates for a long time before they came out into the open. As a more or less public system of thought, the Tantra gathered momentum after 500 or 600 A.D. Its beginnings do, however, go back to the dawn of human history, when an agricultural society was pervaded by magic and witchcraft, human sacrifice and the cult of the mother goddess, fertility rites and chtonic deities. The Tantra is not really a new creation, but the result of an absorption of primitive beliefs by the literary tradition, and their blending with Buddhist philosophy.

The Tantric literature of Buddhism is very bulky, and largely unexplored. Very little has been translated, and the language of the texts is difficult and obscure, often intentionally so. Like the Hindus, the Buddhists distinguish a ' right-handed ' and a ' left-handed ' Tantra. In Hinduism the two groups are distinguished by the fact that the "*right-hand observers*" (*dakshinacarins*) attach greater importance to the male, the "*left-hand observers*" (*vamacarins*) to the feminine principle in the universe. In Buddhism, the difference between the two lies chiefly in their attitude to sex (see p. 195 sq.). It is convenient to reserve the term *Shaktism* for the left-handed form. Hindu Shaktism is associated with Shivaism. Shaiva doctrines had a great influence on Buddhist Shaktism. A Shakti is the creative energy or ' potency,' of a deity, personified as his wife, or consort. In Shivaism Shakti-worship is directed towards Shiva's wife—Parvati or Uma— also known as *The great goddess*, and the *Great Mother*. It is a peculiarity of Shaktism that many deities exist both in a benign and a terrible form. The terrible form of Parvati is Durga, *The Unapproachable*, or Kali, *The Black*. The terrible forms are associated with death and destruction, with necromancy, with animal and human sacrifices. At the same time Shivaism possesses a profusion of feminine deities, of sorceresses, witches and ogresses, many of whom were incorporated into Buddhist Shaktism. The followers of the more extreme Shivaite practices did not always command the respect of their contemporaries. The Shiva magician Bhairavananda sings, in an Indian drama of 900 A.D., the following song:

" *As for black-book and spell—they may all go to hell!*
My teacher excused me from practice for trance.
With drink and with women we fare mighty well,
As on—to salvation—we merrily dance!
A fiery young wench to the altar I've led.
Good meat I consume, and I guzzle strong drink ;
And it all comes as alms—with a pelt for my bed.
What better religion could anyone think ?
Gods Vishnu and Brahm and the others may preach

Of salvation by trance, holy rites, and the Vedies.
'Twas Uma's fond lover alone that could teach
Us salvation plus brandy plus fun with the ladies."

(C. R. Lanman)

The scholarly investigation of the Tantric documents is
still in its beginnings. As far as we can judge at present,
among the multitude of Tantric sects, two great schools
were historically the most important, the left-handed form
of the *Vajra-yana*, and the right-handed form of the
Mi-tsung (*School of Secrets*).   The Vajrayāna is the
Adamantine Vehicle. The Vajra is literally the Thunderbolt
which Indra, like Zeus and Thor, used with great effect
as a weapon. Itself unbreakable, it breaks everything else.
In later Buddhist philosophy the word is used to denote
a kind of supernatural substance which is as hard as a
diamond, as clear as empty space, as irresistible as a thunderbolt. The Vajra is now identified with ultimate reality,
with Dharma and enlightenment. The Vajrayāna
mythologizes the doctrine of emptiness, and teaches that
the adept, through a combination of rites, is reinstated
into his true *diamond-nature*, takes possession of a diamond
body, is transformed into a diamond-being (Vajrasattva).
The beginnings of the Vajrayāna may go back to ca 300
A.D. As it is known to us, the system developed from
ca 600 A.D. onward. The Guhyasamaja-tantra is one of
its earliest scriptures. The Vajrayāna was founded by a
succession of teachers, among whom a second Nagarjuna
(ca 600–650) was one of the first. Their names are recorded
up to about 1,100 A.D. The Vajrayāna originated
apparently in the extreme North of India, both in the
East, in Bengal and in the hills of Assam, and in the West,
in a district called Uddiyana, which may perhaps be the
region round Peshawar. Non-Indian influences had something to do with the shaping of Tantric ideas. The erotic
mysticism and the stress on the female principle owed much
to the Dravidian stratum of Indian culture which, in the
cult of the *Village Goddess* had kept alive the matriarchal
traditions about the *Mother-Goddess* to a greater extent
than the Vedic religion had done. In Bengal, the patronage
of the Pala dynasty (750–1150) enabled the Tantric doctrines

to develop and organise themselves. The official Buddhism
of that period was a mixture of Prajnaparamita and
Tantra. The monks who lived in Nalanda, and in the
settlements founded by the Pala kings—such as Odantapuri,
Vikramasila, Jaggadala, Somarupa—combined metaphysics
and magic, almost like the Gerbert of Rheims and Albert
the Great of mediaeval folklore. Their range of interest
is well typified by Vagisvarakirti, ca A.D. 1,000, about
whom Taranatha says : " *By constantly looking on the face
of the holy Tara, he resolved all his doubts. He erected eight
religious schools for the Prajnaparamita, four for the exposition
of the Guhyasamaja, one each for each one of three other
kinds of Tantra. He also established many religious schools
with provisions for teaching the Madhyamika logic. He
conjured up quantities of the elixir of life, and distributed
it to others, so that old people, 150 years old and more, became
young again.*" This combination of Prajnaparamita and
Tantra has shown an astounding vitality. It was destroyed
in Bengal by the Muslims, but it spread to Java and Nepal,
and in Tibet it still continues as a living tradition.
The right-handed Tantra is chiefly known to us through
the system of Amoghavajra (705–774) which is preserved
in China. This doctrine also claims to descend from
Nagarjuna. The Chinese Mi-tsung school combined two
Tantric systems, each one embodied in a magical circle
(mandala). The *Circle of the Womb* (garbha-dhatu-mandala)
and the *Circle of the Thunderbolt* (vajra-dhatu-mandala)
are said to be, in a higher sense, identical and to represent
different aspects of the supreme reality. The Buddha
Mahavairocana is here the universe. His body is divided
into two complementary constituents, the passive, mental
womb-element, and the active, material *diamond-element*.
The whole world is the Buddha's revelation to himself, and
it is represented in those two mandalas. This doctrine
came to Japan with Kobo Daishi about A.D. 800, and as
the Shin-gon (*True Word*) school it is still one of the largest
Japanese sects, with 8,000,000 members and 11,000 priests
in 1931. Other esoteric doctrines were adopted by the
Ten-dai school, founded by Dengyo Daishi, who supplemented them with a more ' open ' doctrine, founded on

the " *Lotus of the Good Law.*" Shaktism never spread very much in China or Japan. Erotic tendencies developed in the Tachikawa sect of the Shin-gon in the 11th century, but the sect was soon suppressed. In 1132 a reformed Shingon school, Shingi-shingon-shu was established.

Tantric literature consists of treatises, spells, hymns, and descriptions of mythological beings. Tantric deities often bear the same names as those of the bhaktic tradition. The identity of the names hides a profound difference in the function of the pantheon. Bhaktic deities are creatures of the mythological imagination who are loved and implored for help. Tantric deities are personifications of spiritual and magical forces which are conjured up and utilised as steps on the road to salvation.

Tantric Practices

Like all other schools of Buddhism, the Tantra developed a number of practices which are peculiar to it. Essential to the Tantra is the difference between the initiated and the uninitiated, and, corresponding to it, a sharp division between an exoteric and an esoteric doctrine. The Buddha, as he is depicted in the Scriptures of Pali Buddhism, took pride in the fact that he kept nothing hidden " *in his closed fist,*" as far as any item of knowledge conducive to salvation was concerned. The Tantra now, on the contrary, assumes that the really efficacious methods of salvation and their proper use cannot be learned from books, but that they can be taught only by personal contact with a spiritual instructor, called a Guru. Only a Guru, to whom we submit in complete obedience, and who for us stands in the place of the Buddha, can translate the true secrets and mysteries of the doctrine. Small circles of initiates gather around a Guru, and what is taught outside these small circles of initiates is really very far from the truth.

Without initiation one cannot even begin a spiritual training. Initiation in this system of Buddhism has the same decisive importance as it had in the Mystery cults of Greece and Rome. In addition, we may note that initiation has always been important in primitive societies,

and that in this as in many other ways, Tantric Buddhism
is a reversal to primitive ways of thinking and acting.
The Sanscrit word for the initiation ceremony is *Abhisheka*,
which literally means *Besprinkling*. The initiated is
sprinkled with holy water, and there is in this respect
some similarity with Christian baptism. The ceremony
derives from the ancient Indian ritual of the inauguration
of a Crown Prince. In theory, a Crown Prince was, through
that ceremony, transformed into a world ruler. Similarly
in this case, the water of Knowledge is supposed to enable
the devotee to become a spiritual world ruler, i.e. a Buddha.
It would lead us here too far to describe all the varieties
of worship and ritual which were practised by the initiates.
There are three methods, however, with which we must
deal in some detail. They are :

 I. The recitation of spells.

 II. The performance of ritual gestures and dances.

 III. The identification with deities by means of a
    special kind of meditation.

I. With regard to the use of spells, we have to distinguish
three periods. At first the Buddhists, like all the other
inhabitants of India at the time, expected from magical
formulae protection from danger, and furtherance of their
worldly interests. The use of spells for such purposes was
widespread among all nations in the pre-industrial period
of human history. It implied at least two assumptions,
i.e. that diseases and many other misfortunes are due to
the influence of some demonic power, and, that words
have power to deal effectively with the demon, by either
driving him out, or driving him away, or by mobilising
some greater benevolent magical power against him. The
belief in the efficacy of magical words was greatly encouraged by the priests and doctors, who had a kind of
vested interest in them. There were, of course, always
some sceptics, who pointed out, as the famous Buddhist
Vasubandhu did, that very often the herbs or the medicine
are the curative agent, but that the doctors, who fear that
' one will do without us, and we will get no more money,'
claim that the drug is successful only through the *mantra*
(Sanskrit for "spell"), which is their professional secret. A

mantra is an incantation which effects wonders when
uttered. The Buddhists employed for protection not only
the traditional mantras of Brahmanism, but used also
some of the shorter Buddhist sutras as charms. Hiuen-
Tsiang, the Chinese pilgrim, told Hwui-Li, his biographer,
how the *Sutra of the Heart of Perfect Wisdom* helped him
to cross the Gobi desert, by calling forth the aid of
Kwan-Yin, who had taught this sutra. Hiuen-Tsiang,
in the Gobi desert " *encountered all sorts of demon shapes
and strange goblins, which seemed to surround him behind
and before. Although he invoked the name of Kwan-Yin,
he could not drive them all away ; but when he recited this
sutra, at the sound of the words they all disappeared in a
moment. Whenever he was in danger, it was to this alone
that he trusted for his safety and deliverance.*"
From the third century A.D. onward, the Buddhists made
an ever-increasing use of mantras for the purpose of guarding
their spiritual life from interference by malignant deities.
Special chapters on spells are added to some of the best
known Sutras, like the ' *Lotus of the Good Law* ' (Chap. 21),
' *The Lankavatara Sutra* ' (pp. 260–262), etc.

Thirdly, from the seventh century onward, the mantras
become, among a section of the community, the chief
vehicle of salvation. The permissible, but so far subsidiary,
practice of murmuring spells becomes, in the *Mantra-yāna,
The Vehicle of the Mantras*, the very key to emancipation
from the fetters of existence. If applied according to the
rules, there is nothing that the mantras cannot achieve.
Their power " *can confer even Buddhahood—how much more
anything else one may want !* " About 200 B.C. Nagasena
in ' *The Questions of King Milinda*,' (ed. Trenkner p. 150),
had still taught that charms can protect only where they
are unopposed by hostile Karma—evidence being the case
of Maudgalyayana, the disciple of the Buddha, who was
most proficient in magic, and who yet could not protect
himself from being punished for a wrong action in his
remote past by being beaten to death by robbers
(*ibidem*, p. 188). In the Tantra, on the other hand, the
Mantras and Dharanis act infallibly if only the rules,
which are numerous and minute, are strictly observed.

Innumerable mantras were thought out by the Tantric Buddhists, and the whole subject was treated as a most elaborate science, with numerous laws of its own. For instance, a mantra addressed to a male deity must end with HUM or PHAT; if the deity, however, is feminine, the last word should be SVAHA; and if neuter, it should be NAMAH. Leaving these details to look after themselves, we must say a few words about the reasoning which induced the Tantra to assume that the mumbling of usually quite meaningless syllables could produce such great effects in the world. It is, of course, the power of mind which makes the mantras efficacious. The mantra is a means of getting into touch with the unseen forces around us through addressing their personifications. Benevolent higher beings have given us those mantras. The famous ' OM MANI PADME HUM,' for instance, which in Tibet is everywhere—on the rocks, on the houses, in the praying wheels, and on the lips of the people—is one of Avalokitesvara's most precious gifts to this suffering world. The ' *Mahā-Vairocana-Sutra,* in its fourth chapter, explains the power of mantras as follows : ' *Thanks to the original vow of the Buddhas and Bodhisattvas, a miraculous force resides in the mantras, so that by pronouncing them one acquires merit without limits.*' The same text says that ' *success in our plans through mantras is due to their consecration by the Buddha which exerts upon them a deep and inconceivable influence.*' To pronounce a mantra is a way of wooing a deity and, etymologically, the word mantra is connected with Greek words like ' meimao ' which express eager desire, yearning and intensity of purpose, and with the old High German word minn-ia, which means ' making love to.'

In order to appreciate the place of mantras in the ritual of Tantric Buddhism, we may in conclusion describe briefly the four operations which the ' *Mahā-Vairocana Sutra* ' distinguishes in the process of the recitation, or Jāpa, of Mantras. I. The *Contemplative Recitation,* which has four aspects : (a) One recites the mantra while contemplating in one's heart the shape of the letters—this is called the ' *Heart Enlightenment.*' (b) One distinguishes well the sound of the different letters, and (c) Understands well the significance of the phrases. Finally, there is (d) 'The Practice of Breathing,' in which one regulates one's breath in order to contemplate the mutual inter-penetration of the faithful and the Buddha. On that follows, 2 and 3, the recitation, accompanied by offerings to the deity, such as flowers, perfume, etc. Finally, 4, there is the *Recitation of Realisation*, when one attains 'success' (Siddhi), through the power of the mantras.

II. In addition to the sounds of the mantras, ritual gestures are of great importance in the Tantra, which worked out a complicated classification of the magically efficacious positions of the hands. A few of the more common ritual gestures are known from the statues of Buddhas and Bodhisattvas, and they are an important guide to the identification of these statues. This is not the place to go into the details. Dancing is to the Hindus a form of '*singing with the body*'; it gained considerable importance in the North of India and in the countries under Tibetan influence. In any case, according to the Tantric theory, a valid ritual action must involve all the three sides of our being, i.e. body, speech and mind. The body acts through the gestures, the speech through the mantras, and the mind through the trance (Samādhi).

III. The Tantra combines the devotional needs of the masses with the meditational practices of the Yogacara school, and with the metaphysics of the Madhyamikas. In other words, the Tantra took over the vast pantheon of popular mythology, with its bewildering variety of deities, fairies, witches, etc. The Tantrists agreed, however, with the metaphysical assumptions of the Prajnaparamita, according to which only the one reality of emptiness is fully real, whereas any kind of multiplicity would be ultimately unreal, and the fictitious product of our diseased imagination. The multiplicity of Gods would be really nothing but a fiction of the imagination, and not one of those deities would be really there. Our free-thinking modern mind would whole-heartedly agree with that postulate. There is, however, the important difference that, according to our modern assumptions, the multiplicity of things around us is real and the deities a less real fabrication due to the disappointments of our instinctual life when confronted with the hard facts of everyday ' reality.' According to the Tantra, things and Gods alike are equally unreal compared with the one vast emptiness, but on the whole the data of mythology represent a kind of fiction far more worth-while than the data of our everyday practical experience, and when properly handled, can greatly assist us in winning emancipation from the fetters of existence.

The Tantra worked out a system of meditation on deities which is marked by a sequence of four steps :

First of all, there is the understanding of emptiness and the sinking of one's separate individuality into that emptiness.

Secondly, one must repeat and visualise *germ-syllables* (*bija*).

Thirdly, one forms a conception of the external representation of a deity, as shown in statues, paintings, etc.

Fourthly, through identification, one becomes the deity.

1. We remember that, according to the New Wisdom School, emptiness is the one ultimate reality ; the Yogacarins identified this emptiness with Thought, and taught that outside Thought there is nothing in the external world. From its very beginning Buddhism in all its forms regarded the illusion of individuality as the root of sin, suffering and failure. The Tantra now advises the Yogi to " *develop emptiness* " by cultivating the Thought " *I am, in my essential being, of diamond nature.*" A successful cultivation of this thought would finally abolish the individual personality. As the *Sadhana-Mala* puts it : " *Through the fire of the concept of emptiness all the five Skandhas are destroyed without return.*" Once we have identified ourselves, or our self with emptiness, our state of mind is called ' *The Thought of Enlightenment*' (*Bodhi-Citta*).

2. From the Vedas onward sound has been treated far more seriously in India than it has been in the West. Western philosophy is almost throughout dominated by the visual appearance of things, and sound is relegated to a comparatively subordinate position, almost on a level

with smell and taste. We have somehow got the conviction that the visual and tactile appearance of things corresponds more closely to what is really there, than their sound. In the magical tradition of all ages, however, sound comes much nearer to the essence of a force than anything else. Each word can be analysed into its syllables, and according to the Tantra, different syllables not only correspond to different spiritual forces or deities, but a syllable, or letter, can be used to conjure up a deity, and therefore it can, in a sense, be called the ' germ ' of that deity, just as a grain of wheat contains the plant in itself. It seems logical to assume that if one can, as the first step, dissolve oneself into emptiness through concentrated thought, then it must also be possible to conjure up from emptiness the entire world of phenomena. With the help of certain sounds—such as AM, HUM, SVAHA—one does actually create the deities out of the void. In the belief that these deities did not exist objectively before they were created by the Yogin, with the help of sounds, the Tantra seems to be fairly unique, and only the Egyptian priests have credited themselves with a similar power. Most mythological systems would be afraid to rob their deities of objective and independent existence. Normally, it is regarded as derogatory to a deity to say that it is " *not there.*" Here, however, the deities are a mere reflex. The creative imagination is supreme, though restrained by tradition.

3. The indefiniteness and prolixity of individual fantasy is brought into some kind of order by a tradition concerning the visual appearance of the deities. That is described with meticulous care in the so-called *Sādhanas*, some of which go back to about 500 A.D. It was the task of artists to carry out those prescriptions. The overwhelming majority of the Tantric images which have come down to us agree closely with the prescriptions of the Sadhanas. It is only on rare occasions that artists have introduced alterations of their own for artistic reasons, e.g. in order to increase the symmetry of many-armed images. The artistic image is regarded as a basis for visualising the deity. It is a kind of prop which should be dispensed

with in due course, when what we would call the
' hallucination ' of the deity takes its place.

4. It is a commonplace of magic that identification with
a deity allows us to participate in his or her magical powers.
The deity, to be sure, is illusory, and so are the benefits
we derive from them. It is again the emptiness of everything which allows this identification to take place—the
emptiness which is in us coming together with the emptiness
which is the deity. Step three brought about the vision
of the deity. By step four we actually do become the
deity. The subject is actually identified with the object,
the faithful with the object of faith. " *The worship, the
worshipper and the worshipped, those three are not separate.* "
This is the mental state which is known as Yoga,
Concentration (Samādhi), or Trance (Dhyāna).

An important aid to Tantric meditation are the Magical
Circles or *Mandalas*, which are known to all lovers of
Buddhist art. A Mandala is a diagram which shows deities
in their spiritual or cosmic connections, and it is used as
a basis for winning insight into the spiritual law which is
thus represented. A Mandala is either painted on cloth
or paper, or drawn on the ground with coloured rice or
pebbles, or it may be engraved on stone or metal. Each
system of the Tantra had its own Mandalas. The deities
are shown either pictorially, in their visible form, or by
the Sanskrit letters, which form their *germ syllables*, or
by various symbols. Some Mandalas give a detailed,
though condensed, representation of the entire universe,
and they include not only the Buddhas and Bodhisattvas,
but also the Gods and spirits, mountains and seas, the
zodiac and the great heretical teachers. The Mandalas
are in the direct line of the ancient tradition of magic.
The first step of a magician who wishes to conjure up a
magical power has always been to mark off from its profane
surroundings a Charmed Circle, in which the power can
manifest itself. In recent years, C. G. Jung found that
some of his patients spontaneously drew pictures similar
to the Buddhist Mandalas. The circle and the square
are, according to him, the essential elements of a Mandala,
and, although Jung has never really understood the Buddhist

methods of meditation, his attempt to bring together the Tantric tradition and the Psychology of the Unconscious is a fruitful starting point for further work in this field.

Tantric Philosophy

If the Tantra expects salvation from sacred actions, it must have a conception of the Universe according to which such actions can be the lever of emancipation. The cosmos consists of a great number of forces, which are modes of the activity of the world force ; through sacred actions we adapt ourselves to those forces and render them service-able to our purposes, which in themselves are also the purposes of the cosmos. The Buddha is no longer just a transcendent spiritual reality. The omnipresence of the Buddha-nature results from the fact that the Buddha is conceived as a ' *cosmic body.*' The six elements, which are the material of everything : Earth, Water, Fire, Air, Space, and Consciousness, are the substance of that cosmic body, and the actions of body, speech, and mind are its functions. The world is nothing but a reflection of the Buddha's light, more concentrated in one place, and more diffused in another, as the case may be. The Buddha is the secret reality in all things, their heart, the living and central truth in them. We ourselves are not strange elements external to it, and all we have to do is to realise that we ourselves are the Buddha and the cosmos. Logical reasonings and discussions are quite unavailing. Only actions of mystical value can help us to realise our intimate and universal community, or identity with the Buddha.

It is easy to see that this theory is a logical development rendered inevitable by the trends in Buddhism which preceded it. To the Old Wisdom School, Nirvana had been the absolute opposite of this world. The early Mahayana had identified Nirvana and this world in the one Absolute Reality of emptiness. Now, in the Tantra, the world becomes a manifestation of the Dharma-body of the Buddha. And again, the old Buddhist urge for total self-extinction is expressed through the new meta-physical formulation. "*When we consider ourselves, as well as all other beings, as a manifestation of the eternal principle of life, we act in a feeling of our own personal nullity, free from personal and egoistical interests. Then, and only then, can we devote ourselves to earthly work without doing damage to our spiritual progress. For through our changed mental attitude to this world of phenomena, we have practically overcome this world."* (v. Glasenapp.)

Tantric Mythology

From the very beginning the personality of man was interpreted as a complex of the skandhas. The Tantra now transfers this conception to the Buddha himself, and claims that he is composed of five skandhas. The skandhas themselves are Buddhas. In European literature, they are often called *Dhyāni Buddhas*, but this term, introduced by Hodgson about a century ago, is not only faulty Sanscrit: it has never been found in any Tantric text. It is time to discard it. The texts themselves always speak of the '*Five Tathagatas*,' or '*The Five Jinas*.' Jina means ' victor,' or ' conqueror,' and is an old epithet of the Buddha, referring originally to his conquest over passion. The Tibetans always speak of the five Jinas, and I shall follow their example. The five Jinas are ' Vairocana,' *The Illuminator*, or *The Brilliant* ; ' Akshobhya,' *The Imperturbable* ; ' Ratna Sambhava,' *The Jewel-born* ; ' Amitabha,' *The Infinite Light* ; and ' Amoghasiddhi,' *The Unfailing Success*. These five Buddhas were introduced about 750 A.D., and they differ completely from all the other Buddhas known to Buddhism up to then. All the Buddhas one had heard about in the pre-Tantra period had commenced their career as ordinary human beings, or even as animals, and then, through progressive purification, in many millions of lives, had worked their way slowly and gradually up to Buddahood. The five Jinas, on the other hand, always were Buddhas from the very beginning, and had never been anything else.

The five Jinas constitute the body of the Universe. In addition, the Tantra worked out a system according to which these five Jinas ' corresponded ' mystically to the various constituents of the Universe, who severally " participated " in them. Five elements correspond to the five Jinas, five senses and sense-objects, five cardinal points (the centre being the fifth). At the same time there are further correspondences with letters of the alphabet, with parts of the body, with the various kinds of ' vital Breath,' with colours, sounds, etc. This is not all. Each celestial Buddha is reflected in a celestial Bodhisattva, and in a human Buddha, and is united with a feminine force, Shakti. Further, by introducing the idea that each Jina presides over a mystical ' family,' this system can, on principle, group all the other deities under the five Jinas as accessory divinities.

The system of the five Jinas was the most influential, but by no means the only, mythological system of the Tantra. Just as Buddhism could consider the human personality as constituted of five skandhas, without postulating a unifying principle over and above them, just so a reduction of the Universe to the five Tathagatas as its ultimate constituents would satisfy the logical requirements of the majority of Buddhists. It appears, however, that after 800 A.D. a doctrine was propounded, in various places and in varying forms, which tried to derive the five Tathagatas as emanations from one original, first, or primeval Buddha, who is sometimes called the *Adi-Buddha*, and who is the one eternal living principle of the entire Universe.

The traditions about the Adi-Buddha were considered as a particularly secret part of the teaching, and we are at present not in a position to distinguish clearly between the different schools of thought. Many schools seem to have singled out one of the five Jinas, usually Vairocana, as the chief. Others introduced a sixth person to preside over them. This person bears the name sometimes of Mahavairocana, sometimes of Vajradhara, and sometimes he is simply called the Adi-Buddha.

It is at this point that Buddhism at last deviates completely from its original teachings, and prepares the way for its own extinction. It is quite clear that this kind of teaching

must tend in the direction of Henotheism. As we saw
before, it has always been a basic conviction of the Buddhist
tradition that the object of thinking about the world was
escape from it, and not explanation of its origin. As far
as the origin of the appearance of this universe around us
was concerned, one was content to put it down to ignorance
and not to God. The Yogacarins were the first to build
up an extremely complicated and involved system which
was designed to deduce the appearance of a world of external
objects from ignorance as the cause, and from the " Store-
consciousness " as the basis of the universe. 500 years
later, about 950, some Tantric scholars, who lived near
the Jaxartes, came to regard a near-monotheistic cosmogeny as the very centre of the Buddhist doctrine. Up to
then the Tathagata had been the one who delivers the
true teaching about the cause of the universe. Now the
Tathagata himself becomes the cause. In the *Kalacakra
Tantra*, and in some Chinese systems, the Buddha acts as
a kind of creator. As *Lords of the Yogis*, the Buddhas
were transformed into magicians, who created this world
by means of their meditation. All things are their
magical creations. Everything that exists, they see in
their creative meditation. And what they see in their
meditation, must be real because, except for this
meditation, nothing at all exists, and everything, as it
is, is really Thought. It had been usual for many
centuries, in Yogacara circles, to describe ultimate reality
as the "*Womb of the Tathagatas*." It is now from this
Womb of the Tathagatas that the world is said to issue.
The elaboration of this cosmogeny was the last creative
act of Buddhist thought. Once it had reached this stage
of development it could do no more than merge into the
monotheistic religions around it.

Left-handed Tantra

In our historical survey, we have drawn attention to the
difference between the Left-handed and the Right-handed
Tantra (see pp. 177 sq). The chief features of the Left-
handed Tantra are : 1. The worship of *Shaktis*, of female

deities, with whom the male deities are united in the embrace of loving union, and from whom they derive their energy. 2. The presence of vast numbers of demons and terrifying deities, the worship of the God Bhairava (*The Terrible*), and an elaborate ritual connected with the burial ground. 3. The inclusion of sexual intercourse, and other forms of ' immoral conduct,' among the practices which conduce to salvation.

The Left-handed Tantra has met with much disapproval, and moral indignation has prevented most observers from attempting to understand it. Its vitality has, nevertheless, been surprising ; for centuries it has been a historical force of the first magnitude in the East, and we must try to arrive at some appreciation of its three salient features.

1. The Old Buddhism had been a severely masculine system, and only a few quite subordinate feminine deities were admitted. The higher gods are sexless, so are the inhabitants of the Buddha-fields. Femininity was on the whole a bar to the highest spiritual attainment, and on approaching Buddha-hood the Bodhisattva ceased to be reborn as a woman. A woman cannot possibly become a Buddha.

The Prajñaparamita and Tara were the first autonomous Buddhist deities. The cult of Tara seems to have entered Buddhism about 150 A.D. Tārā, from Sanskrit tārayati, is the saviouress who helps us to ' cross ' to the other shore, who removes fear and dread and who grants the fulfilment of all our wishes. Tārā was a creation of the popular mind. The Prajnaparamita, on the other hand, originated among small groups of ascetic metaphysicians. In the Mahayana, the Prajñaparamita was not only a virtue, a book, and a mantra, but also a deity. The personification of transcendental wisdom seems to have started about the beginning of our era. In the Prajnaparamita sutras, she is described as ' *The Mother of all the Buddhas.*' What is the meaning of this phrase ? Just as a child is born of the mother, so the full enlightenment of a Buddha comes forth from the Perfection of Wisdom. It is she who shows them their way about in the world. In this way a feminine principle was placed side by side with the Buddha, and

to some extent even above him. It is interesting to note
that the Prajñaparamita texts, with their emphasis on
the feminine principle in the world, originated in the
South of India, where the Dravidian environment had
kept alive many matriarchal ideas, which the more
exclusively masculine Brahmanism had suppressed in the
North of India. Almost everywhere in ancient thought
we find the notion of a principle which represents both
wisdom and femininity, and which combined motherhood
with virginity. In the Mediterranean world, we meet,
at the same period, with a *Sophia*, who is modelled
on Ishtar, Isis, and Athene; she represents a fusion
between the idea of wisdom and the idea of the Magna
Mater, and is placed by the side of the supreme male
being. Like Ishtar and the Virgin Mary, the
Prajñaparamita was in essence both mother and virgin.
She is the 'Mother of all the Buddhas,' i.e. she is not
barren but fertile, fruitful of many good deeds, and her
images lay great stress on her full breasts. Like a virgin,
on the other hand, she remains '*unaffected, untouched,*'
and the Scriptures emphasise her elusiveness more than
anything else.

While thus Buddhism acknowledged the importance of
feminine attitudes to the world, and personified them into
a multitude of feminine deities, a sexual attitude to
femininity was generally discouraged, and the sexual implications, both of femininity, and of the relation between
the masculine and the feminine principle, were glossed
over. In the Left-handed Tantra, concepts derived from
sexual life were openly introduced into the explanation
of spiritual phenomena. It is, of course, well known to
psychologists that sexuality, almost undisguised, has often
intruded into mystical experiences. Even abstract metaphysical thought is not entirely without its libidinous side.
This has been felt even by a philosopher whom one usually
regards as almost inhuman in his withdrawal from all
normal human affections. Somebody asked Immanuel Kant
why he had never married. Kant replied that all his life
he had had one 'mistress'; that had been metaphysics,
and he had wished to remain faithful to her. Similarly,

the authors of the Prajñaparamita sutras were aware that the pursuit of perfect wisdom could easily assume the character of a love affair with the Absolute. The persistent elusiveness of perfect wisdom on its own would maintain interest to the end. We are, as a matter of fact, told explicitly that a Bodhisattva should think of perfect wisdom with the same intensity and exclusiveness with which a man thinks of a 'handsome, attractive, and beautiful woman' with whom he has made a date, but who is prevented from seeing him.

What, however, is only implied in most treatises on wisdom, is brought out in the open in Shaktism. The highest reality is conceived as a union of a masculine (active) and a feminine (passive) principle. The active principle is called 'skill in means,' the passive principle being 'wisdom.' Only the union of the two can lead to salvation. The one Absolute is a union of the two, and that act of union fills it with the 'highest bliss.' The art of this school, as is well-known, represents the Buddhas and Bodhisattvas in the act of sexual intercourse—called by the Tibetans the Yab-Yum (father-mother) attitude.

2.   The emphasis on the terrifying aspect of the universe is connected with the purpose of Yogic practices in the Left-handed Tantra. The Left-hand path aims at stripping man of his ego, so that he may become completely identified with the divine principle. The object is to bring about a complete and total destruction and obliteration of all the elements which build up the ego, i.e. of our desires and passions. The concentration on self-destruction would, to some extent, account for the appearance of the many terrifying deities, which represent the Yogi's own destructive efforts. As Dr. P. H. Pott puts it, " *the idea of destruction awakens naturally the association with the burial ground where the material body is destroyed. The place where the acts of consecration of the ' left-path ' should be performed is by preference the burial ground. The ritual is inspired by its atmosphere.*" Esoterically, the burial ground stands for the place where the last remaining link between man and his world is severed.

3.   Finally, we must consider the arguments which are

put forward in justification of all kinds of immoral conduct. One does not really expect the followers of any religion to advocate, for instance, " *daily intercourse in out of the way places with* 12-*year-old girls of the Candala caste,*" as a kind of sacred duty. The *Guhyasamaja-tantra*, one of the earliest, and also one of the most sacred, Scriptures of the Left-handed Tantra seems to teach the very opposite of what Buddhist asceticism stood for. It tells us that we will certainly easily attain Buddhahood if we " *cultivate all sensual pleasures, just as we may desire.*" Hardships and austerities fail, where the " *satisfaction of all desires* " succeeds. Just the most immoral, the most tabooed, actions seem to have a particular fascination for the followers of this doctrine. One is enjoined to defy the prohibitions which restrict the food permitted to ascetics. One must feed on the flesh of elephants, horses and dogs, and all food and drink should be mixed with ordure, urine or meat. No wonder that the doctrine has so often been called an aberration of the human mind.

The purpose of these doctrines should be perfectly familiar to anyone who has studied the mentality of mysticism. What is wanted here is to bring the senses purposely into contact with the objects that stimulate them, either by way of strong attraction, or repugnance. On the one hand, one can come to a full realisation and understanding of the vanity and relativity of the pleasures of the senses only by exposing oneself to them. On the other hand, we know also of Christian saints who strove to overcome their sensuous repugnance of disgusting things by putting them into their mouths. Such conduct would be really in keeping with the spirit of asceticism. It is further easy to see that the metaphysics of the Mahayana could very well lead to such conclusions. Nirvana and this world were taught to be one. Then the passions are also not outside Nirvana, ' *the passions are the same as Nirvana.*' Both branches of the Tantra agreed on that. The Right-handed form maintained that the passions had to be sublimated before they could become wings to enlightenment. Sensual love, the love of self, of women, of worldly possessions are justified in so far as they are the starting point of a universal and all-embracing love. The passions, therefore, should not be suppressed, but ennobled and transformed. The Left-handed Tantra, on the other hand, believed that the passions in their direct and unsublimated form could be made into vehicles of salvation. One must further, I think, admit that the objection to immoral practices carried out in the name of religion is not so much a religious, as a social one. It is possible that the Left-hand Yogis lacked in spirituality, but it is certain that they were sadly deficient in respectability. It is equally certain that they did not wish to be respectable. In order to understand this better, we must realise that religion can exist either in an institutionalised, or in a highly individualistic form. In an institutionalised religion, religious doctrine and practice is rarely in conflict with ordinary social morality. The more individualistic mystics, on the other hand, see no real reason why religion and morality should be necessarily tied together. The ordinary morality of the common people is based on little more than social taboos, i.e., essentially on the fear of social isolation which the mystic regards as the ideal breeding ground for spiritual emancipation. While they are still under the influence of the fear of the taboos of society, the Yogis have not gained the ' freedom of the spirit,' which they aim at. During that stage of their spiritual progress, in which they still feel bound to the moral rules of their social environment, they may find that it is salutary to break their attachment to them, and to bear living apart in isolation from the cosy warmth of tribal approval. Such revolt against social restraints is called ' Anti-nomianism.' It has made its appearance at different times in all religions, and in Buddhism it is not confined to the Tantras, but it is also observed among the Amidists, and in the Ch'an. Immoral conduct is therefore a perhaps necessary stage of transition for the attainment of a-moral conduct. We find an almost exact counterpart to Buddhist a-moralism in Ruysbroek's description of the views of certain ' followers of the free spirit.' " *Hence they go so far as to say that so long as man has a tendency to virtues, and desires to do God's very precious will, he is still imperfect, being preoccupied with the acquiring of things. Therefore they think they can never either believe in virtues, or have additional merit, or commit sins. Consequently, they are able to consent to every desire of the lower nature, for they have reversed to the state of innocence, and laws no longer apply to them. They claim indeed to be free, outside of commandments and virtues. Free in their flesh they give the body what it desires. To them the highest sanctity for man-consists in following without compulsion and in all things his natural instinct, so that he may abandon himself to every impulse in satisfying the demands of the body."*

The Control of the Body

It would be misleading, however, to make too much of the disagreement which separates the doctrinal formulations of the Tantra from those of the older Buddhism. In one decisive particular, the Tantra, in all its branches, has remained faithful to the spirit of Buddhist tradition. The physical body is here, as always, regarded as the chief object of all endeavour. We have pointed out before (pp. 97–8) that a mindful discipline of the body is the very cornerstone of Buddhist training. This applies to all schools, in spite of their divergences.

It had been the dignified physical bearing of a monk which had converted Shariputra. The privations of a homeless life demanded a considerable mastery over the body. The monk, as the Buddha said to Shariputra, must be able to endure cold, excessive heat, the pangs of hunger ; he must not fear gadflies, snakes, or attacks from men or beasts ; he must not brood discontentedly on where he will eat or sleep. The work on the body belonged to the essential routine of the Buddhist life which went on quietly, unaffected by doctrinal disputes. The comfort of the skin is consistently disregarded and opposed. Muscular movements are subjected to perpetual *mindfulness*, i.e. one tries to be consciously aware of what one does, when walking, standing, sitting, etc. Rhythmical and mindful yogic breathing controls the lungs and respiratory system. One combats the demands of the alimentary canal by fasting, by the rule that no food must be eaten after mid-day, and by a set meditation on the onerous and disgusting aspects of feeding. The sense organs, as we saw above (p. 99) are rigidly *guarded*. The control and mortification of the body is of the essence of the spiritual life. At the same time, the body, though a burden, should not be despised. The highest trance is, as we saw (p. 101) achieved through the body. It gives great beatitude and complete calm, and since all thought is extinct, the realisation of this state depends on the body. One is said " *to touch the deathless element with one's body.*"

Anyone who has ever tried to meditate must have observed that the weaknesses and disturbances of the body are apt to interfere with continuous meditation. Accordingly, the *Sukhavativyuha* had taught that in Amitabha's Paradise the physical bodies of beings will be " *as strong as the diamond of Narayana.*" The Tantra took up this idea, and adopted many Yogic practices which would transform this body into a *diamond body*, make it into a fit vehicle for the spiritual journey, and render it *ripe*, strong enough to bear the strain imposed upon it by spiritual work. In this connection the physiology of Hathayoga was accepted as authoritative. The body is believed to contain an immense number of nerves, or arteries (nadi), channels of occult force, and four vital centres which are called *nerve-plexuses* (*cakra*) or *lotuses* (*padma*). The lowest centre is in the region of the navel, another in the heart, another just below the neck, and another in the head. Among the innumerable *nerves*, three are the most important : Two by the two sides of the spinal cord, and one in the middle. The left nerve represents Wisdom, the right Skill in Means, and the central Absolute Unity. With the help of esoteric practices, which are quite unintelligible without the guidance of a Guru, the Yogi causes a union of Wisdom and Skill in Means to take place in the lowest nerve centre, thus producing there the *Thought of enlightenment* (*bodhi-citta*). This must then be moved upwards along the middle nerve until it becomes a state of motionless bliss in the highest nerve-centre. Systematic breathing exercises play a big part in this technique, because they are said to regulate the *Vital Winds* which in their turn determine the flow of the occult force in the nerves. All this, as put down here in general terms, sounds quite phantastic, and it would take many pages to make it even vaguely plausible. I must refer the reader to the ample treatises on Hatha Yoga which are available.

In this context we are only concerned to show the seriousness with which the Tantra regarded the body. The truth is within the body, and arises out of it. In the *Hevajra-Tantra* the Lord explains that, although everything is empty, there is need for the existence of a physical body, because the highest bliss could not be gained without it. The ultimate truth resides within the body. "*He is within the house, but you are enquiring about him outside. You are seeing your husband within, yet you are asking the neighbours as to his whereabouts.*" So Saraha, a Tantric poet of Bengal. "*The scholars explain all the Scriptures, but do not know the Buddha residing within the body.*" It was the arduous struggle with his own physical constitution which filled the life of the Tantric Yogin, and any theories he might have were no more than minor by-products of his exertions.

IX

NON-INDIAN DEVELOPMENTS

Survey

THE schools which we have considered so far, had their origin in India, and, although they were accepted outside India, their fundamental tenets were not seriously modified there. Three schools outside India have, however, profoundly modified the Indian impulse. They are, in the Far East, the *Ch'an* (*Zen*) and *Amidism*, in Tibet the *Rnyin-ma-pa*.

Buddhism had spread to China from Central Asia. It was first introduced about 50 A.D. Always suspect to the Confucians, Chinese Buddhism took a great deal of its colour from the native Taoism. It had a great success under the Liang dynasty in the sixth century and during the greater part of the T'ang dynasty (618–907). From ca A.D. 1,000 onward, two schools have drawn to themselves the majority of the Chinese monks. The meditational Ch'an sect is a development of Mahayana metaphysics, of the Prajñaparamita and of the Yogacarins, re-shaped by Chinese and Japanese conditions. Amidism is the form which, in the course of time, the ' Buddhism of Faith ' took in China and Japan.

Monks from Bengal carried, about A.D. 700, the Buddhist religion to Tibet. The native, *Bön*, religion of Tibet had been a form of magical Shamanism. Buddhism did not by any means succeed in superseding it. Until this day, after nearly 1,200 years of Buddhist rule, the Bön religion still remains a vital force. The monks of Tibet have always been sharply divided in their attitude to the indigenous Shamanism. Some absorbed a great deal of it, others much less. After A.D. 1,400 the less magical school, known as the *Yellow Church* has, through the reforms of Tsong-kha-pa, gained the upper hand. Many of the more magical *Red* sects continue to exist, and the Rnyin-ma-pa represent that branch of the Tibetan Tantra which has yielded more than any other to the influence of Bönism.

Ch'an

The word *Ch'an* is the Chinese equivalent of the Sankrit word Dhyana, and means *meditation*. Four stages can be distinguished in the development of the Ch'an school:

1. A *formative period*, which began about 440 with a group of students of Gunabhadra's Chinese translation of the *Lankavatara Sutra*. About 520 we have the legendary figure of Bodhidharma. After that, a few groups of monks round men like Seng-t'san (+ 606), whose poem, called *Hsin Hsin Ming* ("*On believing in mind*") is one of the finest expositions of Buddhism I know of, and Huineng (637–713), of Southern China, who is held up to posterity as an illiterate, practically-minded person, who approached truth abruptly and without circumlocution. Much of the traditions about the early history of Ch'an are the inventions of a later age. Many of the Sayings and Songs of the patriarchs which are transmitted to us are, however, very valuable historical and spiritual documents.

2. After ca 700 A.D. Ch'an establishes itself as a *separate school*. In 734 Shen-hui, a disciple of Hui-neng, founded a school in the South of China. While the Northern branch of Ch'an died out in the middle of the T'ang period (ca 750), all the later developments of Ch'an issue from Shen-hui's school. Whereas so far the Ch'an monks had lived in the monasteries of the Lu-tsung (Vinaya) sect, about 750 Pai-chang provided them with a special rule of their own, and an independent organisation. The most revolutionary feature of Pai-chang's Vinaya was the introduction of manual work. "*A day without work, a day without food*." Under the T'ang dynasty (618–907), the Ch'an sect slowly gained its ascendancy over the other schools. One of the reasons was the fact that it survived the bitter persecution of 845 better than any other sect,

The five Great Masters among Hui-neng's disciples initiated a long series of great T'ang masters of Ch'an, and this was the heroic and creative period of Ch'an.

3. By about 1,000, Ch'an had overshadowed all Chinese Buddhist sects, except Amidism. Within the Ch'an school, the Lin-chi sect had gained the leadership. Its approach was now *systematized*, and to some extent mechanised. In the form of collections of riddles and cryptic sayings, usually connected with the T'ang masters, special text books were composed in the twelfth and thirteenth century. The riddles are technically known as *Kungan* (Japanese *Koan*, literally *official document*). An example is this one : " Once a monk asked Tung-shan : ' What is the Buddha ? ' Tung-shan replied : ' Three pounds of flax.' "

4. The final period is one of *permeation* into the general culture of the Far East, its art and the general habits of life. The art of the Sung period is an expression of Ch'an philosophy. It was particularly in Japan that the cultural influence of Zen made itself felt. Ch'an had been brought to Japan about 1,200 by Eisai and Dogen. Its simplicity and straightforward heroism appealed to the men of the military class. Zen discipline helped them to overcome the fear of death. Many poems were composed testifying to the soldier's victory over death :

> " *Neither heaven nor earth give me shelter.*
> *I rejoice to know that all things are void,—myself and*
>   *the world.*
> *Honour to the sword wielded by the great Yuan swordsmen.*
> *Strike, and it cuts through a spring breeze, like a*
>   *lightning flash.*"

A detailed description of the far-reaching influence of Zen on Japanese painting, and calligraphy, gardening, tea-ceremony, fencing, dancing and poetry would lead us too far here, and I must refer the reader to D. T. Suzuki's excellent works on the subject.

The specific features of Ch'an Buddhism can also be grouped under four headings :

1. The traditional aspects of Buddhism are viewed with hostility. Images and scriptures are held up to contempt, conventions are derided by deliberate eccentricities.

Ch'an evinces a spirit of radical empiricism, very similar to that shown by the Royal Society in England in the seventeenth century. There also the motto was, "*Don't think, try !*" and "*With books they meddle not farther than to see what experiments have been try'd before.*" (Sprat). Ch'an aimed at a direct transmission of Buddhahood outside the written tradition. The study of the scriptures was therefore neglected. In the monasteries they are placed for occasional reference in close proximity to the lavatory. To discuss commentaries, ransack the scriptures, brood over words is regarded like investigating the sand at the bottom of the sea. "*What use is it to count the treasures of other people ?*" "*To see one's own nature is Ch'an.*" By comparison with that, nothing else matters. Historians have often attributed these attitudes to the practical turn in the Chinese national character. This cannot be the whole truth because anti-traditionalism pervaded the whole Buddhist world between 500 and 1,000, and the Indian Tantra in this respect offers many parallels to Ch'an.

2. Ch'an is hostile to metaphysical speculation, averse to theory and intent on abolishing reasoning. Direct insight is prized more highly than the elaborate webs of a subtle thought. The truth is not stated in abstract and general terms, but as concretely as possible. The T'ang masters were renowned for their oracular and cryptic sentences, and for their curious and original actions. Salvation is found in the ordinary things of everyday life. Hsuan-chien was enlightened when his teacher blew out a candle, another when a brick dropped down, another when his leg got broken. This was not an altogether new phenomenon. The Pali *Psalms of the Brethren* and *Psalms of the Sisters* show that also in the Old Wisdom School trivial incidents could easily start off the final awakening. The Ch'an masters flaunt their disapproval of mere tradition in startling actions. They burn wooden statues of the Buddha, kill cats, catch shrimps and fishes. The master assists the pupil not so much by the wise words which issue from his mouth, but by the " direct action " of pulling at his nose, hitting him with the staff (pang), or shouting at him (pang-ho). The Koans, which are the

basis and support of meditation, consist of riddles and puzzling stories which one should think about, until intellectual exhaustion leads to a sudden realisation of their meaning. Again, the Koan is not, as is so often asserted, a peculiar creation of the Chinese genius. It is nothing but the Chinese form of a general Buddhist trend which, at the same time, is clearly visible in Bengal, where the Tantric Sahajiyas taught by riddles and enigmatic expressions, partly to guard the secrets of their thoughts, partly to avoid abstractions by concrete imagery.

3. *Sudden enlightenment* was the distinctive slogan of the Southern branch of Ch'an. Enlightenment according to Hui-neng and his successors is not a gradual, but an instantaneous process. The purport of this teaching has often been misunderstood. The Ch'an masters did not intend to say that no preparation was necessary, and that enlightenment was won in a very short time. They just laid stress on the common mystical truth that enlightenment takes place in a "*timeless moment*," i.e. outside time, in eternity, and that it is an act of the Absolute itself, not our own doing. One cannot do anything at all to become enlightened (p. 112). To expect austerities or meditation to bring forth salvation is like "*rubbing a brick to make it into a mirror*." Enlightenment just happens, without the mediacy of any finite condition or influence, and it is, as we might put it, a totally "*free*" event. It is not the gradual accumulation of merit which causes enlightenment, but a sudden act of recognition. All this teaching is, in its essence, impeccably orthodox. The Ch'an sect deviated from orthodoxy only when it drew the inference that one need not adhere to the minor prescriptions of discipline, and thus cultivated a moral indifference which enabled it to fall in with the demands of Japanese militarism.

4. Like Amidism, the Madhyamikas, and to some extent the Tantra, Ch'an believes that the fulfilment of the Buddhist life can be found only in its negation. The Buddha dwells hidden in the inconspicuous things of daily life. To take them just as they come, that is all that enlightenment amounts to. "*As regards the Ch'an followers,*

*when they see a staff they simply call it a staff. If they want
to walk, they just walk ; if they want to sit, they just sit.
They should not in any circumstances be ruffled and dis-
tracted."* Or : *" How wondrously supernatural ! And how
miraculous this ! I draw water, I carry fuel ! "* Or, once
more :

> *" In spring, the flowers, and in autumn the moon*
> *In summer a refreshing breeze, and in winter the snow.*
> *What else do I have need of ?*
> *Each hour to me is an hour of joy."*

Amidism

The cult of Amitabha had originated in the North West
of India, in the borderland between India and Iran.
Missionaries from the same area had carried it to China
about 150 A.D. About 350 Hui-yuan founded the *Pure
Land School,* which taught an easy way to salvation, based
on the Sukhavati Sutra (p. 146). For a long time the
Buddhism of Faith in China centred round the figures of
Shakyamuni (Shih-chia) and Maitreya (Mi-lo), and a number
of Bodhisattvas like Avalokitesvara (Kuan-yin) and
Kshitigarbha (Ti-tsang) were widely revered. Although
Maitreya has always remained popular, and the cult of
Manjusri (Wen-shu) and Vairocana (Pi-lu-che-na) spread
widely in the eighth century, the inscriptions and images
suggest that Amitabha (O-mi-to) came to the fore about
650 A.D., and Kuan-yin became then firmly associated
with his cult. While in India so far scarcely any portrayals
of Amitabha and none of his Paradise have been found,
China offers an abundance of such images. We do not know
the reasons why just Amitabha's Paradise should have
stirred the imagination of the Chinese to such an extent.
The Egyptian " *Fields of Reeds,*" or the Paradise of Osiris,
the Iranian " *Var,*" and the Greek " *Islands of the Blessed* "
and the " *Gardens of the Hesperidae* " also lie in the West,
and Chinese folklore already possessed the notion of a
fairy palace on the Kun-lun mountains, inhabited by
Hsi-wang-um, " *Royal Mother of the West.*" After 650
Amidism was provided with an elaborate theology.

Tzu-min (680–748) was one of the earliest to concentrate on the mere repetition of the name of Amitabha. The school has retained its popularity until to-day.

In Japan, the ideas of Amidism began to spread after 950 A.D. In the Kamakura period the movement was organised into a number of schools of which two are the most important : Honen founded the " *Pure Land School* " (*Jodo*) in 1175, and one of his disciples, Shinran Shonin (1173–1262) the " *True Sect of the Pure Land* " (*Jodo Shin-shu*). In 1931 the " Pure Land Schools " had in Japan 16 million adherents, with 23,000 priests. Slightly less than one-half of all Japanese Buddhists belonged to them.

It is customary to reckon the sect of Nichiren (1222–1282) as one of the schools of Amidism. It would be more appropriate to count it among the offshoots of nationalistic Shintoism. Nichiren suffered from self-assertiveness and bad temper, and he manifested a degree of personal and tribal egotism which disqualify him as a Buddhist teacher. He did not only convince himself that he, personally, was mentioned in the " *Lotus of the Good Law*," but also that the Japanese were the chosen race which would regenerate the world. The followers of the Nichiren sect, as Suzuki puts it : " *even now are more or less militaristic and do not mix well with other Buddhists*."

From the point of view of Buddhist thought, the chief interest of the Far Eastern development of Amidism lies in its increasing radicalism which reaches its culmination in the Shin sect. The Shin-shu, intent on magnifying the power of faith and of Amida's vows, to cheapen salvation and to simplify the doctrine, rejects all ritualism, philosophy and even the mild asceticism of a monastic life. All men, whether honest or criminal, are, without distinction, admitted to Amida's Paradise. Faith in Amida's grace is the one and only condition of admission. We are all equally sinful, and Amida is a God of compassionate love. Unlike the Christian God, he is not a judge. The idea that morality counts as nothing compared with faith goes back a long time. It is attested already a millenium before Shinran. About 150 A.D. we find in the Divyavadana (pp. 258–9) a story which illustrates how lightly even at that time moral rules might be regarded. Dharmaruci, who lived three aeons ago, had killed his parents, killed an Arhat, and burnt down a monastery. Nevertheless, the future Shakyamuni ordained him with the words: " *Of what use are the rules? Only repeat constantly the formula, ' Homage to the Buddha, Homage to the Dharma ! ' *" The priests of the Shin-shu may marry, and eat fish and meat. They carry to its logical conclusion the old idea that one should accommodate oneself to the world. By doing as the world does, by living like other ordinary people, the priests avoid setting up barriers, and they can meet the laity on easier terms. The Shin sect tends in the direction of the abolition of all specific religious observances. The motive for the abrogation of celibacy is, of course, quite different from that prevalent in the Tantra. There the idea was to utilise the whole body for salvation, and there was no reason why the sexual parts should be left out. Sex was a form of physical drill, and a temptation bravely borne. In the Shin-shu, marriage is a means of sharing the burdens of the low and humble, of observing the customs and duties of the society in which one lives and which it would be presumptuous to reject. The main task is to live like any one else, and to serve both the world and the Buddha. The democratic spirit of the Shin-shu and its sanction of social duties have made for success in the world of to-day. Alone among all Buddhist schools, the Shin sect has during the last 50 years shown that Buddhism can adapt itself to industrial conditions, although such ' adaptation ' of Buddhism could easily be mistaken for its abolition.

The Rnyin-ma-pa

In Tibet the ancient Red sect, whose adherents wear red instead of yellow gowns, preach and practise an esoteric doctrine which was originally introduced by the Indian prince Padma Sambhava about 750 A.D. Padma Sambhava was a wonder-worker who paid no more than two brief visits to Tibet. During the short 18 months of his stay he exerted, however, an influence which is still felt in Tibet to-day, in spite of the fact that the official Yellow Church has combated his doctrine for now five centuries. The chief reason for Padma Sambhava's lasting influence seems to lie in the fact that his interpretation of Buddhism—a form of the Tantra—is very much akin to Bönism, the indigenous religion of Tibet. The followers of Padma Sambhava are usually called the Rnyin-ma-pa, literally " The Ancient Ones." The reason for this epithet is to be found in the fact that their doctrines were introduced roughly between 750 and 850, i.e. in the period before the great persecution of Buddhism by King Glandar-ma (836–41).

It is quite obvious that secret magical doctrines, since they do not claim to be justified by reasoning alone, require some form of inspiration to lend them authority. The Rnyin-ma-pa tradition claims to be based on two sources of authority. The initial foundations of the doctrine were transmitted direct from the Indian masters. In addition, however, the Rnyin-ma-pa chose to believe, like the Hermetic tradition of the Mediterranean world, that the tradition has an additional basis in the discovery of buried texts (gter-ma). Padma Sambhava, and other masters, buried certain texts in out of the way places, which would be found at the appointed time by predestined persons whenever the need for a supplementary revelation should arise. Similarly, the Hermetic texts dealing with astrology, alchemy, magic and so on, do in many cases claim to represent books written by ancient sages, to be ' found ' and edited when the time was ripe. This seems again to confirm our view that a great deal of the Tantra is a fusion between the Egyptian magic in its gnostic form on the one side, and the metaphysics of the Mahayana on the other. The buried texts in Tibet were dug up from ca 1125 onward. Among them are some extremely valuable works.

In its essentials the Rnyin-ma-pa doctrine is a branch of the Left-handed Tantra. The worship of tutelary deities plays an important part, and this system knows of 100 such deities, of whom 58 are serene and 42 angry. In addition, of course, there is the cult of the terrible deities, who are in their essence conceived as the destroyers of the three traditional arch-enemies of our peace of mind, i.e. of greed, hate, and delusion. The physiological practices of Hatha Yoga play an important part. The manipulation of the " Arteries " (see pp. 198–9) and of the semen virile is held to result in the production of happiness, light and thoughtlessness. The different classes of practices are normally performed in the following order ; First, there should be the mental creation of the images of the tutelaries, brought about by reciting formulas and meditating on the visions thus raised. Secondly, comes the physical-mental control of the Arteries and of the semen virile ; and thirdly, a realisation of the true nature of one's own mind which is emptiness itself. The distinctive idea of this School is that it tries to utilise what the Buddhists generally discard, i.e. the emotions of anger and lust, etc. ; and secondly that it tries to employ the material body, a dreaded shackle of the spirit to other Buddhists, as a profitable means to help the spirit. The magical nature of the Rnyin-ma-pa is seen in their doctrine of Thod-gyal, *Surpassing of the Uppermost*, according to which there is a way of salvation or emancipation in which the material body may vanish in the rainbow, or in the manner of the colours of the rainbow.

The doctrines of this School are very involved in their details, and it would be quite impossible to give a short explanation of them. Readers who are interested in this side of Buddhism are referred to some of the texts which Evans-Wentz has made available in English. A particularly fascinating doctrine which the Rnyin-ma-pa have preserved is the doctrine of the *Bardo*. Bardo is the name of the experience a person undergoes in the interval between death and a new rebirth. Many Buddhists assume that a new birth follows instantaneously on death. Others, however, postulate an interval, and the Rnyin-ma-pa School give us a most detailed description of the experiences of the " soul " on the Bardo plane, which has been rendered accessible to us by Evans-Wentz's admirable translation of the *Tibetan Book of the Dead*. Some of the traditions which it contains obviously go back to the Stone Age.

The book gives advice to the soul of the dying man by preparing him for the typical experiences to which he will be exposed. In this work a great deal of Egyptian wisdom lives on until to-day.

European Buddhism

The Jesuit missionaries had, in the 17th and 18th centuries, acquired a fairly accurate knowledge of Chinese and Japanese Buddhism, but it was a German philosopher, Arthur Schopenhauer, who first made Europe acquainted with Buddhism as a living faith. Without any knowledge of the Buddhist Scriptures, guided only by the philosophy of Kant, a Latin translation of a Persian translation of the *Upanishads* and his own disillusionment with life, Schopenhauer had, by 1819, evolved a philosophical system which in its insistence on the " *Negation of the Will to live*," and on compassion as the one redeeming virtue, breathed a spirit very akin to that of Buddhism. The ideas of Schopenhauer, expressed in a lively and readable style, have had a great influence on the Continent. Richard Wagner was deeply impressed by the teachings of the Buddha, and in recent years Albert Schweitzer lived the life which Schopenhauer only recommended.

In the course of the 19th century, the invasion of Asia by European merchants, soldiers and missionaries was accompanied by a slow infiltration of Asiatic ideas into Europe. The infiltration took the two forms of scientific research and popular propaganda. The scholarly investigation of Buddhist writings and art has continued now for 120 years without interruption. The history of Buddhism has, in each generation, attracted a considerable number of scholars of great ability. Many of them, especially at first, studied Buddhism as one watches an enemy, intent on proving the superiority of Christianity. A few were convinced that they had to deal with a faith of supreme purity from which Europe could learn a great deal. The majority investigated the documents with the detachment with which one solves crossword puzzles. As the result of the labours of four generations, the exploration of Buddhism has made great progress, though much remains to be done. Sociologically, 'Orientalism' in Europe was bound up with imperialism. With the decline of European imperialism, Orientalism is at present in the throes of a deep crisis, and one wonders how it will fare in the future. In the U.S.S.R. Buddhist studies seem to have petered out, although Russians had contributed much to Buddhist scholarship in the past. It may be that the mysticism of the Buddhists is not to the taste of the dialectical materialists.

The year 1875 marks an event of great importance. Madame Blavatsky and Colonel Olcott founded the 'Theosophical Society.' Its activities accelerated the influx of knowledge about Asiatic religions, and restored self-confidence in the wavering minds of the Asiatics themselves. At that period, European civilization, a blend of science and commerce, of Christianity and militarism, seemed immensely strong. The latent dynamite of national war and class war was perceived by only a few. A growing number of educated men in India and Ceylon felt, as the Japanese did about the same time, that they had no alternative but to adopt the Western system with all that it entails. The Christian missionaries looked forward to speedy mass conversions. But then the tide turned, rather suddenly and unexpectedly. A few members of the dominant race, white men and women from Russia, America and England, Theosophists, appeared among the Hindus and Ceylonese to proclaim their admiration for the ancient wisdom of the East. Mme. Blavatsky spoke about Buddhism in terms of the highest praise, Colonel Olcott wrote a 'Buddhist Catechism,' and A. P. Sinnett published a very successful book in which all kinds of mysterious, but fascinating, ideas were presented as 'Esoteric Buddhism.' The myth of the Mahatmas located those invisible, wise and semi-divine leaders of mankind in the Himalayas, in Tibet, a Buddhist country, which became surrounded by an aura of superhuman wisdom. By its timely intervention, the Theosophical Society has done a great service to the Buddhist cause. Although later on it became, as an organisation, corrupted by wealth and charlatanism, it has continued to be an impetus to Buddhist studies and has inspired many to seek further. To the ranks of the Theosophists belonged also Edwin Arnold, whose poem, " *The Light of Asia*," has led many hearts to love and admire the Buddha for the purity of his life, and his devotion to the welfare of mankind.

After 1900, a few missionaries were sent from Asia, who laboured, in London and elsewhere, without much success. In the European capitals, in Paris, London and Berlin, small propaganda organisations were established. In England ' The Buddhist Society ' has, under the able leadership of Christmas Humphreys, shown a great deal of initiative in " *beating the drum of the Dharma.*" So far, however, European Buddhism has been unable to find its feet. The organisation of the Samgha has been, as we saw (p. 53) the one permanent and stable element in Buddhist history. Monks and monasteries are the indispensable foundation of a Buddhist movement, which aims at being a concrete, living social reality. A number of European Buddhists who felt drawn to the monastic life have gone to Ceylon, China and Japan. The obstacles to the establishment of Buddhist monasteries in Europe are great, but probably not greater than they were originally in China. As the bankruptcy of our civilisation becomes ever more patent, many more people will be drawn to the wisdom of the past, and some of them to its Buddhist form. It remains to be seen when and where Europeans garbed in the saffron robe will make their first appearance.

The main dates of
BUDDHIST HISTORY

Am. = Amidism, B. = Buddhism, Ch. = China, Chinese, Hi. = Hinayana, MY. = Madhyamika-
Yogacarin, N.W. = New Wisdom, S. = Sarvastivadin, T. = Tantra, Th. = Theravadins,
Y. — Yogocarin, Y.L. = Yogacarin Logic, Z. = Zen (Ch'an).

After Buddha	Before Christ	HISTORY	HINAYANA	MAHAYANA	ART
80	480	**480** Death of Buddha			
		325 Alexander in India			
		315 Candragupta			
260	300	**274** Asoka begins to rule	**246** Mahinda brings B. to Ceylon		
		236 Asoka +	**240** Sthaviravadins and Mahasanghikas split		
360	200	**160** Menandros		Original Prajnaparamita (NW)	**120** Gates at Sanchi
460	100		**80** Pali scriptures written down	**80** Mahayana sutras: Saddharma Pundarika, etc.	**–500 A.D.** Gandhara
					–200 A.D. Mathura
560	A.D.	**25—60** Kadphises I B. spreads to China			Amaravati
		61 Dream of Mingti			
		78—103 Kanishka		Large Prajnaparamita (NW)	Reliquary of Peshawar
			100 Ashvagosha		
660	100		**140** Vibhasha (S) in Kashmir	**160** Sandhinirmocana sutra (Y) Nagarjuna (NW) Aryadeva (NW)	**150–350** Bulk of Amaravati

After Buddha	A.D.	HISTORY	HINAYANA	MAHAYANA	ART
760	200	220 B. spreads to Annam			Buddhist painters in South China 265 First Pagoda in China −600 Gupta Art
860	300	355 Ch. edict permits monkhood 357—385 Fu kien protects B. 372 B. spreads to Korea 385—414 Candragupta II 399—414 Fa hien in India		333 Hui-yüan (Am) ✱ Lankavatara sutra (Y) Maitreyanatha (MY)	Ellora. Ajanta Ku k'ai chih
960	400	 414—455 Kumaragupta I founds Nalanda 438—452 To-pa Tao perse- cutes B. B. spreads to Burma, Java, Sumatra 452 sq. To-pa's protect B.	Vasubandhu (S) 420 Buddhaghosa (Th) 440 Mahavamsa (Th) 460 Dhammapala (Th)	Vasubandhu (Y) Asanga (Y) Kumarajiva (NW) 416 Hui-yüan + Dignaga (YL) 498–561 Bodhidharma (Z) Paramartha (Y)	−500 B. sculpture in N. China 414–520 Grottos of Yun-kang Wei sculpture
1060	500	518 Oldest catalogue of Ch. Tripitaka 552 B. spreads to Japan 572 Shotoku Taishi ✱ 573 Second persecution in China		 560 Sthiramati + 580 Tien tai founded San-lun founded	 Renaissance of Art in China

After Buddha	A.D.	HISTORY	HINAYANA	MAHAYANA	ART
1160	600	B. spreads to Sumatra		Hua-yen founded	
		606—647 Harshavardhana		606 Seng-t-san (Z) +	
		621 Shotoku Taishi +		635 Dharmapala (Y)	Grotto I in Ajanta
		629—645 Hiuen-tsiang in India		637 Hui-neng (Z) * Lu-tsung founded	
		642 sq. Song-tsen-gampo (Tibet)		645–664 Hiuen-tsiang (Y) works in China	Li-szu-hsun
		642 B. spreads to Tibet		650 Chandrakirti (NW)	
		651 First B. temple in Tibet		643 Fa-tsang (Hua-yen) Dharmakirti (L)	
		671—695 I-tsing's Travels		691 Shantideva (NW) *	Nara Temples
1260	700	B. spreads to Annam Mahayana official religion of Srivijaya			
		710—784 Nara period		713 Hui-neng (Z) +	Wu tao tze Java
		711 Sindh lost to Islam		716 Shin-gon founded	–1000 Tun-hu-ang
		720 B. (Hi) spreads to Siam		Shubhakarasimha (T) Vajrabodhi (T) Amoghavajra (T)	
		749 First monastery (Sam-ye) in Tibet	740 Anuruddha, Abhidham- mattha- sangaha	747 Padmasambhava to Tibet (T) Shantarakshita (T)	747 Gigantic Buddha at Nara Borobudur Todaiji
		760 Arabs take Central Asia Odantapuri founded Pala Dynasty		774 Amoghavajra +	
		770—815 Dharmapala			

After Buddha	A.D.	HISTORY	HINAYANA	MAHAYANA	ART
1360	800	Shivaism supersedes B. in Kashmir Mahayana develops in Cambodia 845 Persecution by Wu-tsang 850—1350 Korye Dynasty in Korea		Haribhadra (NW) 805 Dengyo Daishi founds Ten-dai on Mt. Hiei 840 Kobo Daishi (T) +	802 Angkor founded
1460	900	Lang-dharma Islam supersedes B. in Central Asia	920 King Aba Salamevan Kasup V (Ceylon)	Koan system (Z) 949 Yuen-men (Z) + Kuya (Am) 942—1017 Genshin (Tendai) 965 Kala-cakra (T) 980 Atisa ✳	−1300 Korean Art
1560	1000	1000—1200 B. enjoys royal support in Annam 1077 King Anuruddha of Burma + 1086—1112 King Kyanzittha of Burma	1040 Theravadins win Burma	1020 Pi-yen-chi (Z) 1038—1122 Milarepa 1039 Atisa goes to Tibet 1052 Atisa +	1017 Yeishin Sozu +
1660	1100	1180—1205 Dvayavarman VII (Cambodia) 1197 Nalanda destroyed by Islam	1140 Theravadins win Siam	1100 Ryonin (Tendai, Am) 1133 Honen Shonin (Am) ✳ 1173 Shinran (Am) ✳ 1191 Eisai brings Zen to Japan	Art flourishes in Tibet Art of Bayon in Cambodia

After Buddha	A.D.	HISTORY	HINAYANA	MAHAYANA	ART
1760	1200	1202 Shakyapandita arrives in Tibet		1200 Dogen (Z) ✱ Jodo-shu founded (Am)	
				1211 Honen Shonin (Am)+	
				1215 Eisai (Z) + Dogen (1200–53) founds Soto (Z)	
		1227—63 Tokiyori favours Zen		1222 Nichiren ✱	
				1225 Jodo-shin-shu founded	
				1228 Mumon Kwan (Z)	1252 Kamakura Dai Butsu Engakuji Temple
		1251—84 Hojo Tokimune favours Zen	1240 Dhammakitti	1239 Ippen Shonin (Z) ✱	
				1253 Dogen (Z) +	
		1260—94 Kublai Khan favours B. Tea ceremony comes to Japan		1267 Dai-o Kokushi (1235–1308) founds Rinzai (Z), Eison (1202–90) revives Ri-tsu (Vinaya) school	
			1280 Jinacarita	1282 Nichiren +	
				1289 Ippen Shonin (Am)+	
				1288 Bu-ston (T) ✱	

After Buddha	A.D.	HISTORY	HINAYANA	MAHAYANA	ART
1860	1300	*1320* Mahayana declines in Cambodia			
		1340 Laos converted		*1357* Tsong-kha-pa +	
		1360 B. (Hi) official religion of Siam		*1365* Nagarakirtagama (T) in Java	
		1392 B. declines in Korea		*1385* Ryogo Shogei's Jugi (Am)	
				1392 Ge-lug-pa (T) founded	
1960	1400	*−1500* Persecution in Annam		*1419* Tsong-kha-pa +	*1420–1506* Sesshiu (Z)
		1480 Java : Hinduism supersedes B. Sumatra : Islam supersedes B.			
2060		*1576* Kum bum founded		Shi yen ki of Wu Ch'eng-en (Am)	
	1500	*1577* Final conversion of Mongols		*1573* Taranatha ✱	*1582–1645* Miyamoto
				1573–1645 Takuan (Z)	
				1599–1655 Chih-hsu	
2160	1600	*1603* Tokugawa in Japan Decline of B.	*1620* Yogavacara's Manual		
		1642 5th Dalai Lama becomes Priest-King of Tibet			
		1643 Potala built		*1685–1768* Hakuin (Z)	*1643–94* Basho

After Buddha	A.D.	HISTORY	HINAYANA	MAHAYANA	ART
2260	1700	*1718* Mongol armies assist Ge-lug-pa			
		1769 Nepal turns to Hinduism			
		1785 First Burjat monastery			
2360	1800	*1819* Schopenhauer's *Welt als Wille und Vorstellung*			
		1840 Burnouf			
		1850–65 Tai-ping rebellion destroys many monasteries			
		1875 Theosophical Society founded			
		1879 E. Arnold's *Light of Asia*			
		1890 Revival of B. in Japan			
2460	1900	*1891* Mahabodhi Society founded			
		1904 British Epedition to Lhasa			
		1909 Tai Hsu revives Chinese Bu.			
		1926 English Buddhist Society founded		*1924–29* Taisho Issaikyo	
		1928 Amis du Bouddhisme founded			

INDEX

A SELECTION OF BOOKS

INTRODUCTIONS AND SURVEYS

A. DAVID-NEEL, *Buddhism, its Doctrines and Methods*, 1939.

J. B. PRATT, *The Pilgrimage of Buddhism*, 1929.

CH. ELIOT, *Hinduism and Buddhism*, 3 vols., 1921.
Japanese Buddhism, 1934.

E. J. THOMAS, *The Life of Buddha as Legend and History*, 1927.

HAR DAYAL, *The Bodhisattva-Doctrine in Buddhist Sanskrit Literature*, 1932.

J. E. CARPENTER, *Buddhism and Christianity*, 1922.

H. KERN, *Manual of Indian Buddhism*, 1896.

J. BLOFELD, *The Jewel in the Lotus*, 1948 (China).

L. A. WADDELL, *The Buddhism of Tibet*, 1895–1934.

CH. BELL, *The Religion of Tibet*, 1931.

E. STEINILBER-OBERLIN, *The Buddhist Sects of Japan*, 1938.

D. T. SUZUKI, *Essays in Zen Buddhism*, 3 vols., 1926–34.

TEXTS

THERAVADINS:

F. L. WOODWARD, *Some Sayings of the Buddha*, 1925.

A. K. COOMARASWAMY and I. B. HORNER, *The Living Thoughts of Gotama the Buddha*, 1948.

THE DHAMMAPADA, ed., trsl. S. Radhakrishnan, 1950.

SUTTA NIPATA: *Woven Cadences*, trsl. E. M. Hare, 1944.

NYANATILOKA, *Guide through the Abhidhamma-Pitaka*, 1938.

BUDDHAGHOSA, *The Path of Purity*, trsl. P. M. Tin, 3 vols., 1923–31.

SARVASTIVADINS:

E. J. THOMAS, *The Quest of Enlightenment. A Selection of the Buddhist Scriptures;* trsl. from the Sanskrit, 1950.

VASUBANDHU, *Abhidharmakosha, traduit et annotée par L. de la Vallee-Poussin*, 1923–31.

QUOTATIONS

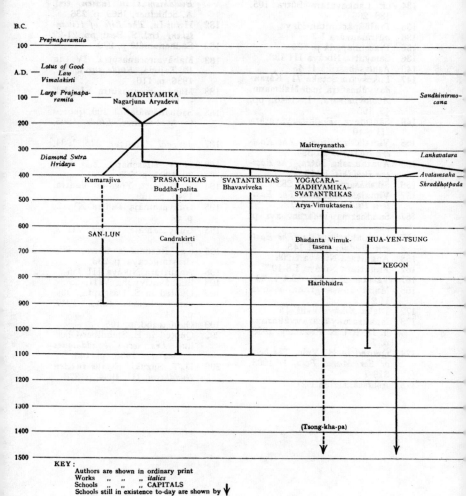

KEY:
Authors are shown in ordinary print
Works   ,,   ,,   ,,   *italics*
Schools   ,,   ,,   ,,   CAPITALS
Schools still in existence to-day are shown by ↓

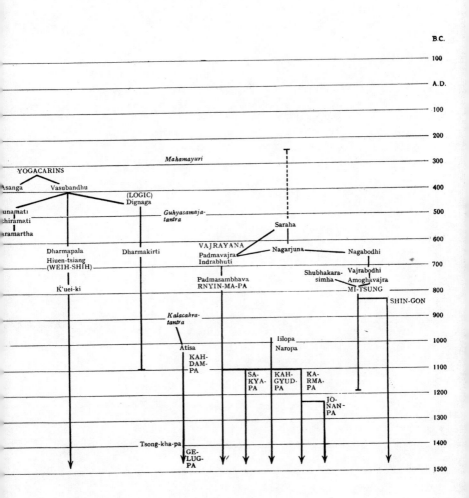

hARPER ✦ tORChbOOKS

HUMANITIES AND SOCIAL SCIENCES

American Studies: General

HENRY STEELE COMMAGER, Ed.: The Struggle for Racial Equality TB/1300
EDWARD S. CORWIN: American Constitutional History. △ Essays edited by Alpheus T. Mason and Gerald Garvey TB/1136
CARL N. DEGLER, Ed.: Pivotal Interpretations of American History TB/1240, TB/1241
A. S. EISENSTADT, Ed.: The Craft of American History: Recent Essays in American Historical Writing
Vol. I TB/1255; Vol. II TB/1256
CHARLOTTE P. GILMAN: Women and Economics ‡ TB/3073
OSCAR HANDLIN, Ed.: This Was America: As Recorded by European Travelers in the Eighteenth, Nineteenth and Twentieth Centuries. Illus. TB/1119
MARCUS LEE HANSEN: The Atlantic Migration: 1607-1860. Edited by Arthur M. Schlesinger TB/1052
MARCUS LEE HANSEN: The Immigrant in American History TB/1120
JOHN HIGHAM, Ed.: The Reconstruction of American History △ TB/1068
ROBERT H. JACKSON: The Supreme Court in the American System of Government TB/1106
JOHN F. KENNEDY: A Nation of Immigrants. △ Illus. TB/1118
LEONARD W. LEVY, Ed.: American Constitutional Law TB/1285
LEONARD W. LEVY, Ed.: Judicial Review and the Supreme Court TB/1296
LEONARD W. LEVY: The Law of the Commonwealth and Chief Justice Shaw TB/1309
RALPH BARTON PERRY: Puritanism and Democracy TB/1138
ARNOLD ROSE: The Negro in America: The Condensed Version of Gunnar Myrdal's An American Dilemma TB/3048
MAURICE R. STEIN: The Eclipse of Community: An Interpretation of American Studies TB/1128
W. LLOYD WARNER: Social Class in America: The Evaluation of Status TB/1013

American Studies: Colonial

BERNARD BAILYN, Ed.: The Apologia of Robert Keayne: Self-Portrait of a Puritan Merchant TB/1201
BERNARD BAILYN: The New England Merchants in the Seventeenth Century TB/1149
CHARLES GIBSON: Spain in America † TB/3077
LAWRENCE HENRY GIPSON: The Coming of the Revolution: 1763-1775. † Illus. TB/3007

PERRY MILLER: Errand Into the Wilderness TB/1139
PERRY MILLER & T. H. JOHNSON, Eds.: The Puritans: A Sourcebook Vol. I TB/1093; Vol. II TB/1094
EDMUND S. MORGAN, Ed.: The Diary of Michael Wigglesworth, 1653-1657: The Conscience of a Puritan TB/1228
EDMUND S. MORGAN: The Puritan Family: Religion and Domestic Relations in Seventeenth-Century New England TB/1227
RICHARD B. MORRIS: Government and Labor in Early America TB/1244
KENNETH B. MURDOCK: Literature and Theology in Colonial New England TB/99
JOHN P. ROCHE: Origins of American Political Thought: Selected Readings TB/1301
JOHN SMITH: Captain John Smith's America: Selections from His Writings. Ed. with Intro. by John Lankford TB/3078
LOUIS B. WRIGHT: The Cultural Life of the American Colonies: 1607-1763. † Illus. TB/3005

American Studies: From the Revolution to 1860

JOHN R. ALDEN: The American Revolution: 1775-1783. † Illus. TB/3011
RAY A. BILLINGTON: The Far Western Frontier: 1830-1860. † Illus. TB/3012
EDMUND BURKE: On the American Revolution. ‡ Edited by Elliott Robert Barkan TB/3068
WHITNEY R. CROSS: The Burned-Over District: The Social and Intellectual History of Enthusiastic Religion in Western New York, 1800-1850 TB/1242
GEORGE DANGERFIELD: The Awakening of American Nationalism: 1815-1828. † Illus. TB/3061
CLEMENT EATON: The Freedom-of-Thought Struggle in the Old South. Revised and Enlarged. Illus. TB/1150
CLEMENT EATON: The Growth of Southern Civilization: 1790-1860. † Illus. TB/3040
LOUIS FILLER: The Crusade Against Slavery: 1830-1860. † Illus. TB/3029
WILLIAM W. FREEHLING, Ed.: The Nullification Era: A Documentary Record ‡ TB/3079
FELIX GILBERT: The Beginnings of American Foreign Policy: To the Farewell Address TB/1200
FRANCIS GRIERSON: The Valley of Shadows: The Coming of the Civil War in Lincoln's Midwest: A Contemporary Account TB/1246
ALEXANDER HAMILTON: The Reports of Alexander Hamilton. ‡ Edited by Jacob E. Cooke TB/3060
JAMES MADISON: The Forging of American Federalism: Selected Writings of James Madison. Edited by Saul K. Padover TB/1126
BERNARD MAYO: Myths and Men: Patrick Henry, George Washington, Thomas Jefferson TB/1108

† The New American Nation Series, edited by Henry Steele Commager and Richard B. Morris.
‡ American Perspectives series, edited by Bernard Wishy and William E. Leuchtenburg.
* The Rise of Modern Europe series, edited by William L. Langer.
** History of Europe series, edited by J. H. Plumb.
¶ Researches in the Social, Cultural and Behavioral Sciences, edited by Benjamin Nelson.
§ The Library of Religion and Culture, edited by Benjamin Nelson.
Σ Harper Modern Science Series, edited by James R. Newman.
o Not for sale in Canada.
△ Not for sale in the U. K.

JOHN C. MILLER: Alexander Hamilton and the Growth of
the New Nation   TB/3057
RICHARD B. MORRIS, Ed.: The Era of the American Revolution   TB/1180
FRANCIS S. PHILBRICK: The Rise of the West, 1754-1830. †
Illus.   TB/3067
TIMOTHY L. SMITH: Revivalism and Social Reform:
American Protestantism on the Eve of the Civil War
                                                  TB/1229
ALBION W. TOURGÉE: A Fool's Errand ‡   TB/3074
GLYNDON G. VAN DEUSEN: The Jacksonian Era: 1828-
1848. † Illus.   TB/3028
LOUIS B. WRIGHT: Culture on the Moving Frontier
                                                  TB/1053

American Studies: The Civil War to 1900

W. R. BROCK: An American Crisis: Congress and Reconstruction, 1865-67 ° △   TB/1283
THOMAS C. COCHRAN & WILLIAM MILLER: The Age of Enterprise: A Social History of Industrial America TB/1054
W. A. DUNNING: Reconstruction, Political and Economic:
1865-1877   TB/1073
HAROLD U. FAULKNER: Politics, Reform and Expansion:
1890-1900. † Illus.   TB/3020
HELEN HUNT JACKSON: A Century of Dishonor: The Early
Crusade for Indian Reform. ‡ Edited by Andrew F.
Rolle   TB/3063
ALBERT D. KIRWAN: Revolt of the Rednecks: Mississippi
Politics, 1876-1925   TB/1199
ROBERT GREEN MC CLOSKEY: American Conservatism in
the Age of Enterprise: 1865-1910   TB/1137
ARTHUR MANN: Yankee Reformers in the Urban Age:
Social Reform in Boston, 1880-1900   TB/1247
WHITELAW REID: After the War: A Tour of the Southern
States, 1865-1866. ‡ Edited by C. Vann Woodward
                                                  TB/3066
CHARLES H. SHINN: Mining Camps: A Study in American
Frontier Government. ‡ Edited by Rodman W. Paul
                                                  TB/3062
VERNON LANE WHARTON: The Negro in Mississippi:
1865-1890   TB/1178

American Studies: 1900 to the Present

RAY STANNARD BAKER: Following the Color Line: American Negro Citizenship in Progressive Era. ‡ Illus.
Edited by Dewey W. Grantham, Jr.   TB/3053
RANDOLPH S. BOURNE: War and the Intellectuals: Collected Essays, 1915-1919. ‡ Ed. by Carl Resek TB/3043
A. RUSSELL BUCHANAN: The United States and World War
II. † Illus.   Vol. I TB/3044; Vol. II TB/3045
THOMAS C. COCHRAN: The American Business System:
A Historical Perspective, 1900-1955   TB/1080
FOSTER RHEA DULLES: America's Rise to World Power:
1898-1954. † Illus.   TB/3021
JOHN D. HICKS: Republican Ascendancy: 1921-1933. †
Illus.   TB/3041
SIDNEY HOOK: Reason, Social Myths, and Democracy
                                                  TB/1237
ROBERT HUNTER: Poverty: Social Conscience in the Progressive Era. ‡ Edited by Peter d'A. Jones TB/3065
WILLIAM L. LANGER & S. EVERETT GLEASON: The Challenge
to Isolation: The World Crisis of 1937-1940 and
American Foreign Policy
            Vol. I TB/3054; Vol. II TB/3055
WILLIAM E. LEUCHTENBURG: Franklin D. Roosevelt and
the New Deal: 1932-1940. † Illus.   TB/3025
ARTHUR S. LINK: Woodrow Wilson and the Progressive
Era: 1910-1917. † Illus.   TB/3023
GEORGE E. MOWRY: The Era of Theodore Roosevelt and
the Birth of Modern America: 1900-1912. † TB/3022
RUSSEL B. NYE: Midwestern Progressive Politics   TB/1202
WILLIAM PRESTON, JR.: Aliens and Dissenters   TB/1287
WALTER RAUSCHENBUSCH: Christianity and the Social
Crisis. ‡ Edited by Robert D. Cross   TB/3059

JACOB RIIS: The Making of an American. ‡ Edited
Roy Lubove   TB/3
PHILIP SELZNICK: TVA and the Grass Roots: A Study
the Sociology of Formal Organization   TB/1
IDA M. TARBELL: The History of the Standard Oil Company. Briefer Version. ‡ Edited by David M. Chalm
                                                  TB/3
GEORGE B. TINDALL, Ed.: A Populist Reader ‡   TB/3

Anthropology

JACQUES BARZUN: Race: A Study in Superstition. Revised Edition   TB/
JOSEPH B. CASAGRANDE, Ed.: In the Company of Man:
Portraits of Anthropological Informants   TB/
W. E. LE GROS CLARK: The Antecedents of Man: Introduction to Evolution of the Primates. ° △ Illus. TB/
CORA DU BOIS: The People of Alor. New Preface by
author. Illus.   Vol. I TB/1042; Vol. II TB/1
RAYMOND FIRTH, Ed.: Man and Culture: An Evaluation
of the Work of Bronislaw Malinowski ¶ ° △   TB/1
DAVID LANDY: Tropical Childhood: Cultural Transmission and Learning in a Puerto Rican Village ¶ TB/1
L. S. B. LEAKEY: Adam's Ancestors: The Evolution
Man and His Culture. △ Illus.   TB/1
EDWARD BURNETT TYLOR: The Origin of Culture. Part
of "Primitive Culture." § Intro. by Paul Radin TB
EDWARD BURNETT TYLOR: Religion in Primitive Culture
Part II of "Primitive Culture." § Intro. by Paul Ra
                                                  TB

Art and Art History

WALTER LOWRIE: Art in the Early Church. Revised Edition. 452 illus.   TB/
EMILE MÂLE: The Gothic Image: Religious Art in France
of the Thirteenth Century. § △ 190 illus.   TB
MILLARD MEISS: Painting in Florence and Siena after the
Black Death: The Arts, Religion and Society in the
Mid-Fourteenth Century. 169 illus.   TB/1
ERICH NEUMANN: The Archetypal World of Henry
Moore. △ 107 illus.   TB/2
DORA & ERWIN PANOFSKY: Pandora's Box: The Changing
Aspects of a Mythical Symbol. Illus.   TB/2
ALEXANDRE PIANKOFF: The Shrines of Tut-Ankh-Amon.
Edited by N. Rambova. 117 illus.   TB/2
JEAN SEZNEC: The Survival of the Pagan Gods △   TB/2
OTTO VON SIMSON: The Gothic Cathedral △   TB/2
HEINRICH ZIMMER: Myths and Symbols in Indian Art and
Civilization. 70 illustrations   TB/2

Business, Economics & Economic History

REINHARD BENDIX: Work and Authority in Industry
                                                  TB/3
THOMAS C. COCHRAN: The American Business System:
Historical Perspective, 1900-1955   TB/1
THOMAS C. COCHRAN & WILLIAM MILLER: The Age of Enterprise: A Social History of Industrial America TB/1
ROBERT DAHL & CHARLES E. LINDBLOM: Politics, Economics, and Welfare   TB/3
PETER F. DRUCKER: The New Society: The Anatomy
Industrial Order △   TB/1
EDITORS OF FORTUNE: America in the Sixties: The Economy and the Society   TB/1
ROBERT L. HEILBRONER: The Great Ascent: The Struggle
for Economic Development in Our Time   TB/3
ROBERT L. HEILBRONER: The Limits of American Capitalism   TB/13
FRANK H. KNIGHT: The Economic Organization TB/12
FRANK H. KNIGHT: Risk, Uncertainty and Profit TB/12
ABBA P. LERNER: Everybody's Business   TB/3
ROBERT GREEN MC CLOSKEY: American Conservatism
the Age of Enterprise, 1865-1910   TB/11
PAUL MANTOUX: The Industrial Revolution in the
Eighteenth Century ° △   TB/1

3

4

G. M. TREVELYAN: British History in the Nineteenth Century and After: 1782-1919. △ *Second Edition* TB/1251

H. R. TREVOR-ROPER: Historical Essays ○ △ TB/1269

ELIZABETH WISKEMANN: Europe of the Dictators, 1919-1945 ** ○ △ TB/1275

JOHN B. WOLF: The Emergence of the Great Powers, 1685-1715. * *Illus.* TB/3010

JOHN B. WOLF: France: 1814-1919: *The Rise of a Liberal-Democratic Society* TB/3019

Intellectual History & History of Ideas

HERSCHEL BAKER: The Image of Man TB/1047

R. R. BOLGAR: The Classical Heritage and Its Beneficiaries △ TB/1125

RANDOLPH S. BOURNE: War and the Intellectuals: *Collected Essays, 1915-1919.* ‡ △ *Edited by Carl Resek* TB/3043

J. BRONOWSKI & BRUCE MAZLISH: The Western Intellectual Tradition: *From Leonardo to Hegel* △ TB/3001

ERNST CASSIRER: The Individual and the Cosmos in Renaissance Philosophy. △ *Translated with an Introduction by Mario Domandi* TB/1097

NORMAN COHN: Pursuit of the Millennium △ TB/1037

C. C. GILLISPIE: Genesis and Geology: *The Decades before Darwin* § TB/51

G. RACHEL LEVY: Religious Conceptions of the Stone Age and Their Influence upon European Thought. △ *Illus. Introduction by Henri Frankfort* TB/106

ARTHUR O. LOVEJOY: The Great Chain of Being: *A Study of the History of an Idea* TB/1009

FRANK E. MANUEL: The Prophets of Paris: *Turgot, Condorcet, Saint-Simon, Fourier, and Comte* TB/1218

PERRY MILLER & T. H. JOHNSON, Editors: The Puritans: *A Sourcebook of Their Writings* Vol. I TB/1093; Vol. II TB/1094

MILTON C. NAHM: Genius and Creativity: *An Essay in the History of Ideas* TB/1196

ROBERT PAYNE: Hubris: *A Study of Pride. Foreword by Sir Herbert Read* TB/1031

RALPH BARTON PERRY: The Thought and Character of William James: *Briefer Version* TB/1156

GEORG SIMMEL et al.: Essays on Sociology, Philosophy, and Aesthetics. ¶ *Edited by Kurt H. Wolff* TB/1234

BRUNO SNELL: The Discovery of the Mind: *The Greek Origins of European Thought* △ TB/1018

PAGET TOYNBEE: Dante Alighieri: *His Life and Works. Edited with Intro. by Charles S. Singleton* TB/1206

ERNEST LEE TUVESON: Millennium and Utopia: *A Study in the Background of the Idea of Progress.* ¶ *New Preface by the Author* TB/1134

PAUL VALÉRY: The Outlook for Intelligence △ TB/2016

W. WARREN WAGAR, Ed.: European Intellectual History since Darwin and Marx TB/1297

PHILIP P. WIENER: Evolution and the Founders of Pragmatism. △ *Foreword by John Dewey* TB/1212

BASIL WILLEY: Nineteenth Century Studies: *Coleridge to Matthew Arnold* ○ △ TB/1261

BASIL WILLEY: More Nineteenth Century Studies: *A Group of Honest Doubters* △ TB/1262

Literature, Poetry, The Novel & Criticism

JACQUES BARZUN: The House of Intellect △ TB/1051

W. J. BATE: From Classic to Romantic: *Premises of Taste in Eighteenth Century England* TB/1036

RACHEL BESPALOFF: On the Iliad TB/2006

R. P. BLACKMUR et al.: Lectures in Criticism. *Introduction by Huntington Cairns* TB/2003

JAMES BOSWELL: The Life of Dr. Johnson & The Journal of a Tour to the Hebrides with Samuel Johnson LL.D: *Selections.* ○ △ *Edited by F. V. Morley. Illus. by Ernest Shepard* TB/1254

ABRAHAM CAHAN: The Rise of David Levinsky: *a documentary novel of social mobility in early twentieth century America. Intro. by John Higham* TB/1028

ERNST R. CURTIUS: European Literature and the Latin Middle Ages △ TB/2015

ÉTIENNE GILSON: Dante and Philosophy TB/1089

ALFRED HARBAGE: As They Liked It: *A Study of Shakespeare's Moral Artistry* TB/1035

STANLEY R. HOPPER, Ed.: Spiritual Problems in Contemporary Literature § TB/21

A. R. HUMPHREYS: The Augustan World: *Society in 18th Century England* ○ △ TB/1105

ALDOUS HUXLEY: Antic Hay & The Giaconda Smile. ○ △ *Introduction by Martin Green* TB/3503

ARNOLD KETTLE: An Introduction to the English Novel △ Volume I: *Defoe to George Eliot* TB/1011 Volume II: *Henry James to the Present* TB/1012

RICHMOND LATTIMORE: The Poetry of Greek Tragedy △ TB/1257

J. B. LEISHMAN: The Monarch of Wit: *An Analytical and Comparative Study of the Poetry of John Donne* ○ △ TB/1258

J. B. LEISHMAN: Themes and Variations in Shakespeare's Sonnets ○ △ TB/1259

ROGER SHERMAN LOOMIS: The Development of Arthurian Romance △ TB/1167

JOHN STUART MILL: On Bentham and Coleridge. △ *Introduction by F. R. Leavis* TB/1070

KENNETH B. MURDOCK: Literature and Theology in Colonial New England TB/99

SAMUEL PEPYS: The Diary of Samuel Pepys. ○ *Edited by O. F. Morshead. Illus. by Ernest Shepard* TB/1007

ST.-JOHN PERSE: Seamarks TB/2002

V. DE S. PINTO: Crisis in English Poetry, 1880-1940 ○ △ TB/1260

ROBERT PREYER, Ed.: Victorian Literature TB/1302

GEORGE SANTAYANA: Interpretations of Poetry and Religion § TB/9

C. K. STEAD: The New Poetic: *Yeats to Eliot* ○ △ TB/1263

HEINRICH STRAUMANN: American Literature in the Twentieth Century. △ *Third Edition, Revised* TB/1168

PAGET TOYNBEE: Dante Alighieri: *His Life and Works. Edited with Intro. by Charles S. Singleton* TB/1206

DOROTHY VAN GHENT: The English Novel TB/1050

E. B. WHITE: One Man's Meat TB/3505

BASIL WILLEY: Nineteenth Century Studies: *Coleridge to Matthew Arnold* ○ △ TB/1261

BASIL WILLEY: More Nineteenth Century Studies: *A Group of Honest Doubters* ○ △ TB/1262

RAYMOND WILLIAMS: Culture and Society, 1780-1950 △ TB/1252

RAYMOND WILLIAMS: The Long Revolution. △ *Revised Edition* TB/1253

MORTON DAUWEN ZABEL, Editor: *Literary Opinion in America* Vol. I TB/3013; Vol. II TB/3014

Myth, Symbol & Folklore

JOSEPH CAMPBELL, Editor: Pagan and Christian Mysteries. *Illus.* TB/2013

MIRCEA ELIADE: Cosmos and History: *The Myth of the Eternal Return* § △ TB/2050

MIRCEA ELIADE: Rites and Symbols of Initiation: *The Mysteries of Birth and Rebirth* § △ TB/1236

THEODOR H. GASTER: Thespis △ TB/1281

DORA & ERWIN PANOFSKY: Pandora's Box: *The Changing Aspects of a Mythical Symbol.* △ *Revised Edition. Illus.* TB/2021

HELLMUT WILHELM: Change: *Eight Lectures on the I Ching* △ TB/2019

HEINRICH ZIMMER: Myths and Symbols in Indian Art and Civilization. △ *70 illustrations* TB/2005

Philosophy

G. E. M. ANSCOMBE: An Introduction to Wittgenstein's Tractatus. ○ △ *Second Edition, Revised* TB/1210

Political Science & Government

Psychology

9

HAROLD F. BLUM: Time's Arrow and Evolution   TB/555
JOHN TYLER BONNER: The Ideas of Biology. Σ △ Illus.
TB/570
A. J. CAIN: Animal Species and their Evolution. △ Illus.
TB/519
WALTER B. CANNON: Bodily Changes in Pain, Hunger,
Fear and Rage. Illus.   TB/562
W. E. LE GROS CLARK: The Antecedents of Man: Intro. to
Evolution of the Primates. ᵒ △ Illus.   TB/559
W. H. DOWDESWELL: Animal Ecology. △ Illus.   TB/543
W. H. DOWDESWELL: The Mechanism of Evolution. △ Illus.
TB/527
R. W. GERARD: Unresting Cells. Illus.   TB/541
DAVID LACK: Darwin's Finches. △ Illus.   TB/544
ADOLF PORTMANN: Animals as Social Beings. ᵒ △ Illus.
TB/572
O. W. RICHARDS: The Social Insects. △ Illus.   TB/542
P. M. SHEPPARD: Natural Selection and Heredity. Illus.
TB/528
EDMUND W. SINNOTT: Cell and Psyche: The Biology of
Purpose   TB/546
C. H. WADDINGTON: How Animals Develop. △ Illus.
TB/553
C. H. WADDINGTON: The Nature of Life: The Main Prob-
lems and Trends in Modern Biology △   TB/580

Chemistry

J. R. PARTINGTON: A Short History of Chemistry. △ Illus.
TB/522

Communication Theory

J. R. PIERCE: Symbols, Signals and Noise: The Nature
and Process of Communication △   TB/574

Geography

R. E. COKER: This Great and Wide Sea: An Introduction
to Oceanography and Marine Biology. Illus.   TB/551
F. K. HARE: The Restless Atmosphere △   TB/560

History of Science

MARIE BOAS: The Scientific Renaissance, 1450-1630 ᵒ △
TB/583
W. DAMPIER, Ed.: Readings in the Literature of Science.
Illus.   TB/512
A. HUNTER DUPREE: Science in the Federal Government:
A History of Policies and Activities to 1940 △   TB/573
ALEXANDRE KOYRÉ: From the Closed World to the Infinite
Universe: Copernicus, Kepler, Galileo, Newton, etc. △
TB/31
A. G. VAN MELSEN: From Atomos to Atom: A History of
the Concept Atom   TB/517
O. NEUGEBAUER: The Exact Sciences in Antiquity. △ TB/552
HANS THIRRING: Energy for Man: From Windmills to
Nuclear Power △   TB/556
STEPHEN TOULMIN & JUNE GOODFIELD: The Architecture of
Matter ᵒ △   TB/584
STEPHEN TOULMIN & JUNE GOODFIELD: The Discovery of
Time ᵒ △   TB/585
LANCELOT LAW WHYTE: Essay on Atomism: From Democ-
ritus to 1960 △   TB/565

Mathematics

E. W. BETH: The Foundations of Mathematics: A Study
in the Philosophy of Science △   TB/581
H. DAVENPORT: The Higher Arithmetic: An Introduction
to the Theory of Numbers △   TB/526
H. G. FORDER: Geometry: An Introduction △   TB/548
S. KÖRNER: The Philosophy of Mathematics: An Intro-
duction △   TB/547
D. E. LITTLEWOOD: Skeleton Key of Mathematics: A
Simple Account of Complex Algebraic Problems △
TB/525
GEORGE E. OWEN: Fundamentals of Scientific Mathe-
matics   TB/569
WILLARD VAN ORMAN QUINE: Mathematical Logic TB/558
O. G. SUTTON: Mathematics in Action. ᵒ △ Foreword by
James R. Newman. Illus.   TB/518
FREDERICK WAISMANN: Introduction to Mathematical
Thinking. Foreword by Karl Menger   TB/511

Philosophy of Science

R. B. BRAITHWAITE: Scientific Explanation   TB/515
J. BRONOWSKI: Science and Human Values. △ Revised and
Enlarged Edition   TB/505
ALBERT EINSTEIN et al.: Albert Einstein: Philosopher-
Scientist. Edited by Paul A. Schilpp   Vol. I   TB/502
Vol. II   TB/503
WERNER HEISENBERG: Physics and Philosophy: The Revo-
lution in Modern Science △   TB/549
JOHN MAYNARD KEYNES: A Treatise on Probability. ᵒ △
Introduction by N. R. Hanson   TB/557
KARL R. POPPER: Logic of Scientific Discovery △ TB/576
STEPHEN TOULMIN: Foresight and Understanding: An
Enquiry into the Aims of Science. △ Foreword by
Jacques Barzun   TB/564
STEPHEN TOULMIN: The Philosophy of Science: An In-
troduction △   TB/513
G. J. WHITROW: Natural Philosophy of Time ᵒ △   TB/563

Physics and Cosmology

JOHN E. ALLEN: Aerodynamics: A Space Age Survey △
TB/582
STEPHEN TOULMIN & JUNE GOODFIELD: The Fabric of the
Heavens: The Development of Astronomy and Dy-
namics. △ Illus.   TB/579
DAVID BOHM: Causality and Chance in Modern Physics.△
Foreword by Louis de Broglie   TB/536
P. W. BRIDGMAN: The Nature of Thermodynamics
TB/537
P. W. BRIDGMAN: A Sophisticate's Primer of Relativity △
TB/575
A. C. CROMBIE, Ed.: Turning Point in Physics   TB/535
C. V. DURRELL: Readable Relativity. △ Foreword by Free-
man J. Dyson   TB/530
ARTHUR EDDINGTON: Space, Time and Gravitation: An
Outline of the General Relativity Theory   TB/510
GEORGE GAMOW: Biography of Physics Σ △   TB/567
MAX JAMMER: Concepts of Force: A Study in the Founda-
tion of Dynamics   TB/550
MAX JAMMER: Concepts of Mass in Classical and Modern
Physics   TB/571
MAX JAMMER: Concepts of Space: The History of
Theories of Space in Physics. Foreword by Albert
Einstein   TB/533
G. J. WHITROW: The Structure and Evolution of the Uni-
verse: An Introduction to Cosmology. △ Illus. TB/504